essentials

AppTech

PUBLISHER 2000

SALLY PRESTON
WASHTENAW COMMUNITY COLLEGE

ROBERT FERRETT
EASTERN MICHIGAN UNIVERSITY

JOHN PRESTON
EASTERN MICHIGAN UNIVERSITY

Prentice
Hall

Upper Saddle River, New Jersey

Publisher 2000 Essentials

International Standard Book Number: 0-13-026198-X

03 02 01 00   4 3 2 1

Interpretation of the printing code: the rightmost double-digit number is the year of the book's printing: the rightmost single-digit number, the number of the book's printing. For example, a printing code of 00-1 shows that the first printing of the book occurred in 2000.

Trademark Acknowledgments

Editor-in-Chief:
Mickey Cox

Managing Editor:
Melissa Whitaker

Development Editor:
Susan Hobbs

Technical Editor:
Ash Patel

Assistant Editor:
Kerri Limpert

Director of Strategic Marketing:
Nancy Evans

Marketing Manager:
Kris King

AVP/Director of Production & Manufacturing:
Michael Weinstein

Manager, Production:
Gail Steier de Acevedo

Project Manager:
Tim Tate

Manufacturing Buyer:
Natacha St. Hill Moore

Associate Director, Manufacturing:
Vincent Scelta

Book Designer:
Louisa Klucznik

Full Service Composition:
Graphic World Inc.

About the Authors

Sally Preston is President of Preston & Associates, a computer software-training firm. She uses her extensive business experience as a bank vice president in charge of branch operations along with her skills in training people on new computer systems. She provides corporate training through Preston & Associates and through the Institute for Workforce Development at Washtenaw Community College, where she also teaches computer courses part-time. She has co-authored nearly 20 books on Access, Excel, PowerPoint, Word, and WordPerfect, including the *Learn 97* and *Learn 2000* series, as well as the *Office 2000 Essentials* and *Access 2000 Essentials* books. She has an MBA from Eastern Michigan University.

Robert L. Ferrett is the Director of the Center for Instructional Computing at Eastern Michigan University. His center provides computer training and support to faculty at the university. He has authored or co-authored more than 30 books on Access, PowerPoint, Excel, Word, and Word Perfect and was the editor of the *1994 ACM SIGUCCS Conference Proceedings*. He is a series editor for the *Learn 97* and *Learn 2000* books and has been designing, developing, and delivering computer workshops for nearly two decades. He has a BA in Psychology, an MS in Geography, and an MS in Interdisciplinary Technology from Eastern Michigan University. He is ABD in the Ph.D. program in Instructional Technology at Wayne State University.

John Preston is an Associate Professor at Eastern Michigan University in the College of Technology, where he teaches microcomputer application courses at the undergraduate and graduate levels. He has been teaching, writing, and designing computer training courses since the advent of PCs and has authored and co-authored more than thirty books on Microsoft Word, Excel, Access, and PowerPoint. He is a series editor for the *Learn 97* and *Learn 2000* books. He has received grants from the Detroit Edison Institute and the Department of Energy to develop Web sites for energy education and alternative fuels. He has also developed one of the first Internet-based microcomputer applications courses at an accredited university. He has a BS from the University of Michigan in Physics, Mathematics, and Education, and an MS from Eastern Michigan University in Physics Education. He is ABD in the Ph.D. degree program in Instructional Technology at Wayne State University.

Acknowledgments

The authors acknowledge the indispensable contribution of the hard working and talented team of editors and management personnel who kept watch for errors and made valuable suggestions for improvement. Special thanks and credit go to:

Susan Hobbs . . . . Development Editor

Asit Patel . . . . Technical Editor

Melissa Whitaker. . . . . Managing Editor

Tim Tate . . . . Project Manager

The authors would also like to thank Paul Majeske, a faculty member in the Communication Technology program at Eastern Michigan University, who gave us valuable advice about the commercial printing aspects of publication design.

In addition to the editing and production team listed on the credits page, the authors want to acknowledge the contributions of the students in the technical writing program at Eastern Michigan University. These students, under the instruction and guidance of their professor, Dr. Ann Blakeslee, provided a valuable review and usability test of the manuscript for this book. The following students participated in this project:

Angie Broadus	Lolo Lord
Elizabeth Donoghue Colvin	John Moreau
Emily Hamlin	Jennifer Podgorny
Jennifer Hutchison	Lori Shifflett
Ryan Kilyanek	Lisa Tallman
Barbara Lauter	Matthew Thompson
Mark Lockwood	

Contents at a Glance

Table of Contents

Introduction

Essentials courseware from Prentice Hall is anchored in the practical and professional needs of all types of students. This edition of the *Publisher 2000 Essentials* benefits from painstaking usability research by the publisher, authors, editors, and students. Practically every detail—by way of pedagogy, content, presentation, and design—was the object of continuous online (and offline) discussion among the entire team.

The *Essentials* series has been conceived around a "learning-by-doing" approach, which encourages you to grasp application-related concepts as you expand your skills through hands-on tutorials. As such, it consists of modular lessons that are built around a series of numbered, step-by-step procedures that are clear, concise, and easy to review. Explicatory material is interwoven before each lesson and between the steps. Additional features, tips, pitfalls, and other related information are provided at exactly the place where you would most expect them. They are easily recognizable elements that stand out from the main flow of the tutorial. We have even designed our icons to match the Microsoft Office theme. The end-of-chapter exercises have likewise been carefully graded from the routine Checking Concepts and Terms to tasks in the Discovery Zone that gently prod you into extending what you have learned into areas beyond the explicit scope of the lessons proper. Below, you will find out more about the rationale behind each book element and how to use each to your maximum benefit

How to Use This Book

Typically, each *Essentials* book is divided into seven or eight projects, concerning topics such as working with frames, adding graphics, and building a Web site. A project covers one area (or a few closely related areas) of application functionality. Each project is then divided into seven to nine lessons related to that topic. For example, a project on using special features is divided into lessons explaining how to add and format tables, create mailing lists, and use the Mail Merge feature. Each lesson presents a specific task or closely related set of tasks in a manageable chunk that is easy to assimilate and retain.

Each element in *Publisher 2000 Essentials* is designed to maximize your learning experience. Here is a list of the *Essentials* project elements and a description of how each element can help you:

- **Project Objectives.** Starting with an objective gives you short-term, attainable goals. Using project objectives that closely match the titles of the step-by-step tutorials breaks down the possibly overwhelming prospect of learning several new features of Publisher into small, attainable, bite-sized tasks. Look over the objectives on the opening page of the project before you begin and review them after completing the project to identify the main goals for each project.

- **Key Terms.** This book includes a limited number of useful vocabulary words and definitions, such as *frame*, *AutoFlow*, *placeholder*, and *sidebar*. Key terms introduced in each project are listed in alphabetical order immediately after the objectives on the opening page of the project. These key terms are shown in bold italic and defined during their first use within the text. Definitions of key terms are also included in the glossary.

- **Why Would I Do This?** You are studying Publisher so that you can accomplish useful tasks in the real world. This brief section tells you why these tasks or procedures are important, what you can do with the knowledge, or how these application features can be applied to everyday tasks.

- **Visual Summary.** This opening section graphically illustrates the concepts and features you will learn in the project. Several figures, with ample callouts, show the final result of completing the project. This road map to your destination keeps you motivated as you work through the individual steps of each task.

- **Lessons**. Each lesson contains one or more tasks that correspond to an objective on the opening page of the project. A lesson consists of step-by-step tutorials, their associated data files, screenshots, and the special notes described below. Although each lesson often builds on the previous one, the lessons (and the exercises) have been made as modular as possible.

- **Step-by-Step Tutorial.** The lessons consist of numbered bolded step-by-step instructions that show you how to perform the procedures in a clear, concise, and direct manner. These hands-on tutorials, which are the "essentials" of each project, let you "learn by doing." Short paragraphs between the steps clarify the results of each step. Also, figures are introduced after key steps for you to check against the results on your screen. To revise the lesson, you can easily scan the bold, numbered steps. Quick (or impatient!) learners may likewise ignore the intervening paragraphs.

- **Need to Know.** These sidebars provide essential tips for performing the task and using the application more effectively. You can easily recognize them by their distinctive icon and bolded headings. It is well worth the effort to review these crucial notes again after completing the project.

- **Nice to Know.** Nice to Know comments provide extra tips, shortcuts, alternative ways to complete a process, and special hints about using the software. You may safely ignore these for the moment to focus on the main task at hand; or you may pause to learn and appreciate these tidbits. Here, you will find neat tricks and special insights that will impress your friends and co-workers!

- **If You Have Problems...** These short troubleshooting notes help you anticipate or solve common problems quickly and effectively. Even if you do not encounter the problem at this time, make a mental note of it so that you know what to do if this problem occurs in the future.

- **Summary.** This provides a brief recap of the tasks learned in the project. The summary will guide you to places where you can expand your knowledge, which may include references to specific Help topics or the Prentice Hall *Essentials* Web site (www.prenhall.com/essentials).

- **Checking Concepts and Terms.** This section offers optional true/false, multiple choice, screen ID, and discussion questions designed to check your comprehension and assess retention. If you need to refresh your memory, the relevant lesson number is provided after each true/false and multiple choice question. For example, [L5] directs you to review lesson five for the answer. Lesson numbers may be provided, but only where relevant, for other types of exercises as well.

- **Skill Drill Exercises.** This section enables you to check your comprehension, evaluate your progress, and practice what you have learned. The exercises in this section mirror and reinforce what has been learned in each project. Generally, the Skill Drill exercises include step-by-step instructions.

- **Challenge Exercises.** This section provides exercises that expand on or relate to the skills practiced in the project. Each exercise provides a brief narrative introduction followed by instructions. At least one of the exercises requires you to use Help, to learn how to learn on your own. Although the instructions are usually written in a step-by-step format, the steps are not as detailed as those in the Skill Drill section. Providing less detailed steps helps you learn to think on your own. These exercises foster "near transfer" of learning.

- **Discovery Zone Exercises.** These exercises require advanced knowledge of project topics or application of skills from multiple lessons. In addition, these exercises may require you to research topics in Help or on the Web to complete them. This self-directed method of learning new skills emulates real-world experience. We provide the cues, you do the exploring!

- **Learning to Learn.** Throughout this book, you will find lessons, exercises, and other elements highlighted by this icon. For the most part, they involve using or exploring the built-in Help system or Web-based Help also accessible from the application. However, their significance is much deeper. Microsoft Office has become so rich in features catering to such diverse needs that it is no longer possible to anticipate and teach you everything you might need to know. It is becoming increasingly important that, as you learn from this book, you also "learn to learn" on your own. These elements help you identify related, perhaps more specialized, tasks or questions and show you how to discover the right procedures or answers by exploiting the many resources already within the application.

- **Task Guide.** The task guide that follows the last project lists all the procedures and shortcuts you have learned in this book. It can be used in two complementary ways to enhance your learning experience. You can refer to it, while progressing through the book, to refresh your memory on procedures learned in a previous lesson. Or you can keep it as a handy real-world reference while using the application for your daily work.

- **Glossary.** Here you will find the definitions—collected in one place—of all the key terms defined throughout the book and listed in the opening page of each project. Use it to refresh your memory.

Typeface Conventions Used in This Book

We have used the following conventions throughout this book to make it easier for you to understand the material:

- Key terms appear in ***italic and bold*** the first time they are defined in a project.

- Text that you type, as well as text that appears on your computer screen as warning, confirmation, or general information, appears in a special `monospace` typeface.

- Hotkeys, the underlined keys onscreen that activate commands and options, are also underlined in this book. Hotkeys offer a quick way to bring up frequently used commands.

How to Use the CD-ROM

The CD-ROM accompanying this book contains all the data files for you to use as you work through the step-by-step tutorials, Skill Drill, Challenge, and Discovery Zone exercises provided at the end of each textbook project. The CD contains separate parallel folders for each project. The filenames correspond to the filenames called for in the textbook. Here is how the files are named: The first three characters represent the software (such as Pub for Publisher 2000 Essentials). The last four digits indicate the project number and the file number within the project. For example, the first file used in Project 1 would be 0101. Therefore, the complete name for the first file in the Publisher book is Pub-0101.

Files on a CD-ROM are read-only; they cannot be modified in any way. To use the provided data files while working through this book, they must first be transferred to a read-write medium where you may modify them. There are several ways to do this. This book assumes that you are working with file(s) that are stored on a hard drive or other high capacity storage device such as an Iomega zip disk. Ordinary floppy disks do not have enough storage capacity for these exercises.

- **Using the Save As menu option**. For most programs (excluding Access), you can use the Save As menu option to move a file from the CD-ROM to a hard disk or a zip disk. Find the file you need on the CD-ROM and double-click on the file-name to open it. Choose File, Save As from the menu. Give the file a new name, choose a folder on a hard drive or zip drive, and then click Save. This procedure also removes the read-only status of the file, enabling you to make changes to the file.

- **Copying to a hard drive or zip disk**. First, select the files on the CD that you want to copy. Right-click on the selection and choose Copy from the shortcut menu. Go to the appropriate folder on the hard drive or zip disk, right-click in the folder, and choose Paste from the shortcut menu. After copying, select the copied files and right-click the selection with the mouse again. This time choose Properties, choose the General tab on the Properties dialog box, then uncheck the Read-only attribute at the bottom of this page. Because the original files on the CD-ROM were read-only, the files were copied with this attribute turned on. You can rename files copied in this manner after you have turned off the read-only attribute.

  Although you can use the same method to copy the entire CD contents to a large-capacity drive, it is much simpler to use the installation routine in the CD-ROM for the purpose. This will automatically remove the read-only attribute while transferring the files.

- **Installing to a hard drive or zip drive**. The CD-ROM contains an installation routine that automatically copies all the contents to a local or networked hard drive, or to a removable large-capacity drive (for example, an Iomega zip drive). If you are working in the classroom, your instructor has probably already installed the files to the hard drive and can tell you where the files are located. You will be asked to save or copy the file(s) you need to your personal work area on the hard drive or to a high-capacity work disk.

  Otherwise, run the installation routine yourself to transfer all the files to the hard drive (for example, if you are working at home) or to your personal zip drive. You may then work directly and more efficiently off these high-capacity drives.

CD-ROM Installation Routine

If you have been instructed to install the files on a lab computer, or if you are installing them on your home computer, simply insert the CD-ROM into the CD-ROM drive. When the installation screen appears, follow these steps:

1. From the installation screen, click the Install button.

2. The Welcome dialog box is displayed. Click the Next button.

3. The Readme.txt appears. The Readme.txt gives you important information regarding the installation. Make sure you use the scrollbar to view the entire Readme.txt file. When you are finished reading the Readme.txt, click the Next button.

4. The Select Destination Directory is displayed. Unless instructed otherwise by your instructor, the default location is recommended. Click Next.

5. The Ready to Install screen appears. Click Next to begin the installation.

   A directory will be created on your hard drive where the student files will be installed.

6. A message box appears confirming that the installation is complete.

The installation of the student data files allows you to access the data files from the Start menu. To access the student data files from the Start menu, click Start, click Programs, and then click the Essentials title you installed from the list of Programs. The student data files are in subfolders arranged by project.

Uninstalling the Student Data Files

When you have completed the course, you might decide you do not need the student data files anymore. If that is the case, you have the ability to uninstall them. The following steps walk you through the process:

1. Click on the Start button and select Programs.
2. Click the Essentials title that you installed.
3. Click Uninstall.
4. Click one of the Uninstall methods listed:
   - Automatic—This method deletes all files in the directory and all shortcuts created.
   - Custom—This method enables you to select the files you want to delete.
5. Click Next.
6. The Perform Uninstall dialog box appears. Click Finish. The Student data files and their folders will be deleted.

Instructor Resources

The Web site www.prenhall.com/essentials contains suggested solution files that show how the students' files should look at the end of a tutorial, answers to the Checking Concepts sections, and solution files for the Skill Drill, Challenge, and Discovery Zone exercises that accompany each project. For students, the Web site also contains the data files that are found on the CD-ROM that comes with each textbook.

Project 1

Getting Started with Publisher

Objectives

In this project, you learn how to

➤ **Choose a Design from the Catalog**

➤ **Create a Publication Using a Wizard**

➤ **Update Personal Information**

➤ **Explore the Publisher Screen and Navigate Your Publication**

➤ **Work with Frames**

➤ **Add and Remove Pages**

➤ **Print a Publication**

➤ **Save a Publication**

➤ **Get Help Using the Office Assistant**

Key terms introduced in this project include

- Catalog
- clip art frames
- docked toolbars
- floating toolbars
- frame
- grouped
- masthead
- Office Assistant
- page navigation controls
- picture frames
- placeholder
- ScreenTip
- selection handles
- table frames
- text frames
- wizard
- WordArt frames

Why Would I Do This?

All word processors have some desktop publishing features. Microsoft Publisher, a desktop publishing program, is the type of software you'll want for more sophisticated publications, enabling advanced layout. This would include publications with multiple stories or articles on the same page, stories that might be placed in two or more locations in a publication (e.g., columns continued on another page), or publications that contain many graphics and columns that you want to move around.

Desktop publishing packages are designed to create specific types of publications. Some of the more common ones are newsletters, flyers, banners, brochures, and greeting cards. The more advanced desktop publishers include ways to create Web pages. They also enable you to gather information created in other applications. For example, Microsoft Publisher has the capabilities to import a chart from Excel, text from Word, a table from Access, and graphics from PhotoDraw.

One of the strengths of a desktop publishing package is the capability to move objects around in the publication. With a desktop publishing program, every object is contained in a *frame,* and the frames are easily moved or resized using the pointer. If you think of the blank publication as a checkerboard and the framed objects (e.g., text, pictures, clip art, and tables) as checkers, you can visualize moving the checkers anywhere on the board, even overlapping each other. The rules of desktop publishing are much less restrictive, however, than the rules of checkers!

Microsoft Publisher is a full-featured desktop publishing package. It enables you to create everything from a one-page flyer to a multiple-page publication formatted to be sent to a commercial printer. Because this is an introduction to the program, some of the features are addressed only briefly or not at all. If you are interested in learning more about Publisher, you will be shown how to explore the help that comes with Publisher and try things out. You will be amazed at what you can produce with a little effort!

Some of the projects in this book require that you have the capability to store files on your computer's hard disk or a storage device that has more capacity than a floppy disk. This book assumes that you are using the My Documents folder, but you can use any other folder that you choose.

In this project, you use the **Catalog** to select the type of publication you want to produce, and you also select the publication design. The Catalog is a visual directory of publication types and designs. You also use a wizard to select specific characteristics of the publication. You look at the various elements of the Publisher screen and learn how to navigate through the publication. Finally, you preview, print, and save your publication.

Visual Summary

When you have completed this lesson, you will have used the Microsoft Publisher Catalog to select a newsletter wizard with a preset design. You will have used the wizard to create a four-page newsletter. The first page will look like the one shown in Figure 1.1.

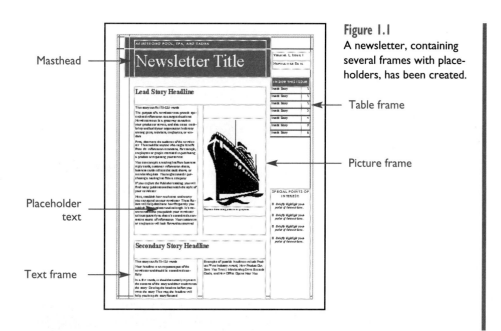

Figure 1.1
A newsletter, containing several frames with place-holders, has been created.

Masthead

Table frame

Picture frame

Placeholder text

Text frame

Lesson 1: Choosing a Design from the Catalog

When you launch Publisher, the first window you see is always the Catalog. If you are starting from scratch, the Catalog enables you to choose the type of publication you want to produce. It also provides many design options.

The Catalog enables you to create a set of different publications—a newsletter, brochure, flyer, shipping labels and business cards, for example—all with the same design. You can also create a publication from a blank page. Finally, you can click on an Existing Files button and select a publication that has already been created.

In this lesson, you explore the Publisher Catalog.

To Choose a Design from the Catalog

1 Click the Start button, select Programs from the Start menu, and select Microsoft Publisher.
When you launch Microsoft Publisher, the Catalog window displays (see Figure 1.2). The Publications by Wizard tab is selected by default. Two other tabs—Publications by Design and Blank Publications—are available. You can also choose to open a file by clicking the Existing Files button at the bottom of the window.

2 Click the Publications by Design tab. Select the Bars option from the Master Sets design set. Use the scrollbar on the right edge of the Catalog window to scroll down to see the different types of publications available.
Notice that nearly every type of publication you might need to run a business is included, from an inventory list to a newsletter (see Figure 1.3). Many of these publication types can also be used for other types of organizations, or even for personal use.

continues ▶

To Choose a Design from the Catalog (continued)

Figure 1.2
The Publisher Catalog gives you a visual directory of publication types and designs.

Publications by Wizard tab

Publications by Design tab

Blank Publications tab

Existing Files button

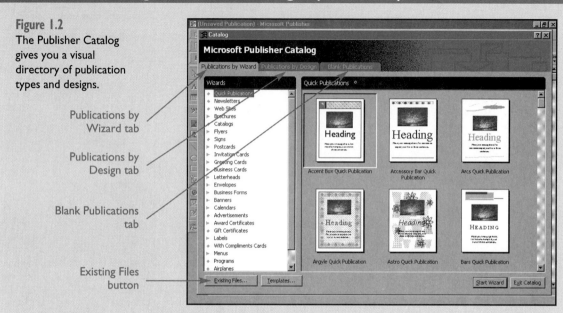

Figure 1.3
The Publications by Design tab gives you the opportunity to create many different business publications with a similar theme.

Publications by Design tab

Master Sets

Related business publications

Bars option

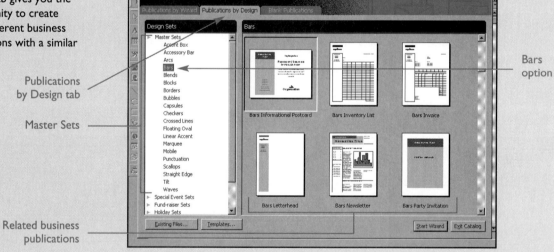

> ☒ If you cannot see the list of Master Sets options, click Master Sets once. The list of available designs is displayed.

3 **Click the Blank Publications tab and scroll down through the options.**
Notice that the number of options is limited.

4 **Click the Publications by Wizard tab.**
A publication Wizard is a short program that asks you questions about how you want to design something, and then creates a publication based on your answers.

5 **Click the Newsletters option in the Wizard section.**
The Newsletters Wizard is selected, and newsletter designs are displayed in the Newsletters area.

6 **Use the vertical scrollbar on the far right to scroll down in the Newsletters panel. Click the Crossed Lines Newsletter design once to select it.**

Your screen should look like Figure 1.4. Leave Publisher open for the next lesson.

Newsletters Wizard option

Start Wizard button

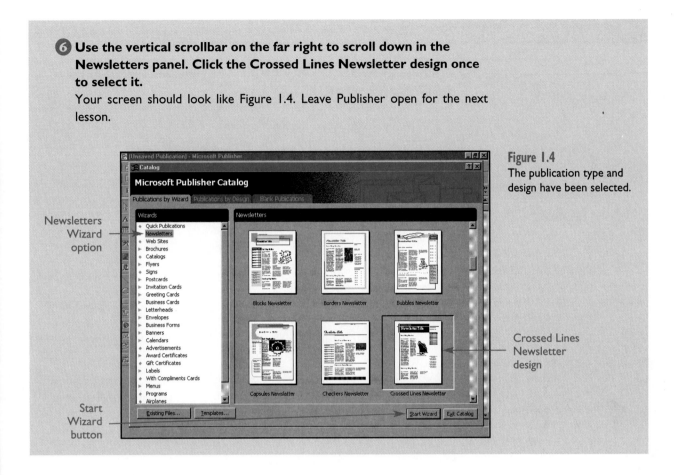

Figure 1.4
The publication type and design have been selected.

Crossed Lines Newsletter design

 Design Set Names
The names you see used for the various Design Sets loosely describe the general look of the page decorations. For example, the Bars design has a dark green bar on every publication type, and the Floating Oval design has a title surrounded by a black oval.

 Automatic Save Prompts
If you take your time going through this project, a dialog box will probably pop up to remind you that it is time to save your publication. These reminders are displayed after a set number of minutes (15 minutes by default). If you get this reminder, click the No button—you will save the publication in Lesson 8.

Lesson 2: Creating a Publication Using a Wizard

Once you have selected a publication type and design, you launch a wizard. A **wizard** is an Office help feature that asks questions and then uses your answers to set something up for you; in this case, a publication. When you choose a newsletter, as you did in Lesson 1, the wizard's questions will relate to newsletter design—what color combination do you want, will the pages be printed back-to-back, and how many columns of text do you want on each page? When you run the wizard to set up your Web site in Project 7, "Building a Web Site with Publisher," the questions will be completely different.

To Create a Publication Using a Wizard

1 **With the Crossed Lines Newsletter design still selected, click the Start Wizard button.**

The Newsletter Introduction window displays. Notice that a four-page newsletter has been set up by default, and a preview of the first page of the newsletter is shown (see Figure 1.5). Read the Introduction text.

Figure 1.5
A default newsletter contains four pages.

Introduction text

Newsletter preview

Four pages have been created

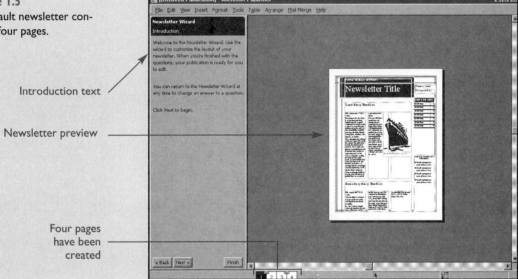

X If you are using the Publisher program for the first time, you will be asked if you want to enter personal information. Click the No button. You will enter this information in the next lesson.

2 **Click the Next button to begin setting up your newsletter.**

The first Newsletter Wizard dialog box asks you to choose a color scheme for your newsletter (see Figure 1.6). Many newsletters use the default black and white option, but if you are able to print the newsletter in color, Publisher offers many color schemes. The first of the five color boxes is the color of the text; the other four are the accent colors of the other elements on the page.

X If the Next button does not appear at the bottom of the screen, it means that someone has turned the wizard questions off. Choose Tools, Options from the menu. Click the User Assistance tab; then click the Step through wizard questions check box. Click OK. Close Publisher without saving your changes and restart the process.

(i) **Moving Quickly to the Publication**
You can move directly to the publication at any time while you are running the wizard. To skip answering questions about the layout of the publication, click the Finish button in the wizard dialog box. This will enable you to immediately begin editing.

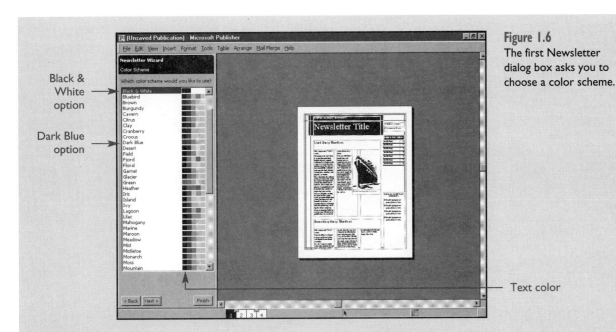

Black & White option

Dark Blue option

Text color

Figure 1.6
The first Newsletter dialog box asks you to choose a color scheme.

❸ Select the Dark Blue color scheme (you may have to scroll up) and click the Next button.

The second Newsletter Wizard dialog box asks you to choose the number of columns. The default is three columns.

❹ Select the 2-column option and click the Next button.

The third Newsletter Wizard dialog box asks you if you want to reserve a space for a mailing address.

❺ Click the Yes button.

The program tells you that the change has been made and that you can see this change on page 4 of the newsletter.

❻ Click the OK button to acknowledge that you have read the message.

❼ Click the Next button.

The fourth Newsletter Wizard dialog box asks you if you want to print on one side of the page or on both sides. If you are going to print the pages back-to-back, the program will make certain formatting changes. For instance, the page numbers will appear on the left side of the left-hand pages, and on the right side of the right-hand pages.

❽ Choose Double-sided and click the Next button.

The fifth (and final) Newsletter Wizard dialog box displays. It asks you which personal information set you would like to use for this newsletter (see Figure 1.7).

❾ Make sure the Primary Business option is selected.

Leave the Newsletter Wizard dialog box open for the next lesson, where you will change the Primary Business information.

continues ▶

To Create a Publication Using a Wizard   (continued)

Figure 1.7
The final Newsletter Wizard dialog box asks which personal information set you would like to use.

Personal Information set options

Update button

The newsletter uses two columns for text

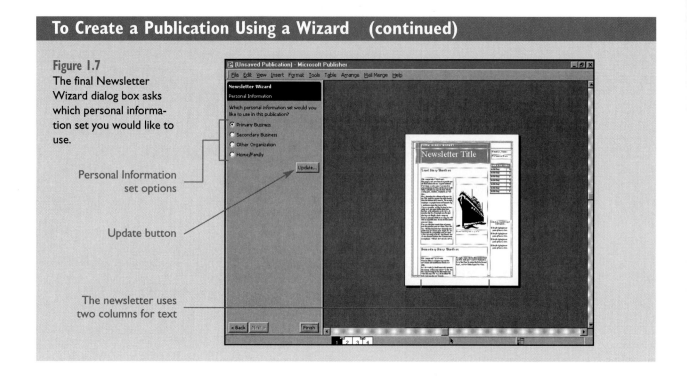

 If you use the 3-column option in the Newsletter Wizard, you will actually end up with four columns on the first page because an extra column is reserved for the table of contents and other information. On a standard sheet of paper, four columns, plus the space between the columns, leave only about $1\frac{1}{2}$" for text in each column. This looks very cluttered and can make your newsletter hard to read.

Lesson 3: Updating Personal Information

Publisher stores personal information for you so that you do not have to reenter it every time you start a new publication. In fact, you can store up to four different information sets: one for your Primary Business, one for a Secondary Business, one for some Other Organization, and one for Home/Family information. You might use the first set of information for use in a retail business and the secondary business set for a wholesale operation affiliated with your primary business. The other organization might be a charity or club, and you might use the last information set for your holiday newsletters and other family publications.

In this lesson, you set up the personal information for a primary business.

To Update Personal Information

❶ Click the Update button in the Publication Wizard Personal Information dialog box.
A Personal Information dialog box displays (see Figure 1.8).

The information in your Personal Information dialog box will not match the one in the figure. If Publisher is being used on your machine for the first time, the text will be similar but the Name and Job or position title will display the name of the person or organization that was entered when the program was installed. If you are using a computer in a lab, this dialog box will display the information that was entered by the last person to make changes to the information set.

Personal Information set to edit →

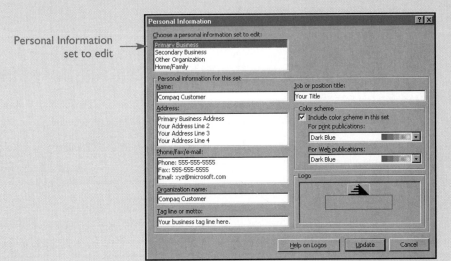

Figure 1.8
The Personal Information dialog box enables you to enter personal information for all four category sets.

2 **Make sure the Primary Business option is selected at the top of the dialog box and then highlight the entry in the Name text box.**

3 **Type your name in the Name text box, then fill in the rest of the information as shown in Figure 1.9.**
Make sure that the Include color scheme in this set check box has been selected and that the Dark Blue option is selected for both print and Web publications (see Figure 1.9). Do not enter anything in the Logo area.

Include color scheme check box

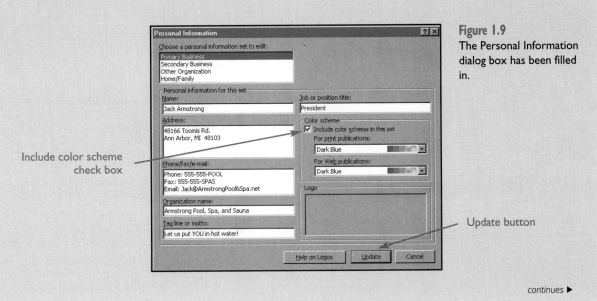

Figure 1.9
The Personal Information dialog box has been filled in.

Update button

continues ▶

To Update Personal Information   (continued)

4 **Click the Update button to update your Primary Business personal information.**
The Personal Information dialog box closes, and you return to the last Publication Wizard dialog box.

5 **Click the Finish button to complete the Publication Wizard.**
You are now ready to work on your new publication. Leave the publication open for the next lesson.

Lesson 4: Exploring the Publisher Screen and Navigating Your Publication

Now that you have created a publication, you need to understand the functions of the various components of the Publisher window, including the menu, toolbars, rulers, scrollbars, status bar, and work area. You also need to know how to move from page to page and how to zoom in and out on the active page. Finally, you need to know how to turn the wizard on and off.

In this lesson, you explore the various components of the Microsoft Publisher 2000 screen and learn how to move around in a publication.

To Explore the Publisher Screen and Navigate Your Publication

1 **Click the Hide Wizard button at the bottom of the Wizard window.**
The Wizard window is hidden, and the Hide Wizard button changes to a Show Wizard button (see Figure 1.10). This gives you a larger area to work in. There are three toolbars on the screen: the Standard toolbar, the Formatting toolbar, and the Objects toolbar. A title bar, which contains the name of the publication, and a menu bar are also present. The page navigation controls are at the bottom-left corner of the window. Notice that the Formatting toolbar has no active buttons because nothing is selected.

 Your screen may not look exactly like the screen shown in Figure 1.10. The toolbars are shown in the default locations. However, if the last person to use Publisher moved one or more of them, they may appear in different locations. The location of the toolbars is not important.

 Hiding the Taskbar
It is usually a good idea to hide the taskbar so that you will have a larger work area. If the taskbar is displayed on your screen, right-click on an open space anywhere on the taskbar. Select Properties from the shortcut menu. Click the Taskbar Options tab in the Taskbar Properties dialog box, if necessary, and click the Auto hide check box. When you want to use the taskbar, move the mouse pointer to the bottom of the screen and it will pop up.

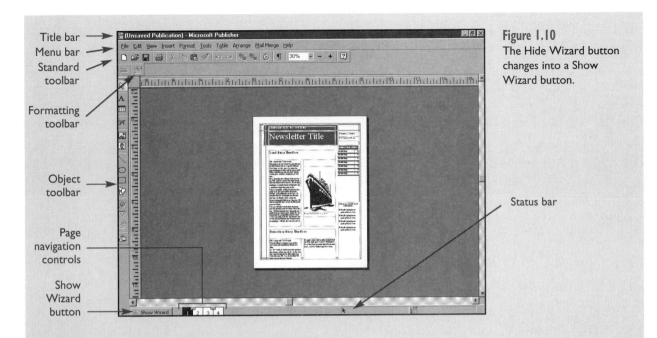

Title bar
Menu bar
Standard toolbar
Formatting toolbar
Object toolbar
Page navigation controls
Show Wizard button
Status bar

Figure 1.10
The Hide Wizard button changes into a Show Wizard button.

2 **Click on the block of text shown in Figure 1.11 and watch the Formatting toolbar.**

Notice that the buttons on the Formatting toolbar have changed (see Figure 1.11). The Formatting toolbar is context sensitive. This means it changes to fit the type of object selected. Also, notice that little squares are displayed around the edges of the selected object. These are called *selection handles* and indicate what object is selected.

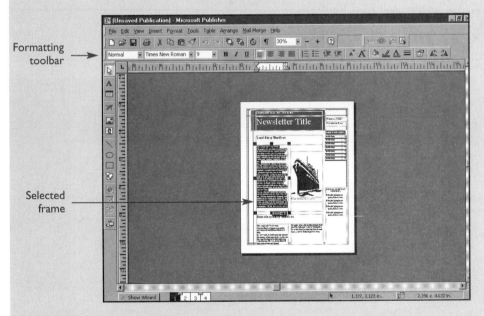

Formatting toolbar

Selected frame

Figure 1.11
The Formatting toolbar changes depending on the type of object selected.

3 **Move the mouse pointer over several of the toolbar buttons but do not click the mouse button.**

Notice that a *ScreenTip* pops up, telling you the name of each button (see Figure 1.12). This helps you identify the button you are looking for and gives you some idea of the purpose of each button.

continues ▶

To Explore the Publisher Screen and Navigate Your Publication (continued)

Figure 1.12
A ScreenTip is displayed.

ScreenTip

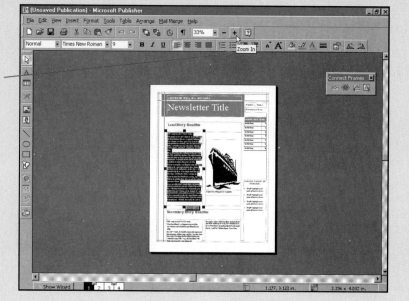

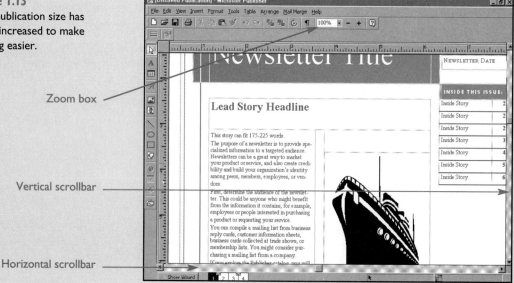 **4** **Click the Zoom In button on the Standard toolbar.**
The size of the publication increases, and the selected object (in this case, the text frame) remains centered in the work area.

5 **Keep clicking the Zoom In button until the Zoom box shows 100%.**
The selected text is still centered in the work area, but the text is much larger and will be easier to work with (see Figure 1.13). Generally, you will zoom in to edit, and zoom out to move things around on the page.

Figure 1.13
The publication size has been increased to make editing easier.

Zoom box

Vertical scrollbar

Horizontal scrollbar

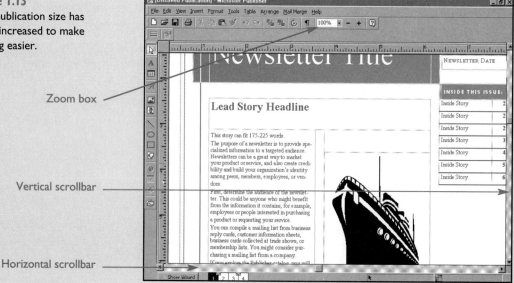

6 **Click the down arrow at the bottom of the vertical scrollbar.**
This enables you to look farther down in your publication. The arrow at the top of the vertical scrollbar moves the publication in the other direction.

7 **Click the right arrow at the right side of the horizontal scrollbar.**
This moves the document so that you can see the right side of your publication. The left arrow in the horizontal scrollbar moves the publication in the other direction.

8 **Click the page navigation control for page 4 of the newsletter.**
The *page navigation controls* are used to move from page to page. In this case, the fourth page of the newsletter displays, in the same relative location that you were in on the first page (see Figure 1.14). Notice that the mailing label you asked for when you ran the wizard is displayed here.

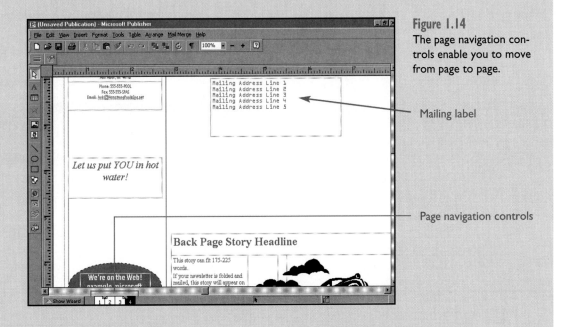

Figure 1.14
The page navigation controls enable you to move from page to page.

Mailing label

Page navigation controls

X If you move the pointer too close to the bottom of the screen, the taskbar will pop up and cover the page navigation controls. It will take a little practice to use these buttons without activating the taskbar.

9 **Click the page 1 page navigation control button to return to the first page of your newsletter.**
Leave the newsletter open for the next lesson.

Lesson 5: Working with Frames

Every object on a Publisher page is contained in a frame. Different frame types are available for different types of objects. **Text frames** work like miniature word processing windows, whereas **table frames** hold information in a row-and-column format, similar to the structure of a worksheet. There are also **clip art frames** for clip art images provided with Publisher, **picture frames** for digitized images, and **WordArt frames** for fancy text created with a special program. These frames can be moved, resized, copied, and pasted. Each part of a frame can be formatted. For example, you can change the background color of a text frame or add a border around a clip art frame.

When you create a publication using a wizard, frames are created automatically. Each type of frame that is added contains a graphic representation, called a ***placeholder,*** of the object that belongs in that frame. Placeholders cannot be edited, but are replaced by the user. Once the placeholder text has been selected, you can replace it by typing in new text or by importing a text file created in another program.

In this lesson, you resize and move a frame. You also use the Undo button to undo your changes.

To Work with Frames

❶ On page 1 of the newsletter, scroll until you can see the Lead Story Headline title. Click on the headline.

Selection handles appear around the perimeter of the text frame, and a light gray line shows you the edges of the frame (see Figure 1.15).

Figure 1.15
Selection handles are displayed around the text frame.

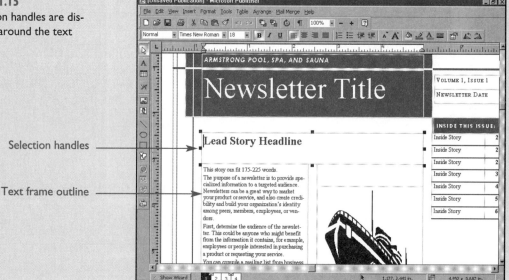

Selection handles

Text frame outline

❷ Click on the clip art image of the ship and release the mouse button, but leave the pointer over the image.

The picture frame is selected, the pointer changes to a Move pointer, and a ScreenTip identifies the type of frame and gives you a hint on how to modify the frame (see Figure 1.16).

❸ Use the vertical scrollbar to display the entire ship image. Move the pointer to the center selection handle on the top edge of the picture frame.

The pointer changes to a Resize pointer.

❹ Click and drag the image down about an inch and a half.

Use the vertical ruler on the right of the screen to judge the height to which you want to resize the clip art image. The image is resized, but it is not resized in proportion (see Figure 1.17). You will learn more about resizing frames in Project 2, "Adding Graphics."

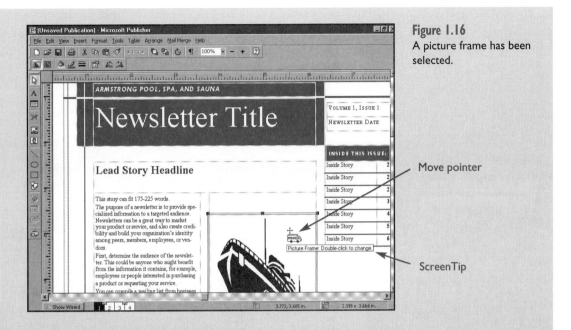

Figure 1.16
A picture frame has been selected.

Move pointer

ScreenTip

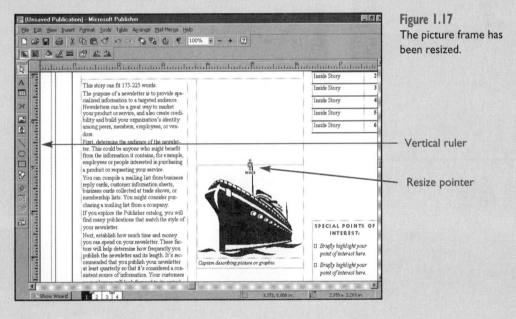

Figure 1.17
The picture frame has been resized.

Vertical ruler

Resize pointer

X If the rulers are not turned on, click <u>V</u>iew in the menu and select <u>R</u>ulers from the drop-down menu. If the <u>R</u>ulers option is not displayed, hold the mouse button above the menu for a couple of seconds until the menu expands.

---

5 Move the pointer into the middle of the clip art image.
The pointer changes to a Move tool.

6 Click the clip art image and drag it up until it is at the top of the col-umn, but don't release the mouse button.
An empty box shows the new location of the image until you release the mouse button.

continues ▶

To Work with Frames   (continued)

7 **Release the mouse button.**

The clip art image is placed at the top of the column. Notice that a text frame is attached to the bottom of the picture frame and moves when you move the picture frame (see Figure 1.18). When two or more frames are attached, they are said to be *grouped*.

Figure 1.18
The picture frame has been resized and moved.

Grouped frames

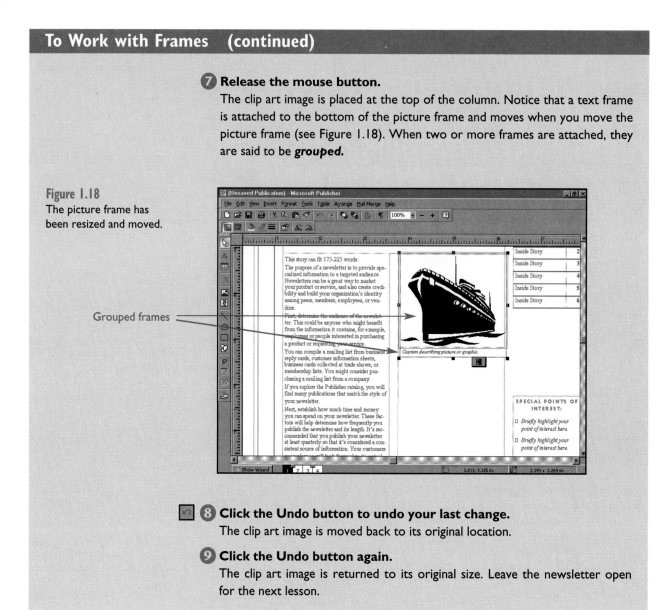

8 **Click the Undo button to undo your last change.**

The clip art image is moved back to its original location.

9 **Click the Undo button again.**

The clip art image is returned to its original size. Leave the newsletter open for the next lesson.

  Copying and Pasting Frames

You can use Copy and Paste or Cut and Paste to move frames in the same way you move objects in other Office programs. Select the frame, click the Cut (or Copy) button, move to the new page, and click the Paste button.

Lesson 6: Adding and Removing Pages

Because it is often difficult to gauge how much information you have for a publication, there will be times when you decide that you need to add an extra page or two or need to remove an existing page. You can add or remove pages from many different types of publications, including newsletters and Web pages (see Project 7).

In this lesson, you add a new blank page to your newsletter, then you delete one of the original pages.

To Add and Remove Pages

1 **Click the page navigation control button to move to page 4.**
You will insert a blank page before this page.

2 **Choose Insert, Page from the menu.**
The Insert Pages dialog box displays (see Figure 1.19). Because this is a double-sided publication, the program displays a right and left page. You can choose a page type for each page. If you were to click OK at this point (do not do so at this time), two pages would be added to your publication.

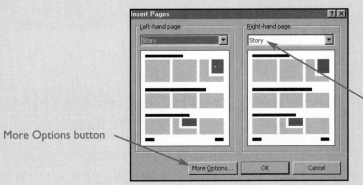

Figure 1.19
The Insert Pages dialog box enables you to add a pair of pages to a double-sided newsletter.

Choose page type here

More Options button

3 **Click the More Options button.**
A second Insert Pages dialog box provides several more options, such as how many pages you want to add and where you want the new pages placed.

4 **Select the Before current page option, and make sure Insert blank pages is selected.**
Your dialog box should look like Figure 1.20.

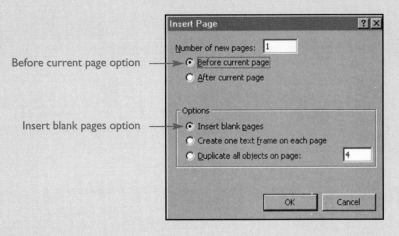

Figure 1.20
The Second Insert Pages dialog box offers several options.

Before current page option

Insert blank pages option

5 **Click OK. Click the list arrow in the Zoom box and select 33%. Use the scrollbars to center the pages on the screen.**
Your publication now has five pages, including a blank page 4 (see Figure 1.21).

continues ▶

To Add and Remove Pages   (continued)

Figure 1.21
The newsletter now has
five pages.

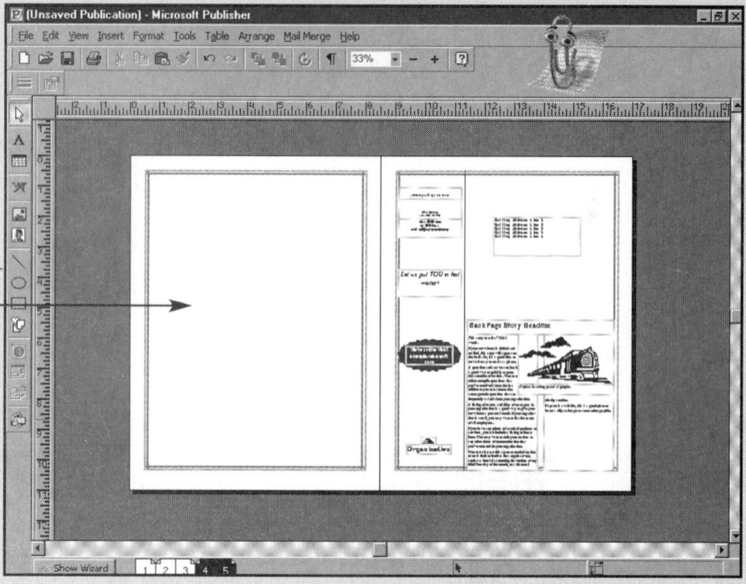

New blank page ⎯⎯⎯⎯⎯⎯⎯⎯→

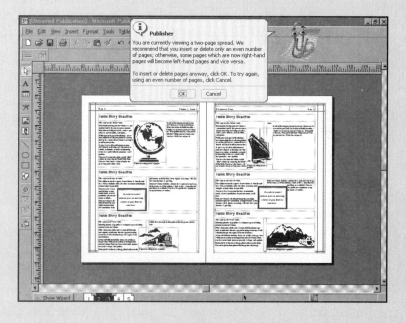

6 Click the page navigation control button to move to pages 2 and 3.

7 Choose **E̲dit, Delete Page** from the menu.
The Delete Page dialog box displays.

8 Select the **R̲ight page only** option and click **OK**.
A warning message tells you that you are working with double-sided pages and should probably delete two matched pages at a time (see Figure 1.22). If the Office Assistant is not turned on, the message appears in a dialog box.

Figure 1.22
The program suggests
deleting matched pages
in a double-sided
publication.

9 Click **OK**.
This overrides the program's suggestion and deletes the selected page. Leave the publication open for the next lesson.

Lesson 7: Printing a Publication

When you are finished making changes to your publication, you will want to print it. There are two ways to print a publication: You can click the Print button, or you can use the Print option from the File menu. The Print button prints the entire publication, whereas the menu option gives you more control over the printing process.

In this lesson, you print the entire newsletter using the Print button, then you print a single page of the newsletter using the menu.

To Print a Publication

❶ Click the Print button on the Standard toolbar.
The entire publication prints.

> **✗** If your publication does not print, check to make sure the printer is turned on. If you are working in a lab, Publisher might not be set up to print to the correct printer. Check with the lab manager to set up the printer.

❷ Choose File, Print from the menu.
The Print dialog box displays (see Figure 1.23).

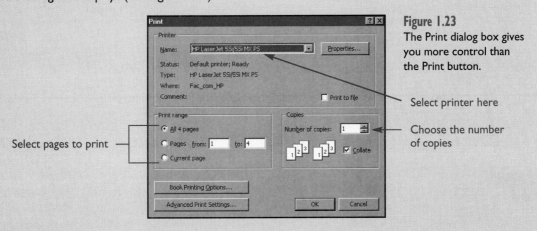

Select pages to print

Figure 1.23
The Print dialog box gives you more control than the Print button.

Select printer here

Choose the number of copies

❸ Type 1 in the from and to boxes in the Print range section of the Print dialog box to print just the first page.

❹ Make sure the correct printer is selected in the Name box in the Printer area. If you are unsure which printer to use, ask your instructor.
You could also select the number of copies of each page to print. For this lesson, you need to print only one page, which is the default.

❺ Click OK.
The first page of the newsletter prints. Leave the newsletter open for the next lesson.

Lesson 8: Saving a Publication

While you were working on this project, you were probably prompted to save your work at least once. Publisher is set up to automatically prompt you to save your changes at regular intervals. It is always a good idea to save your work regularly in case something happens to the computer.

In this lesson, you use the Save button to save the newsletter you have been working on.

To Save a Publication

1 Click the Save button in the Standard toolbar.
If you have not yet saved your publication, the Save As dialog box displays (see Figure 1.24).

Figure 1.24
The Save As dialog box enables you to choose a location and name for your publication.

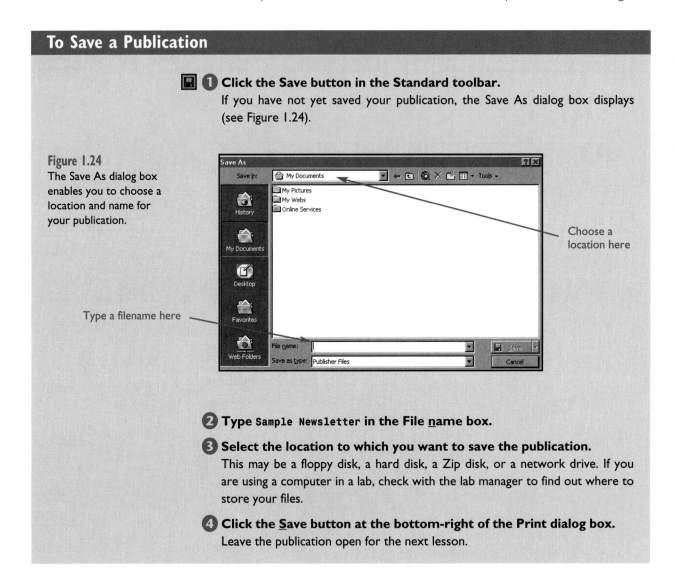

Type a filename here

Choose a location here

2 Type Sample Newsletter in the File name box.

3 Select the location to which you want to save the publication.
This may be a floppy disk, a hard disk, a Zip disk, or a network drive. If you are using a computer in a lab, check with the lab manager to find out where to store your files.

4 Click the Save button at the bottom-right of the Print dialog box.
Leave the publication open for the next lesson.

Lesson 9: Getting Help Using the Office Assistant

At some point, you may encounter problems as you work with Publisher. If you need a quick solution to a Publisher problem, you can use the program's Help feature. The Help system makes it easy to search for information on particular topics. In this lesson, you use the **Office Assistant,** which is an animated guide that helps you search for help.

The Office Assistant is a flexible help feature included with all Microsoft Office applications. It enables you to ask questions, search for terms, or look at context-sensitive tips.

To Get Help Using the Office Assistant

1 **If the Office Assistant is not displayed on your screen, select <u>H</u>elp, Show the <u>O</u>ffice Assistant from the menu.**

The Office Assistant displays on the screen. It can be moved by clicking and dragging it to a new location. The default Office Assistant is an animated paperclip called Clippit.

2 **To get help on a topic, click once on the Office Assistant.**

A small dialog box is displayed, asking you what you would like to do (see Figure 1.25).

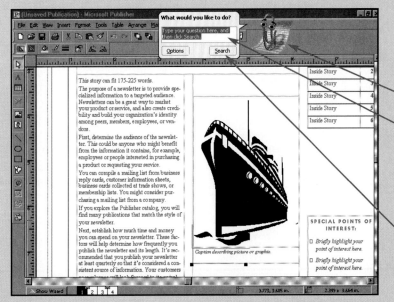

Figure 1.25
The Office Assistant is displayed on the Publisher screen.

Office Assistant

Type your question here

Search button

3 **Type How do I add new pages in the Office Assistant box.**

The Office Assistant will look for key words in your question and try to come up with answers. You do not have to add a question mark to your question.

> ☒ If you start to type a question in the Office Assistant and change your mind, you can remove the dialog box from the screen by clicking anywhere in the publication outside of the dialog box or by pressing the Escape button.

4 **Click the <u>S</u>earch button.**

The Office Assistant looks at your question and anticipates possible answers. The most likely group of answers is shown on the screen (see Figure 1.26). If the topic you are searching for does not appear in this list, click the See more arrow. The most likely answer to your question appears at the top of the list. Notice that by the end of the list the topics are getting pretty far from what you wanted.

continues ▶

To Get Help Using the Office Assistant   (continued)

Figure 1.26
A list of possible topics is displayed.

Topic buttons

Question

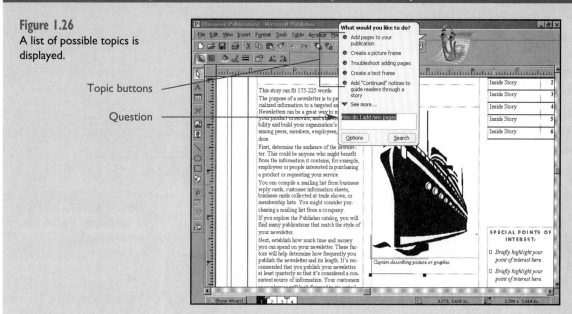

5 **Click the button for the Add pages to your publication topic.**
Several things happen. The work area decreases in size and a Publisher Help window displays on the screen (see Figure 1.27). Notice that some of the text is in blue. This means that the text is hyperlinked and more help is available if you click the word or phrase. You can use the vertical scrollbar to move down the Help window. There is also a Show button that can be used to activate other types of help.

Figure 1.27
A Publisher Help window is displayed on the right side of the screen.

Show button

Hyperlinked text

Publisher Help window

Vertical scrollbar

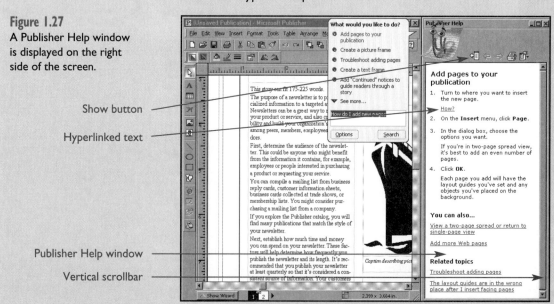

X   Your Publisher Help window may not look exactly like the one shown in the figure. The size and position of the window depends on how it was left the last time it was used. When you expand the Help window in the next step, part of it may be hidden behind the Publisher window. If this happens, click on the Help window to bring it to the foreground.

6 **Click the Show button.**

The Publisher Help window expands to include different types of help (see Figure 1.28). The Index enables you to type a word and see if it matches a predefined topic, whereas the Contents section reads like a book with chapters and topics. The Answer Wizard works just like the Office Assistant; you type a question and the wizard displays a list of related topics. To move between these features, simply click the tabs at the top of the window. The Show button has also changed to a Hide button. If you click the Hide button, the additional Help panel is removed from the screen.

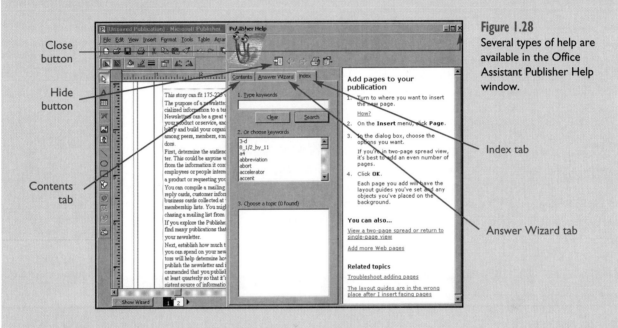

Close button

Hide button

Contents tab

Index tab

Answer Wizard tab

Figure 1.28
Several types of help are available in the Office Assistant Publisher Help window.

7 **Click the Close button to close the Office Assistant Publisher Help window.**

The publication again appears full-size, and the Office Assistant remains on the screen.

8 **Close the publication and exit Publisher.**

Changing or Hiding the Office Assistant

If you don't like the look of the Office Assistant, you can change it. Click the Office Assistant Options button and click the Gallery tab. Click the Next and Back buttons to view your options, and click OK when you find one you like.

Some people do not like to have the Office Assistant on the screen at all. You can hide the Office Assistant by choosing Help, Hide the Office Assistant. To turn it off completely, click once on the Office Assistant and click the Options button. Click the check box for the Use the Office Assistant option at the top of the dialog box.

Unexpected Visits from the Office Assistant
Occasionally, when you are typing a publication or trying to perform a procedure, the Office Assistant appears, even though you have not called for it. Don't worry—the Office Assistant is just trying to be helpful. Read through the comment, and if it looks like it might be helpful, follow the onscreen instructions. If you do not want this help, you can simply close the Help window. If you do not like these hints appearing on your screen, click the Office Assistant <u>O</u>ptions button and turn off the check boxes for the Show tips features.

Summary

In this project, you created a sample newsletter by using the Catalog and answering questions posed by the Newsletter Wizard. You updated personal information and navigated the Publisher window. You were also introduced to the concept of working with frames, and you learned how to use the Publisher Office Assistant. You added and removed pages from the newsletter, and you printed and saved your publication.

There are many ways you can increase your understanding of the Publisher program. One way is to open the program and move the pointer over the buttons to see the ScreenTips and identify what types of buttons are available. You might also want to go back to the Office Assistant, click the Show button, and try using the Index and Contents tabs.

Checking Concepts and Terms

True/False

For each of the following statements, check *T* or *F* to indicate whether the statement is true or false.

__T __F **1.** You can import information from Excel or Word files into a Publisher publication. [Intro]

__T __F **2.** When you launch Publisher, the first window you see is the first Newsletter Wizard dialog box. [L1]

__T __F **3.** The default number of pages for a newsletter created by a wizard is two. [L2]

__T __F **4.** You can skip to the end of a wizard by clicking the Finish button at any time. [L2]

__T __F **5.** There are four personal information sets you can use in Publisher. [L3]

__T __F **6.** If you place the pointer over a button, a ScreenTip pops up in about a second. [L3]

__T __F **7.** A picture frame created in a wizard contains a placeholder, which you can replace with a graphic of your own. [L3]

__T __F **8.** When you move the pointer over a picture frame, it turns into a Move pointer. [L5]

__T __F **9.** To remove a page from a publication, you go to the <u>F</u>ile, Page Set<u>u</u>p option in the menu. [L6]

__T __F **10.** Clicking the Print button on the Standard toolbar prints the entire publication. [L2]

Multiple Choice

Circle the letter of the correct answer for each of the following questions.

1. You might want to use a desktop publishing program rather than a word processor if _____. [Intro]
   a. you are going to have multiple stories on the same page
   b. some stories will have to be continued on other pages
   c. several graphics will be used
   d. all of the above

2. If you choose to set up the pages of a newsletter so that they can be printed back-to-back, the Newsletter Wizard will _____. [L2]
   a. automatically alternate page numbers so that they appear on the outside edge of each page
   b. make the inside margin wider than the outside margin
   c. place page borders around each page
   d. set up the color scheme as black and white only

3. By default, Publisher automatically reminds you to save your work every _____. [L1]
   a. 15 minutes
   b. 10 minutes
   c. 5 minutes
   d. time you make a significant change

4. When you click the Hide Wizard button, _____. [L4]
   a. the wizard is turned off and must be reopened using the File, Show Wizard option in the menu
   b. the Wizard window disappears and the Hide Wizard button changes to a Show Wizard button
   c. the Office Assistant asks if you would also like to close the program
   d. none of the above

5. You use these to move between Publisher pages: [L4]
   a. the Go button on the Standard toolbar
   b. First Page, Previous Page, Next Page, and Last Page buttons
   c. page number controls
   d. page navigation controls

6. Different frame types used in Publisher include _____. [L5]
   a. text frames
   b. table frames
   c. WordArt frames
   d. all of the above

7. When you move the pointer over a handle on a selected frame, it _____. [L9]
   a. turns into a Resize pointer
   b. turns into a Move pointer
   c. changes to a four-way arrow
   d. changes to cross hairs

8. Which one of the following enables you to read help information like a book? [L9]
   a. the Office Assistant
   b. the Index tab of the Help window
   c. the Contents tab of the Help window
   d. the Answer Wizard tab of the Help window

9. To add a page to a newsletter, use the _____. [L6]
   a. Insert Page button
   b. Format, Document menu option
   c. Insert, Page menu option
   d. File, Page Setup menu option

10. If you click the Save button to save a publication for the first time, the program _____. [L8]
    a. saves the publication using the default name
    b. displays a warning box telling you to use the File, Save menu option
    c. displays the Save As dialog box
    d. none of the above; the save button is inactive until you have given the publication a filename

Screen ID

Label each element of the Publisher screen shown in Figures 1.29 and 1.30.

Figure 1.29

A. Move pointer

B. Save button

C. Help topic

D. Office Assistant

E. Text frame

F. ScreenTip

G. Show button

H. Page navigation control

I. Print button

J. Selection handle

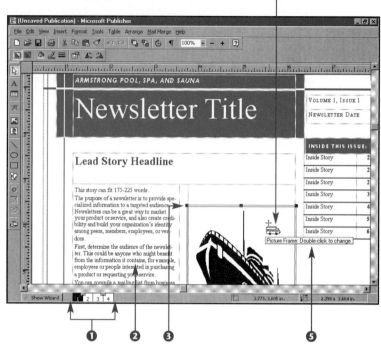

1._____   3._____   5._____

2._____   4._____

Figure 1.30

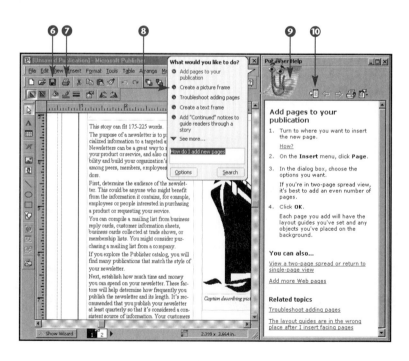

6._____   8._____   10. _____

7._____   9._____

Discussion Questions

1. If you have used Microsoft Word or another word processing program, how do you think Publisher will compare? What might be easier to do in Word? What would make more sense to do in Publisher?

2. One of the options in the Catalog is to open a blank publication instead of using a wizard or a Design Set. When might you want to use a blank publication?

3. In the Why Would I Do This? section at the beginning of this project, it was mentioned that you can import things created in Word, Excel, and several other programs. What type of objects might you want to bring into a newsletter?

4. To get help with a Publisher problem, you can activate the Office Assistant. You can also use the Index, the Contents feature, and the Answer Wizard. Why do you think there are so many different types of help available? Which help feature do you think you are most likely to use?

5. You can turn off the automatic Save reminder if you want to. You saw how this feature works while you were working on this project. Do you think turning it off is a good idea, or do you like the idea of a regular reminder, and why?

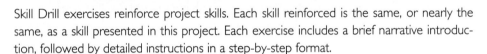

Skill Drill

Skill Drill exercises reinforce project skills. Each skill reinforced is the same, or nearly the same, as a skill presented in this project. Each exercise includes a brief narrative introduction, followed by detailed instructions in a step-by-step format.

Your new marketing manager at Armstrong Pool, Spa, and Sauna Company has suggested that a follow-up thank you card should be sent to each customer who buys a pool, spa, or sauna from your store. In this section, you create a greeting card using the Catalog and the Greeting Card Wizard. You work with the frames in the card, then you explore navigating the card and getting help. Finally, you print and save your publication.

1. Using the Catalog and Wizard to Create a Greeting Card

In this exercise, you use the Catalog to choose the Greeting Card template and run the Greeting Card wizard to set up the card.

To use the Catalog and wizard to create a greeting card:

1. Click the Start button, select Programs from the Start menu, and choose Microsoft Publisher.

2. With the Publications by Wizard tab of the Catalog selected, select the Greeting Cards option in the Wizards section.

3. Click the Thank You greeting card type.

4. Use the vertical scrollbar to scroll down until you can select the Crossed Lines Thank You Card option in the Thank You Cards section. This will keep your publications consistent, because you used this design for your newsletter.

5. Click the Start Wizard button.

6. Read the introductory material in the Greeting Card Wizard, then click Next to begin.

7. Select the Dark Blue color scheme, if necessary, then click Next.

8. Click the Browse button to use one of the built-in verses.

9. Choose Thanks for your business from the Suggested Verse dialog box. Notice that both a Front message and an Inside message are displayed.

10. Click OK, then click Next. Leave the publication open for the next exercise.

2. Updating Personal Information

As a salesperson for the Armstrong Pool, Spa, and Sauna Company, you want to customize these thank you cards to show your name.

To update Personal Information, complete the following steps:

1. Make sure Primary Business is selected in the Personal Information screen of the Greeting Card Wizard.
2. Click the Update button.
3. Type your name in the Name text box.
4. Type `Sales Representative` in the Job or position title text box.
5. Click the Update button.
6. Click the Finish button to finish the Greeting Card Wizard.

3. Navigating Your New Publication

Now you'd like to navigate around your greeting card and see what the wizard created.

To navigate your publication, complete the following steps:

1. Click the Hide Wizard button to give yourself more room to work.
2. Click the page navigation control to see to pages 2 and 3. Notice that a default logo has been placed on the page.
3. Click the page navigation control to see to page 4.
4. Click the Zoom In button until the Zoom box reads 100%.
5. Leave the publication open for the next exercise.

4. Resizing and Moving Frames

You are going to replace the logo placeholder with your company logo, but you would like to get it set up in the right position and the right size.

To resize and move frames, complete the following steps:

1. Click the page navigation control to see page 3.
2. Use the vertical scrollbar to center page 3 on the screen.
3. Move the pointer over the logo until it turns into a Move button.
4. Click and drag the logo to the left until it is centered on the page.
5. Move the pointer to the selection handle in the upper-left corner of the logo. When the pointer changes to a Resize pointer, click and drag the image up and to the left. Increase the height by about $\frac{1}{4}$".
6. Repeat step 5, but choose the selection handle in the upper-right corner of the logo. Your page should look like Figure 1.31.
7. Leave the publication open for the next lesson.

5. Using the Office Assistant

A greeting card needs to be printed on both sides of the sheet of paper so that it can be folded into the proper format. There is help available to show you how to do this.

To use the Office Assistant, complete the following steps:

1. Click on the Office Assistant, or select Help, Microsoft Publisher Help from the menu. If you have turned off the Office Assistant, you will need to select Help, Show the Office Assistant.
2. Type `How do I print two-sided pages`. Click Search.
3. Read the instructions on printing two-sided pages, then close Help.
4. Leave the publication open for the next lesson.

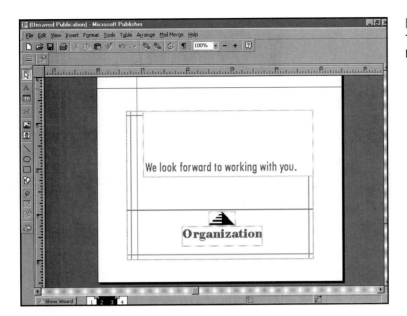

Figure 1.31
The logo placeholder has been moved and resized.

6. Saving and Printing Your Publication

In this exercise, you save the greeting card you have been working on and then send it to the printer.

To save and print your publication, complete the following steps:

1. Click the Save button on the Standard toolbar, or select File, Save from the menu.

2. Type **Sample Greeting Card** in the File name box.

3. Select 3 1/2 Floppy (A:) from the Save in box.

4. Click the Save button at the bottom-right corner of the Save As dialog box.

5. Click the Print button to print your publication on one page.

6. Fold the page in quarters and notice that the card is set up properly, with the your return address and an area for a mailing label and a stamp on the back. All you need to do is modify the text, add your logo, and add the mailing labels.

7. Close the publication, and close Publisher.

Challenge

Challenge exercises expand on or are somewhat related to skills presented in the lessons. Each exercise provides a brief narrative introduction, followed by instructions in a numbered step format that are not as detailed as those in the Skill Drill section.

In the following exercises, you create a calendar that matches the design of the newsletter and greeting card you created earlier in this project. You add a page to the calendar and update the date of the page. You also use special Publisher tools and search for online help.

1. Choosing the Calendar Design from the Design Set

You have created a consistent design for two of the company publications. Now you want to set up a calendar that matches the look of the other publications.

1. Launch Publisher and select the Publications by Design tab in the Catalog.

2. Select the Crossed Lines design set and choose the Crossed Lines Calendar.

3. Start the wizard. Choose the same color combination (Dark Blue) that you used for the other publications in this project.

4. Set the calendar up in landscape mode, and have the calendar pages display by month.

5. Change the dates so that the calendars begin with July 2000 and end with September 2000.

6. Do not include a schedule of events, and use the Primary Business information set.

7. Finish the publication, and save it as **Sample Calendar**. Leave the publication open for the next exercise.

2. Adding Calendar Pages

If you decide you want to add more months to your calendar, reactivate the Calendar Wizard. When you add months to a calendar, it does not affect information on the calendar pages that already exist.

1. If you hid the wizard after the first exercise to look at your calendar, click the Show Wizard button.

2. In the top pane of the Calendar Wizard, select the Date option.

3. Click the Change Dates option button.

4. Choose to have your calendar end with December 2000.

5. Your calendar should now have six pages.

6. Take a look at the new pages to make sure the appropriate months were added. Leave the publication open for the next exercise.

[?] 3. Getting Help Online

The Office Assistant is not the only way to get help in Publisher. An online help feature is also included with the program. You must have a connection to the Internet and a Web browser, such as Netscape or Internet Explorer, installed for the online help to work.

1. Select Help, Microsoft Publisher Web Site from the menu.

2. Look at the Welcome screen and see what kind of information is available.

3. Click the Downloads button and see what kinds of clip art, templates, and other add-ons are available for Publisher.

4. Click the Assistance button to see what kind of help and additional resources are available.

5. Click the Microsoft Technical Support for Publisher option.

6. Go to the frequently asked questions section and see what kind of topics people are contacting Microsoft about.

7. Close your browser when you are finished browsing this Web site.

4. Turning Off Automatic Save Prompts

Some people do not like the automatic save reminders popping up on their screens. You can easily turn these off. If you are using a lab machine, you might want to turn the feature off, but reverse the process and turn it back on before you leave. Ask the lab administrator how you should handle this.

1. Select Tools, Options from the menu.

2. Look through the features you can control on the four Options dialog box tabs.

3. When you are finished, select the User Assistance tab.

4. Turn off the check box for Remind to save publication.

5. Click OK. The reminders will no longer appear.

6. If you are in a lab, go back to the User Assistance tab and turn the Remind to save publication check box back on.

5. Using Floating Toolbars

By default, all Publisher toolbars are connected (**docked toolbars**) to one of the edges of the Publisher window. You can move them away from the edges, where they become free-standing windows known as **floating toolbars.** Use the available help to find out how to detach docked toolbars and how to resize floating toolbars. Move the Objects toolbar away from the edge, and resize it so that it contains three rows of buttons.

If you are working in a lab or if you do not like the way the toolbar looks, move it back into a docked position. If you have completed this lesson, close the calendar and close Publisher. If not, leave the publication open for the first exercise in the Discovery Zone.

Discovery Zone

Discovery Zone exercises help you gain advanced knowledge of project topics and/or application of skills. These exercises focus on enhancing your problem-solving skills. Numbered steps are not provided, but you are given hints, reminders, screen shots, and/or references to help you reach your goal for each exercise.

1. Changing the Wizard Layout Options After the Publication Has Been Created

When you finish creating a publication using a wizard, you may find that you are not satisfied the design you have chosen. There is a way to change the options that you selected while running the wizard.

Goal: Change several of the options you chose while running the Calendar Wizard.

The new calendar should do the following:

- Use the Floating Oval design.
- Contain a Schedule of Events.
- Display in Portrait mode.
- Use the Red color scheme.

Hint: This exercise can all be done using the Wizard window.

Name the revised calendar `Sample Calendar 2`. Your calendar should look like Figure 1.32. Print the first month of the calendar.

Figure 1.32
Several of the Design options have been changed.

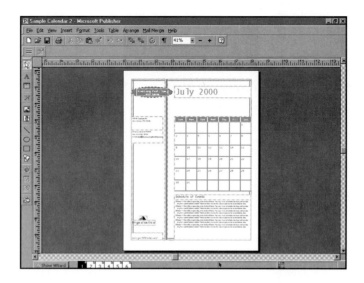

2. Creating a Newsletter from a Blank Publication

Some people have very specific ideas about what should go into a newsletter. For example, most people agree that a **masthead,** which usually contains a title, background, and volume number, is a necessary part of the first page of a newsletter. They will often find that the newsletters created by the Publisher Newsletter Wizard are too "busy" and hard to use. You can start with a blank publication, add only the elements you want, and place them exactly where you want them on the page. You will be working with a few of these elements in later projects.

Goal: Create a one-page order form from a blank publication.

For this exercise, you should do the following:

- Select Full Page from the Blank Publication tab.
- Find the Design Gallery button or the Design Gallery Object menu option.
- Add a Crossed Lines Masthead and move it to the top of the page.
- Add the Reply Form called Order Form (Square) and resize it until it is about $6\frac{1}{2}$" on each side.
- Name the order form `Sample Order Form,` which should look like Figure 1.33. Print the first month of the calendar, then close the publication and close Publisher.

Figure 1.33
An order form and a masthead have been added to a blank publication.

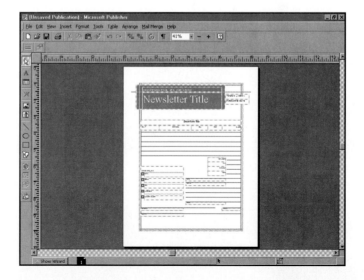

Project 2

Adding Graphics

Objectives

In this project, you learn how to

➤ **Open an Existing Publication**

➤ **Insert a Clip Art Image**

➤ **Resize and Move Frames**

➤ **Insert a Graphic from a File**

➤ **Crop Pictures**

➤ **Create a Heading Using WordArt**

➤ **Modify a WordArt Graphic**

➤ **Use Drawing Tools**

➤ **Layer Objects**

Key terms introduced in this project include

- background
- clip art
- crop
- drawing tools
- layer
- WordArt

Why Would I Do This?

Pictures and graphics draw the readers' attention and increase the overall appeal of any publication. We often look at pictures first; they become the hook that draws us into reading a story or article. How many times has a picture caught your eye and made you want to read the corresponding story? Publisher enables you to add images to your publication in creative ways that increase the visual appeal of the finished product.

Publisher has many graphic tools you can use to illustrate your publications. This includes a wide assortment of *clip art,* which is a collection of photographs or drawings and other such graphics that can be "clipped" from the collection and inserted into your publication. *Drawing tools* can be used to create your own drawings using lines, circles, rectangles, and other shapes. *WordArt* is a program that enables you to transform text into fancy letters that can be manipulated like a graphic object. You can also add pictures of your own to any publication. This is particularly helpful when you want to include images that are specific to your business, such as pictures of employees, events, customers, products, or company locations.

There are several techniques for working with the graphics in your document. You can *layer* images on top of each other and control which image is on the top or bottom of a stack of graphic shapes. You can place images into the *background* so that they appear on every page of a multiple-page document. You can also change the size, shape, or color of an image.

In this lesson, you open an existing file and add the finishing touches by adding clip art, WordArt, and pictures. You work with various drawing tools and learn some of the techniques that are available in Publisher for working with graphic objects.

Visual Summary

When you have completed this lesson, you will have created a flyer for a summer picnic for the Armstrong Company. In it you add clip art, a picture, and WordArt. You also learn how to work with drawing tools and how to layer graphics. Figure 2.1 shows what you will have created at the end of this project.

Figure 2.1
A flyer announces the Armstrong Company Picnic.

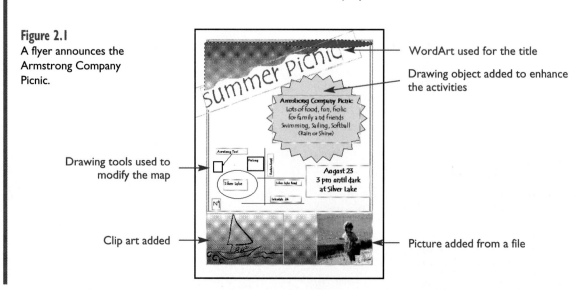

WordArt used for the title

Drawing object added to enhance the activities

Drawing tools used to modify the map

Clip art added

Picture added from a file

Lesson 1: Opening an Existing Publication

When you create a new publication, you can start with an existing publication and modify it to suit your needs. You will also find that you might begin a publication one day and finish it later. You may not have all of the information you need to complete the work, you may be waiting for feedback from others, or you may just run out of time. For various reasons, you need to know how to find and open existing files.

In this lesson, you open a flyer that has already been started. You locate the file on the CD-ROM that came with your book and save it to a new location with a new name.

To Open an Existing Publication

❶ Launch Publisher and click the Existing files button at the bottom of the Catalog dialog box.

The Open Publication dialog box displays just like any other Open dialog box in a Microsoft application. You change the Look in box to the location containing your file, then select the file and click the Open button.

❷ Place the CD-ROM that came with your book in the CD-drive. Click the down arrow at the end of the Look in box and select the CD-drive for your computer.

The CD-drive is generally identified by the letter D or E, depending on the configuration for your computer. A list of the folders contained on the CD is displayed on the screen.

❸ Double-click the Student folder; then double-click the Project02 folder.

The files for this project are listed as shown in Figure 2.2.

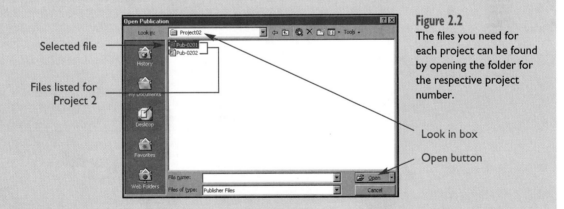

Selected file

Files listed for Project 2

Figure 2.2
The files you need for each project can be found by opening the folder for the respective project number.

Look in box

Open button

 Location of Files
The files that you use for this book might be located on a network drive or on your hard drive. If you need assistance locating the files, consult with your lab administrator or instructor.

❹ Select the Pub-0201 file and click the Open button.

The file opens showing the flyer for a summer picnic (see Figure 2.3). This flyer uses the waves design and the aqua color scheme to convey the idea of a picnic at a lake.

continues ▶

To Open an Existing Publication   (continued)

Figure 2.3
The text for the flyer for
the company picnic has
already been added.

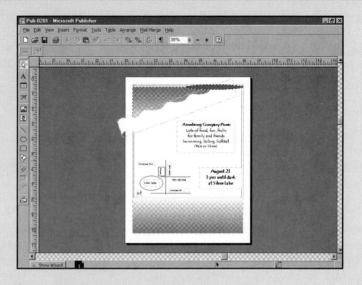

5 **Choose File, Save As from the menu.**
The Save As dialog box opens.

6 **The Save in box displays the My Documents folder located on the
hard drive of your computer.**
You should plan to save the files for this book on the hard drive or some
other high-capacity drive because most files that you create with Publisher
will exceed the capacity of a floppy disk.

 Saving Files
Some of the files created in this book could be saved to a disk, but in
general, the graphics used in Publisher result in files that are larger than
the capacity of a 1.44-MB disk. Therefore, you need access to a storage
location on the hard drive, network, or a high-capacity drive. You may
want to create your own folder on the hard drive or network to store
your files. To do this, click the Create New Folder button in the Save
As dialog box and type your name as the new name for the folder.
Double-click the folder to open it and save your files in this folder.

7 **Change the name in the File name box to Company Picnic.**
The filename is changed to identify its purpose (see Figure 2.4).

Figure 2.4
The file will be saved with
a new name.

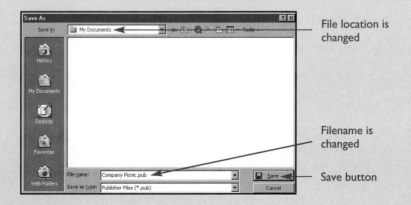

8 **Click the Save button.**
The file is renamed and saved. The name of the new file shows in the title bar, and the Catalog wizard closes. Leave the file open for the next lesson.

 File Extensions
The file extension for Publisher is .pub. The extensions may be turned off on your machine, which means that you will not see the .pub extension displayed. This is nothing to be concerned about. To turn file extensions on or off, you need to open Windows Explorer and then choose View, Folder Options from the menu. Click the View tab, and look for the Hide file extensions for known file types option. A check mark indicates this option is selected and that the extensions will be hidden.

Lesson 2: Inserting a Clip Art Image

Publisher comes with a large collection of drawings, images, and photographs that can be "clipped" and added to your document. These images are found in the Clip Gallery. Approximately 10% of the images are loaded to the hard drive when Publisher is installed. The rest are available on the installation disc and can be accessed by inserting the disc when you want to use clip art. You can also use clip art from other programs or software that you own.

In this example, you add a clip art image to the bottom of the company picnic flyer. The summer picnic is being held at a nearby lake, so you are going to add some images to invoke the idea of lake and beach activities. You first change the zoom so that you can better see the part of the flyer that you need to work with.

To Insert a Clip Art Image

1 **Click the arrow next to the Zoom box and select 50% from the drop-down list.**
The flyer increases in size and the middle of the page is onscreen. You are going to add a clip art image to the bottom of the screen, so you need to scroll down to see that portion of the flyer.

2 **Use the vertical scrollbar on the right side of the window to scroll down until you see the bottom of the flyer.**

3 **Click the Clip Gallery Tool button on the Objects toolbar at the left of the screen.**
The mouse pointer changes to a cross hair shape.

4 **Move the mouse pointer to the aqua area on the bottom-left side of the flyer. Click and drag diagonally to draw a box that is approximately 2" on each side as shown in Figure 2.5.**
Use the horizontal and vertical rulers to help you size the box.

continues ▶

To Insert a Clip Art Image (continued)

Figure 2.5
First, you draw a frame that is the approximate size you want for the clip art image.

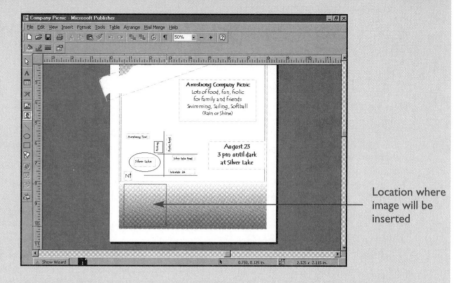

Location where image will be inserted

5 **Release the mouse button.**

When you release the mouse button, the Insert Clip Art window opens. Pictures are sorted into categories. You click a category button to see the images that are available. If you are uncertain where to look, you can type keywords in the Search for clips box and search for images related to the topic you want.

6 **Use the scrollbar on the right side of the dialog box to scroll down the list of categories and click the Sports & Leisure category to select it.**

Images related to sports and leisure activities are displayed.

7 **Click the boating image to select it.**

A pop-up bar displays as shown in Figure 2.6. The top button on this bar inserts the image.

Figure 2.6
When the image you want is selected, use the pop-up menu to insert it.

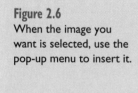

Selected image

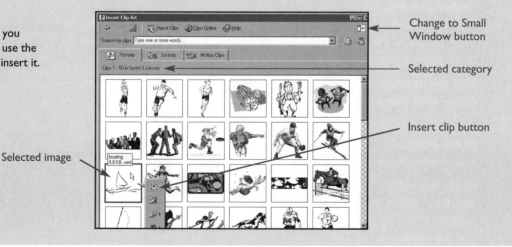

Change to Small Window button

Selected category

Insert clip button

⑧ Click the Insert clip button on the pop-up toolbar.

The clip art image is inserted, but the Insert Clip Art window remains open. You can shrink the window by clicking the Change to Small Window button on the upper-right side of the window. This allows you to see the image that has been inserted in the publication. Then, if you want to change the image, you can expand the window and select a different one.

⑨ Click the Change to Small Window button.

The Insert Clip Art window shrinks to a panel on the left side of your screen and you can now see how the image you selected looks in your flyer (see Figure 2.7).

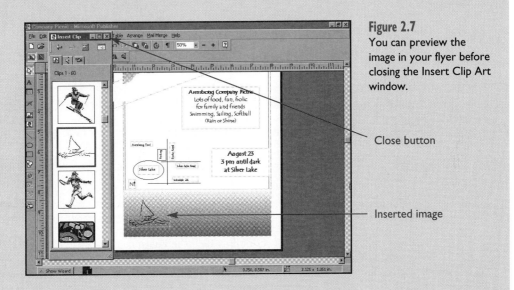

Figure 2.7
You can preview the image in your flyer before closing the Insert Clip Art window.

Close button

Inserted image

⑩ Click the Close button to close the Insert Clip Art window.

⑪ Click the Save button to save your work.

Leave the file open for the next lesson.

 Insert Clip Art Window Size

The Insert Clip Art window opens in the same configuration as when it was last used. Therefore, if you wanted to insert another image, the Insert Clip Art window would now open as a panel on the left side of your window. You can expand the window by clicking the Change to Full Window button located in the upper-right corner of the window.

Location of Clip Art

The standard installation of Microsoft Office 2000 leaves most of the available clip art images on the installation disc. If you are working in a lab setting, the clip art images may be installed on a network for easy access. When working with clip art, it is a good idea to have the Office 2000 installation disc available. If you select an image that is not installed, you will get a message telling you the file is located on a disc, as well as the name of the disc. Insert the appropriate disc and click the Retry button.

Lesson 3: Resizing and Moving Frames

A clip art image that you insert in a publication might be the wrong size or in the wrong location. It is easy to resize or move a clip art image. The techniques for moving an object in Publisher are the same, regardless of the type of object. When an object is selected, small black selection handles appear around the edge of its frame. These selection handles are used to resize an image. When an image is selected, the mouse pointer takes on one of two shapes. When the mouse pointer is placed on the image, the pointer changes to the shape of a truck with the word *MOVE* on the side. This icon indicates that you can move the image. If you place the mouse pointer over one of the square selection handles, the mouse pointer icon becomes a resize icon, which is used to increase or decrease the size of the image.

In this lesson, you move and resize the clip art image so that you can insert another image in the aqua area at the bottom of the flyer.

To Resize and Move Frames

① **If necessary, click the boating image to select it.**
You can tell whether an object is selected because the selection handles are displayed around the parameter of the frame.

② **Move the mouse pointer over the selection handle in the lower-left corner as shown in Figure 2.8.**
The mouse pointer changes to a resize icon. The direction of the arrows indicates the direction in which the image can be resized.

Figure 2.8
The mouse pointer changes to a resize icon when placed over a selection handle.

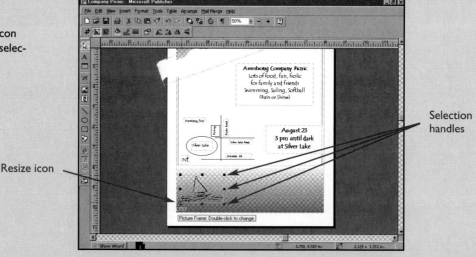

Resize icon

Selection handles

③ **Click and drag the lower-left selection handle down and to the left. Release the mouse button, and then click and drag the upper-right selection handle up and to the right to increase the size of the frame as shown in Figure 2.9.**
If necessary, use another corner selection handle to resize the figure until it is approximately half the width of the aqua area at the bottom of the flyer.

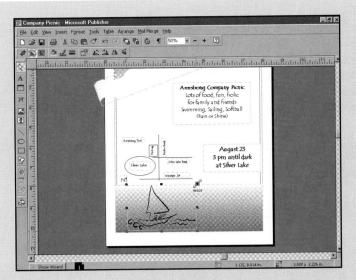

Figure 2.9
The boating image is one of two images that you insert in the bottom portion of the flyer.

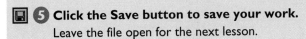 **Selection Handles**
The corner selection handles are used to resize the image proportionally. If you use one of the handles along the side of an image, the image is distorted when you click and drag. If you do not like how the image has been resized, click the Undo button and start over.

4 **Move the mouse pointer onto the image until it changes to a Move icon. Click and drag the image to the left side of the aqua area.**
Make sure the edge of the frame does not extend beyond the left or bottom edge of the aqua area. Your resized and moved boat should look like the one in Figure 2.10.

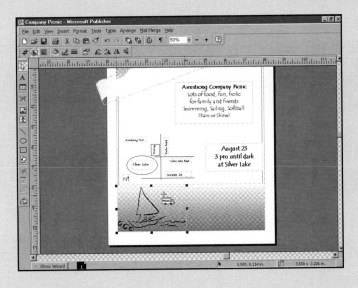

Figure 2.10
The boating image is moved to make room for another image in the bottom-right corner.

5 **Click the Save button to save your work.**
Leave the file open for the next lesson.

Selecting Objects

When working with any object in Publisher, it is important to make sure you select the intended object. For instance, if you were to click to the right of the boating image, you would select the aqua rectangle that is part of the overall design of the flyer. At first glance, you might think that you have selected the boating image because selection handles appear along the left side of the image. However, the other selection handles are located around the larger rectangle.

 Other Resizing Techniques

You can resize an object to precise measurements by choosing Format, Size and Position from the menu. Under Size, enter the measurement for the height and width of the object; then click OK.

Lesson 4: Inserting a Graphic from a File

In addition to using the Clip Art Gallery to illustrate your publications, you may want to use pictures or other graphics that you have on file. In the case of a newsletter, pictures of employees, store locations, or events can be used to attract reader interest. Usually, people are interested in seeing pictures of themselves or others they know.

A company may have a logo that must appear on all printed material. Companies are strongly identified by their logos, and they spend a lot of marketing dollars in carefully developing and refining corporate logos. If you are using a company logo, make sure that you use it appropriately in your publication. Often, companies have rules and guidelines that must be followed when their logo is used. Such guidelines may cover the size, placement, color, or other aspects of the image.

A number of file protocols for images are commonly used and recognized by computers. Publisher recognizes many image files. The file formats are identified by their extensions. Table 2.1 shows some of the image formats used in Publisher. You can find a complete list in Microsoft Publisher Help.

Table 2.1   Partial Listing of Image Formats Recognized by Microsoft Publisher

Picture File Format	Extension
Windows Bitmap	.bmp
CorelDRAW!	.cdr
Graphics Interchange Format	.gif
Joint Photographics Expert Group	.jpeg or .jpg
PC Paintbrush	.pcx
Macintosh Picture	.pict
TIFF, Tagged Image File Format	.tif
Windows Metafile	.wmf
WordPerfect Graphics	.wpg

In this example, you add a picture of a child on the beach to illustrate family and beach activities. This picture was taken at the beach and scanned to create a computer image.

To Insert a Graphic from a File

1 **Click the Picture Frame Tool on the Objects toolbar.**
The mouse pointer changes to cross hairs.

2 **Move the mouse pointer to the lower-right corner of the flyer and click and drag a box approximately 1½" square.**
The size of the frame is not critical at this point because you will crop and move it later.

3 **From the menu, choose Insert, Picture, From File.**
The Insert Picture dialog box opens. You use this dialog box to find the location of the file you want to insert (see Figure 2.11).

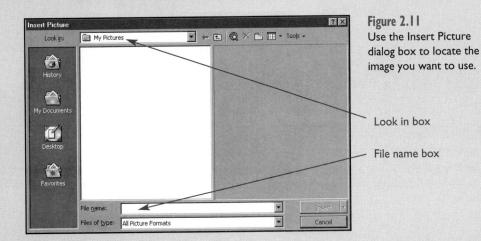

Figure 2.11
Use the Insert Picture dialog box to locate the image you want to use.

Look in box

File name box

4 **Change the Look in box to the folder that contains the files for this project.**
A list of images for this project is displayed.

5 **Click the file named Beach.**
A preview of the picture is displayed on the right side of the dialog box.

6 **Click the Insert button.**
The image is inserted in the picture frame, and the dialog box closes (see Figure 2.12). Notice that the frame adjusted to fit the dimensions of the picture.

7 **Change the zoom to 100% to view the image better.**

8 **Click the Save button to save your work.**
Next, you crop the figure to hide some of the sky and sand; then you resize and move the picture. Leave the file open for the next lesson.

continues ▶

To Insert a Graphic from a File   (continued)

Figure 2.12
The image you selected is inserted in the picture frame.

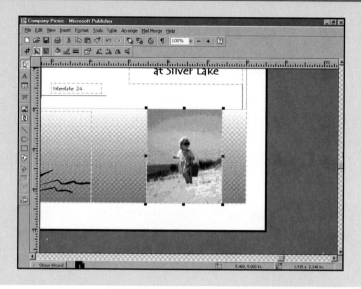

 Another Way to Insert Pictures
Once you draw a picture frame, you can right-click on the empty frame and choose Change Picture, Picture, From File from the shortcut menu.

Lesson 5: Cropping Pictures

Sometimes, pictures you use contain extraneous parts that you do not want to include. You can **crop** the picture using the cropping tool to hide parts of the picture that you do not want to use. This is useful to reduce the overall size of a picture, or simply to focus on the part of the picture that is related to the context of your publication.

In this lesson, you crop the beach picture so that there is less sky and sand.

To Crop Pictures

1 **With the beach image selected, click the Crop Picture button on the Formatting toolbar.**
The Crop Picture button displays only when a picture is selected. At first, it seems as though nothing has changed, but when you place the mouse pointer on one of the selection handles, the mouse pointer changes to a cropping icon that looks like two pairs of scissors.

2 **Position the mouse pointer over the bottom-middle selection handle as shown in Figure 2.13.**
The mouse pointer changes to a cropping icon with the word *CROP* displayed.

3 **Click and drag up to reduce the amount of sand showing in the picture.**
As you drag, you can see a faint line indicating where the image will be cropped (see Figure 2.13).

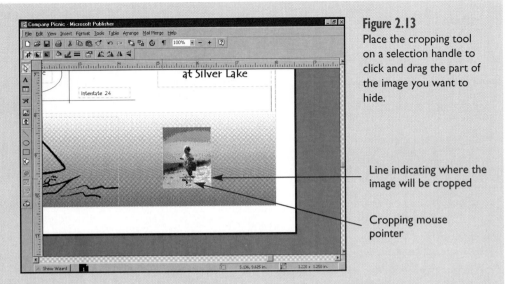

Figure 2.13
Place the cropping tool on a selection handle to click and drag the part of the image you want to hide.

Line indicating where the image will be cropped

Cropping mouse pointer

4 **Release the mouse button. Move the mouse pointer to the top-middle selection handle and click and drag down to reduce the amount of sky that is shown.**

The cropping tool remains active until you click the Crop Picture button a second time.

5 **Position the cropping tool over the middle handle on the right side of the picture and click and drag to remove about ½" of the image as shown in Figure 2.14.**

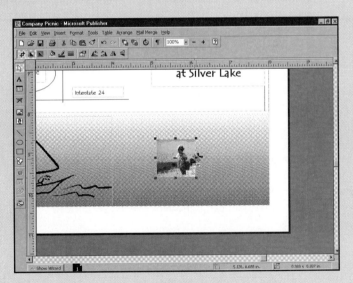

Figure 2.14
The picture is cropped on three sides.

6 **Click the Crop Picture button again to deselect the cropping tool.**

Next, you resize the image to fill the right side of the aqua area.

continues ▶

To Crop Pictures   (continued)

7 **Move the mouse pointer over one of the corner selection handles and click and drag to increase the size of the image.**
You may need to use more than one selection handle to maximize the image for the space available. The final height should be approximately the same as that of the boating image.

8 **Click and drag the image to the lower-right corner of the flyer as shown in Figure 2.15.**
Make sure the image does not go beyond the right or bottom edge of the aqua rectangle.

Figure 2.15
The image has been cropped, resized, and moved to its final location on the flyer.

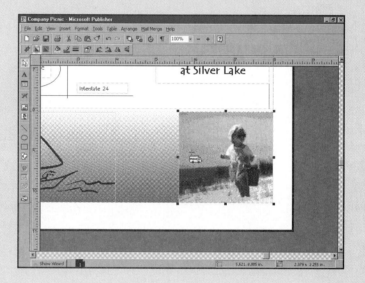

 9 **Click the Save button to save your work.**
Leave the file open for the next lesson.

ⓘ **Undoing Changes**
If you do not like the last change you made when resizing or cropping a picture, click the Undo button to undo the most recent change. You can click the Undo button repeatedly to return the image to its original condition. If you do not like the image at all and want to use another, you can right-click the image, choose Delete Object, and then start over.

Lesson 6: Creating a Heading Using WordArt

To create a heading for your publication that makes an impact, you can use WordArt. WordArt is a program that turns text into fancy letters that are treated like a graphic object. You can alter the direction of the text or slant it at an angle. You can change the color, add shading, change the spacing, or rotate the text. Various special effects used with WordArt make it an ideal choice for titles or headings that you want to stand out from the body of your publication.

In this lesson, you add a heading to the flyer using WordArt; you then rotate the image so that it will fit in the angled box at the top of the flyer.

To Create a Heading Using WordArt

1 **Change the zoom to 50% and scroll to the top of the flyer.**

2 **Click the WordArt Frame Tool.**
The mouse pointer changes to cross hairs.

3 **Click and drag to create a box that is approximately 1" high by 5" long as shown in Figure 2.16.**
When you release the mouse, a text box displays with the words *Your Text Here*. A small dialog box also opens, which is actually where you type the text for your heading. Notice that the toolbar at the top has also changed. This is the WordArt toolbar.

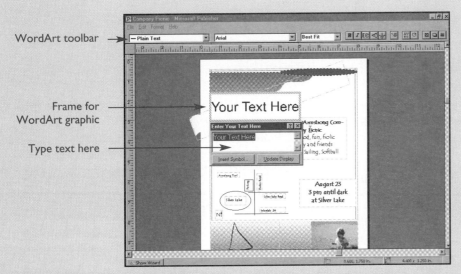

WordArt toolbar ⟶

Frame for
WordArt graphic ⟶

Type text here ⟶

Figure 2.16
The first step in adding a WordArt image is to draw a frame.

4 **Type** `Summer Picnic`. **Make sure you capitalize the "S" in Summer and the "P" in Picnic.**
The insertion point is automatically placed in the dialog box. As you type, the highlighted words in the dialog box are replaced. The new title is inserted in the WordArt Frame only after you click the Update Display button.

5 **Click Update Display and then click the Close button to close the WordArt dialog box.**
The WordArt graphic should look like Figure 2.17.

continues ▶

To Create a Heading Using WordArt   (continued)

Figure 2.17
The words you type are converted to a graphic image when you click the Update Display button.

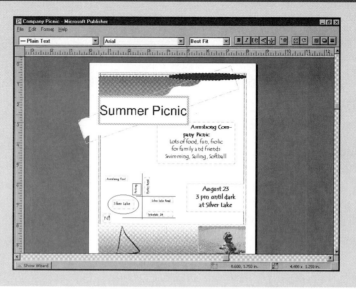

In the next section, you learn how to modify the WordArt graphic using some of the special effect tools.

To Modify a WordArt Graphic

❶ **Click the arrow next to the Font box and select Tempus Sans ITC or a similar font style.**

❷ **Choose Forma_t_, _S_hading from the menu.**
The Shading dialog box opens. Here you can select a foreground and a background color to achieve the color tone that you want for your WordArt.

❸ **Change the _F_oreground to Blue and the _B_ackground to Navy. In the _S_tyle area, select the second option in the second row (see Figure 2.18) and then click OK.**
You use the _S_tyle area to select a pattern for your WordArt. In this example, the goal is to make the text clearly blue, similar in tone to the oval at the top of the flyer, but bright enough to stand out.

Figure 2.18
The Shading dialog box is used to change the color of a WordArt graphic.

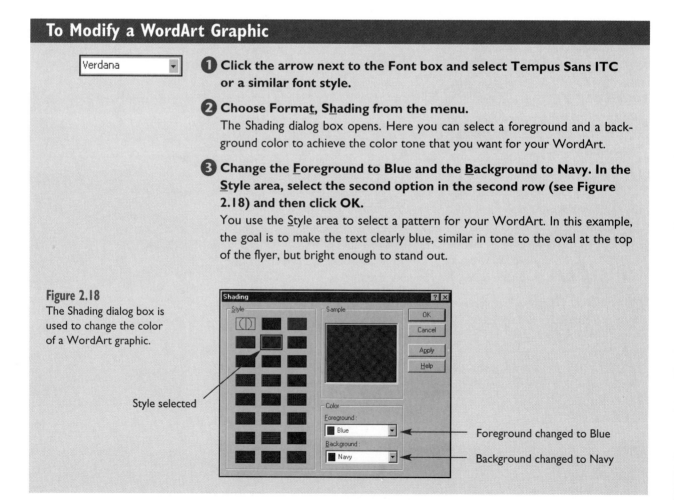

Ee **4** **With the WordArt heading still selected, click the Even Height button.**
This makes the letters all the same height and adds a playful, fun appearance to the text.

5 **Click in an open area of the flyer to close the WordArt program.**
The WordArt toolbar closes and the regular Publisher toolbars display.

6 **Click to select the WordArt frame.**
Selection handles appear around the edge of the WordArt frame, but the WordArt toolbar is no longer displayed. Now you will rotate the frame.

7 **Click the Custom Rotate button.**
The Custom Rotate dialog box opens. You can click either one of the buttons or type the angle that you want to use (see Figure 2.19).

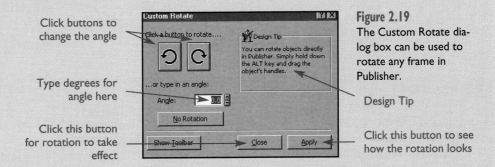

Click buttons to change the angle

Type degrees for angle here

Click this button for rotation to take effect

Figure 2.19
The Custom Rotate dialog box can be used to rotate any frame in Publisher.

Design Tip

Click this button to see how the rotation looks

X You want to make sure you select the WordArt frame and not one of the frames that it overlaps. Check the selection handles to ensure that they surround the Summer Picnic graphic.

8 **Type 20 in the Angle box and click Apply. Click the Close button to close the dialog box.**
The WordArt frame is angled at the same degree as the banner at the top of the flyer.

X If you click the Close (X) button in the corner of the dialog box, it negates the rotation. You must click the Close button for the rotation to take effect.

9 **Move the WordArt graphic so that it is in the banner area. Resize the frame as needed so that it fits the banner area as shown in Figure 2.20.**
The finished heading is placed in the banner area at the top of the flyer.

10 **Save your changes.**
Leave the flyer open for use in the next lesson.

continues ▶

To Modify a WordArt Graphic (continued)

Figure 2.20
The WordArt appears as a banner at the top of the flyer.

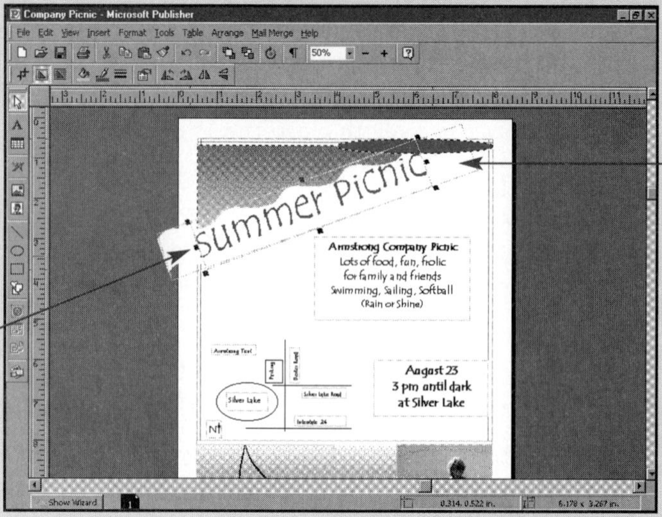

WordArt frame is at a 20-degree angle

Banner area

> ⚠ **WordArt Tools**
> Many of the WordArt tools are toggle buttons—they are used to turn an effect on or off. Unfortunately, there are no ScreenTips for the buttons on the WordArt toolbar, so it is often hard to tell what a particular button might do. However, you can simply click on a button, see the results and then click the button again the remove the effect.

> ⓘ **Rotating WordArt Text**
> Rotating a WordArt frame is different from rotating WordArt Text. To change the orientation of the text within a frame, you use the Special Effects tool in the WordArt program. This changes the orientation of the text, which is not the same as the angle of the frame in which the text is displayed.

Lesson 7: Using Drawing Tools

The Objects toolbar includes basic drawing tools—a line, oval, and rectangle—as well as drawing shapes. These tools can help you draw maps, create directional arrows, or add shapes to a publication.

In this lesson, you finish the map to the picnic by adding a rectangle to represent a tent and adding an arrow pointing to the tent.

To Use Drawing Tools

 1 **Change the zoom to 75%, and scroll down until the map on the flyer is centered on the screen.**
You will add a small rectangle to the map to represent a tent.

 2 **Click the Rectangle Tool button. Click and drag a small rectangle as shown in Figure 2.21.**

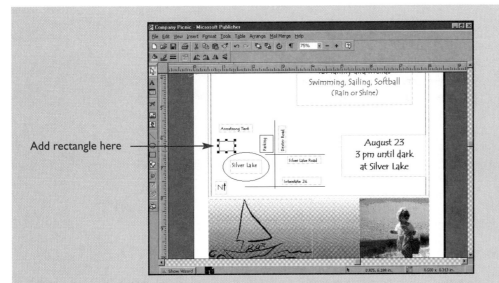

Figure 2.21
A map has been included on the flyer using basic drawing tools.

Add rectangle here →

❸ Click the Line Tool and draw a line at an angle from the Armstrong Tent label to the new rectangle you just added.

Notice that when the line is selected, additional formatting tools appear. These can be used to change the color or thickness of the line or to add an arrowhead to one or both ends of the line (see Figure 2.22).

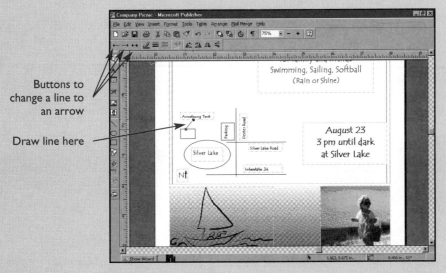

Figure 2.22
A line is drawn from the label to the tent.

Buttons to change a line to an arrow

Draw line here

❹ Click the Add/Remove Left Arrow button.

An arrowhead is added to the end of the line that points to the tent.

❺ Save your changes.

Leave the file open for the next lesson.

Red and Blue Lines
If you happen to click on other drawing objects that are part of this map, you may see red or blue lines surrounding objects or parts of the map. These indicate a grouped relationship between the objects. You will learn how to work with grouped objects in Project 4, "Working with Frames."

 Other Drawing Tools
More extensive drawing tools are available by selecting Insert, Picture, New Drawing from the menu. This opens the Microsoft Draw program and places a drawing frame on your page. It also opens the AutoShapes toolbar, which gives you access to a much wider variety of drawing tools. When you finish, click anywhere else on the publication to exit Microsoft Draw.

Lesson 8: Layering Objects

In addition to lines, ovals, and rectangles, the Objects toolbar has a collection of custom shapes. You can use these shapes to further illustrate or enhance a drawing or to create a shape behind a text box. In Publisher, you can select where an object will be placed in a stack of objects. This is known as *layering*. An object might be on the bottom, middle, or top of a stack of objects. Usually, you can see how objects are layered by the way they overlap. You can also make the object on top transparent so that the object underneath shows through. This is useful when placing a text frame on top of another colored object. You can also place graphics or text in the background of a publication. This is useful for multiple-page publications such as a newsletter, in which you might want a company name, logo, or page numbers to appear on every page.

In this lesson, you add a custom shape on top of the activities information. You then change the color of the shape and send it to the back. This allows the text to appear on top of the shape and adds the finishing touch to our flyer.

To Layer Objects

❶ Scroll up until the Armstrong Company Picnic text box is visible and then change the zoom to 50%.
Next you add a sunlike shape over this text box.

❷ Click the Custom Shapes button on the Objects toolbar.
A palette showing various shapes is displayed as shown in Figure 2.23.

Figure 2.23
A variety of custom shapes are available.

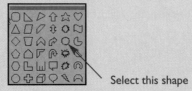
Select this shape

❸ Click the fifth shape in the third row.
The mouse pointer changes to cross hairs and the palette closes.

4 **Starting above and to the left of the text box, click and drag down and to the right to open the sun shape.**

Do not be concerned if the shape does not cover the text box. You can re-size and move it as needed.

5 **Resize and move the sun shape as shown in Figure 2.24 so that it covers the text area.**

The same techniques that you used to change the size and shape of other objects are used here.

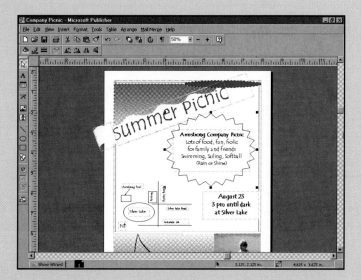

Figure 2.24
A sun shape has been added to the flyer.

6 **Click the Fill Color button and select More Colors (see Figure 2.25).**

Depending on the colors last used, a yellow color may already be displayed on the Fill Color toolbar. If yellow is showing, you can click it to change the sun shape to yellow and continue with step 8.

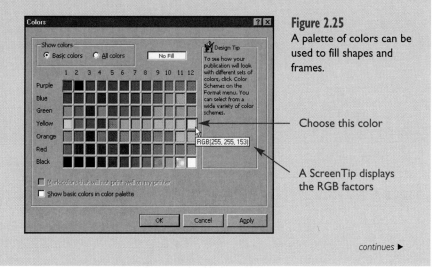

Figure 2.25
A palette of colors can be used to fill shapes and frames.

Choose this color

A ScreenTip displays the RGB factors

continues ▶

To Layer Objects   (continued)

 What is an RGB Factor?
RGB stands for red, blue, green. This is the color model that is used by Publisher to display colors on your computer screen. Each number represents the intensity or amount of these three colors that are used to create the color you see. You learn more about color models and commercial printing of colors in later projects.

7 **Select the yellow at the right-end of the yellow row and click Apply. Click OK to close the Colors dialog box.**
The sun shape changes to yellow. Of course, now you cannot read the list of fun activities available at the picnic.

 If you mistakenly click the More Color Schemes button in the Fill Color toolbar, the Color Scheme dialog box will open. This is used to change the overall colors on the flyer. This is not what you want to do. Simply click the Close button on the dialog box, and try again.

8 **Click the Send to Back button. Click outside of the sun shape to de-select it.**
The shape is placed in back of the text box, and you can now read the list of activities.

9 **Change the zoom to Whole Page so that you can see how the finished product looks.**
Your flyer should look like the one in Figure 2.26

Figure 2.26
The finished flyer for the summer picnic.

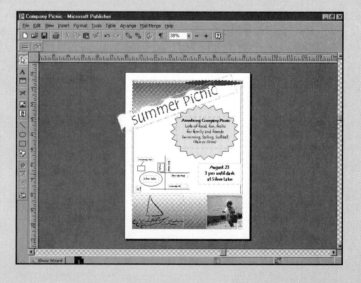

10 **Save your changes and click the Print button.**
The final changes are saved, and the document is printed.

11 **Choose File, Close to close the file.**
If you are finished working, click the Close button to close Publisher; otherwise, continue on to the exercises.

Summary

In this project, you worked with several graphic tools to help illustrate a flyer for a company picnic. You learned how to insert, move, and resize clip art. You learned how to insert a picture from a file and how to crop the picture to hide unwanted parts. You also learned how to create a WordArt graphic; change the font, color, and height of the text; and then rotate the frame. You worked with drawing tools to add the finishing touches to a map. Finally, you added a custom shape, changed the fill color, and moved it to the bottom of a layer of objects.

Many more effects can be achieved with the graphic tools that are provided. The Help program provides brief tutorials on layering and using the background. It has extensive information about using WordArt effects and the Microsoft Draw program. Explore any or all of these topics in Help to learn more about the concepts covered in this project.

Checking Concepts and Terms

True/False

For each of the following statements, check *T* or *F* to indicate whether the statement is true or false.

__T __F **1.** WordArt is a program that turns text into fancy letters. [L6]

__T __F **2.** To open an existing publication, you have to first close the Publisher Catalog. [L1]

__T __F **3.** When you crop a picture, you hide part of the image. [L5]

__T __F **4.** Ninety percent of the clip art images are loaded to your computer when you install Publisher. [L2]

__T __F **5.** The drawing tools available in Publisher are limited to the ones shown on the Objects toolbar. [L7]

__T __F **6.** The technique for resizing a frame is the same regardless of the type of frame. [L3]

__T __F **7.** To move an object, you click and drag on the edge of the object. [L3]

__T __F **8.** To rotate the frame of a WordArt graphic, you must be in the WordArt program. [L6]

__T __F **9.** Objects can be placed in the background when you want them to appear on every page of a publication. [L8]

__T __F **10.** Picture files that you insert into a Publisher document must be in the .jpg, .bmp, or .pcx format. [L4]

Multiple Choice

Circle the letter of the correct answer for each of the following questions.

1. To insert a clip art image, you click the Clip Gallery Tool and _____. [L2]

a. select a category

b. choose Open ClipArt

c. draw a picture frame

d. none of the above

2. If you are uncertain which clip art category to use, the best solution is to _____. [L2]

a. check each category until you find one you like

b. type a keyword in the Search for clips box

c. look at Clips Online first

d. ask someone who is more familiar with Publisher

3. In Publisher, which of the following are not supported picture file formats? [L4]

   a. .jpg, .bmp, .pcx

   b. .gif, .tif, .pict

   c. .cdr, .wmf, .wpg

   d. all of the above are supported

4. Because of the size of Publisher files, it is best to save the files to what kind of storage device? [L1]

   a. a floppy disk so that you can take the file with you

   b. a high-capacity disk

   c. the hard drive on your computer

   d. b or c

5. To use drawing tools that are not on the Objects toolbar, choose _____. [L7]

   a. View, Microsoft Draw

   b. Tools, Microsoft Draw

   c. Insert, Picture, New Drawing

   d. the Other Tools button

6. You can modify WordArt in all of the follow ways except _____. [L6]

   a. changing the text color

   b. making the letters all the same height

   c. underlining it

   d. making it bold

7. How do you resize an image so that it maintains the same proportions? [L3]

   a. Click and drag one of the corner selection handles.

   b. Hold down (Alt) and click and drag one of the selection handles.

   c. Click and drag one of the side selection handles.

   d. Hold down (◆Shift) and click and drag any one of the selection handles.

8. To have a colored shape appear behind a text box, _____. [L8]

   a. click the Send to Back button

   b. choose Format, Background

   c. select the text box and click Bring Forward

   d. choose Placement, Back

9. To add an arrow to a drawing, you draw a line and then _____. [L7]

   a. click the Arrow button

   b. choose Format, Line, Arrow

   c. choose Insert, Arrow

   d. none of the above

10. To change the color of a WordArt graphic, you _____. [L6]

    a. click the Text Color button

    b. choose Format, Shading

    c. choose Format, Text

    d. click the Fill Color button

Screen ID

Label each element of the Access screen shown in Figure 2.27.

Figure 2.27

A. Crop Picture button

B. Fill Color button

C. WordArt graphic

D. Used to change the picture size

E. Custom shape

F. Rectangle tool

G. Line Tool

H. Clip Gallery Tool

I. Picture Frame Tool

J. WordArt Frame Tool

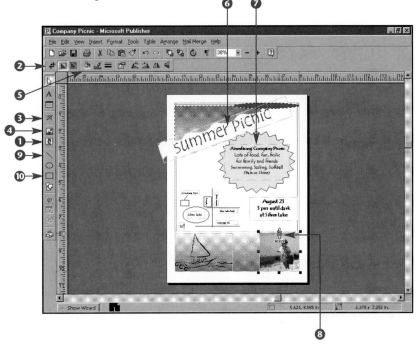

1._____   5._____   9._____

2._____   6._____   10. _____

3._____   7._____

4._____   8._____

Discussion Questions

1. What do you see as the major advantages and disadvantages of using clip art images versus file pictures? When is it appropriate to use each?

2. In what situations would you use WordArt rather than using the text formatting tools that you may be familiar with from a word processing program?

3. Some of the graphic tools that you have seen in this project are also available in word processing programs. What techniques have you learned that are different from things you know how to do with a word processor?

4. The designs available in the wizard are a collection of preformatted graphics. From what you know of Publisher and other Microsoft products, how would you change an element in a design that you wanted to modify?

5. What is the value of adding graphics to a publication? Can there be too many graphic elements? How would you determine whether the number of graphics were excessive?

Skill Drill

Skill Drill exercises reinforce project skills. Each skill reinforced is the same, or nearly the same, as a skill presented in this project. Each exercise includes a brief narrative introduction, followed by detailed instructions in a step-by-step format.

In the Skill Drill exercises, you create publications for a not-for-profit organization. Whether a charity or educational, hospital, or government organization, nonprofit organizations have many of the same needs as for-profit businesses. The examples in this book use a community service organization called Helping Hands. In the following exercises, you create a flyer to announce a walkathon to raise funds for a Helping Hands project.

1. Adding WordArt

The flyer for the annual walkathon held by Helping Hands has been started. The design and color scheme have been chosen, and the text announcing the event has been entered. You will add the graphics to the flyer, starting with the WordArt. As you work through these exercises, refer to Figure 2.28 to see how the final product should look.

To add WordArt to a flyer, complete the following steps:

1. Open the Pub-0202 file from the CD-ROM and save it as `Walkathon`.

2. Click the WordArt Frame tool and draw a box on the left side of the flyer. Type `Walkathon` in the Enter Text Here dialog box. Click Update display and close the dialog box.

3. Change the font to Lucida Sans.

4. Click the Custom Rotate button and change the rotation to 90 degrees so that the text appears sideways.

5. Click in an open area on the flyer to return to the Publisher window.

6. Resize the WordArt frame to fill the vertical space to the left of the text box and above the map, as shown in Figure 2.28.

7. Click the Fill button and choose the Accent 2 (Avocado) color from the available colors.

8. Click the Custom Rotate button and change the angle to 358 degrees. Click the Close button to save the change.

9. With the WordArt selected, click the Send to Back button.

10. Save the changes and leave the publication open for the next exercise.

2. Adding a Picture

You have a picture of the park to use in the flyer. You add this to create interest in the walk, which is scheduled to take place in a nice wooded area.

To add a picture to the flyer, complete the following steps:

1. Click the Picture Frame tool and draw a frame that fills the open area underneath the text to the right of the WordArt.

2. Choose Insert, Picture, From File. Select the Park picture located on the CD-ROM and click the Insert button.

3. Resize the figure until no whitespace is visible at either side of the image.

4. Click the Send to Back button.

5. Save the changes and leave the publication open for the next exercise.

3. Adding ClipArt

Something else is needed to complete the flyer. To fill the empty whitespace on the right at the bottom of the flyer, you will add a clip art image.

To add clip art to the flyer, complete the following steps:

1. Click the Clip Gallery Tool. In the lower-right corner, draw a frame approximately 1" wide by 3" high.

2. Type footsteps in the Search for clips text box. An image of footsteps is shown.

3. Click the image and click the Insert clip button from the pop-up menu. Close the Clip Art gallery.

4. Increase the size of the image vertically by clicking on the middle selection handle at the top or bottom of the image. Adjust it horizontally as needed. (Use Figure 2.28 as a guide to see how much to enlarge the image.)

5. Right-click the image and choose Change Picture, Recolor Picture from the shortcut menu.

6. Click the down arrow next to the Color box and select the Accent 2 (Avocado) color from the Scheme colors. Click OK to apply the color and close the dialog box.

7. With the image still selected, click the Rotate button, type 25.0 in the Angle box, and click Apply to see how this looks. (If necessary, click the title bar of the dialog box and drag it out of the way so that you can see the effect of the rotation.) Adjust the rotation slightly if needed. When you are satisfied, click the Close button to save the change in rotation.

8. Enlarge the image again, if needed, until it slightly overlaps the pathway in the woods as shown in Figure 2.28.

9. Save your changes and leave the publication open for the next exercise.

4. Working with Drawing Tools

The map on the flyer needs to be completed. To see this part of the flyer, you will change the zoom before you use the drawing tools to add the rest of the items needed on the map.

To complete the map using the drawing tools, complete the following steps:

1. Change the zoom to 75% and scroll to the bottom of the flyer.

2. Click the Line tool and draw a line for N. Territorial Road as shown in Figure 2.28. (Hold down ⬆Shift while drawing the line to ensure it is straight.)

3. Click the Rectangle Tool and draw a box around the word *Park*.

4. Use the line tool to draw a short vertical line to the right of the N at the bottom of the map. This is to indicate the direction of north on the map.

5. Click the appropriate arrow button to show that north is up on the map. (If you select the wrong arrow, simply click on the other single-directional arrow button.)

6. Save the changes and leave the publication open for the last exercise.

5. Adding a Custom Shape to Your Publication

Next, you add a custom shape around the map to give it a border. In this example, you change the line color and thickness of the shape that you add.

To add a custom shape to your publication, complete the following steps:

1. Click the Custom Shapes tool to open the palette of shapes.

2. Click the first shape in the first row and click and drag the shape around the objects that are in the map. (Refer to Figure 2.28 for guidance.)

3. With the shape still selected, click the Line/Border Style button on the toolbar. Select the thickest line that displays on the drop-down menu.

4. With the shape still selected, click the Line Color button on the toolbar. Click the More Colors button and choose the fourth color in the fourth row (RGB 102, 102, 51).

5. Choose File, Print from the menu and print a copy of the finished flyer.

6. Save the file and then close it. Close Publisher.

Figure 2.28
The completed flyer for the Helping Hands Walkathon.

WordArt added with selected special effects

Lines added to map

Picture from file added

Clip art added, rotated, and recolored

Challenge

Challenge exercises expand on or are somewhat related to skills presented in the lessons. Each exercise provides a brief narrative introduction, followed by instructions in a numbered step format that are not as detailed as those in the Skill Drill section.

You create several publications in the Challenge section.

Challenge 1. Using Different Special Effects Tools in WordArt

The WordArt window has its own set of tools that can be used for special effects. In this Challenge exercise, you use Help to identify the different buttons and then design a WordArt image of your name using various special effects.

1. Launch Publisher, close the Microsoft Publisher Catalog, and hide the wizard.

2. Draw a WordArt frame and type your name in the Enter Your Text Here dialog box. Update the display and close the text box.

3. Open Help and type **tools and buttons** in the index box. (*Hint:* The Help you want to open is the WordArt Help program, which is activated when the WordArt graphic is still selected.) Open the topic Tools and buttons. The Help topic **Using WordArt effects** should display. This topic identifies the tools and buttons on the WordArt toolbar. Use this information to help you in designing your own signature WordArt for you name. Keep track of the effects you choose.

4. Click the list arrow at the end of the Shape Box and select a shape you like for your name.

5. Change the font. Make sure the end result is still in letters.

6. Use the Shading button to select a different color for your name.

7. Experiment with other tools on the WordArt toolbar to modify your name design. Try adding a shadow or changing the thickness of the line using the border tool.

8. Add a clip art image or other graphic to your name design to illustrate your personality.

9. Save the file as **My Name**.

10. Print the file. Write on the printout the effects that you used to design your name.

11. Close the file and close Publisher.

[?] 2. Understanding the Layers in Design Templates

A template is a model used as a basis for creating a new publication. A template usually contains some basic layout and formatting for a publication and may include text or graphics. Many designs available in the Quick Publication Wizard can be selected for use with a publication. Designs consist of frames that include drawing tools, clip art, and other images that are arranged, shaded, and layered to create a particular effect. In this Challenge exercise, you use Help to learn more about design templates and then you dissect one to understand its components.

1. Launch Publisher and close the Catalog.

2. Use Help and read the information that is available about how to change a template, what is a template, and layering objects.

3. Click the Design button on the Quick Publication Wizard panel. The names of the available designs are listed in the lower half of this panel.

4. Click through the designs to view them. When you select a design, it is displayed on the blank page on the right side of the window. In particular, look at Border Flowers, Pinwheel, Starfish, Wallpaper, and others that sound interesting to you.

5. Select Retro and click Color Scheme to see how other color schemes look with this design. Click several different color schemes until you find one you like.

6. Hide the Wizard and click on the template design. How many different panels are used to create the background? Change the background color of each panel to a contrasting color. Use a different color for each panel. Print the page.

7. This design has a number of images in the background. Increase the zoom and examine the images. What are the primary tools that were used to create these images? What pop-up label displays when one of these images is selected? Write your answers on your printout of the Retro design. Save the file as **Retro**.

8. Click the Show Wizard button and change the design template to Border Flowers.

9. Double-click on one of the flower images. When the Clip Art Gallery opens, change the image to a different one and close the Clip Art Gallery.

   10. Click the Bring to Front button to display the new flower image on top.

   11. Print the design, and then close it. Save the file as **Border Flowers**. Close Publisher.

[?] 3. Cropping a Picture on Four Sides

When you use pictures from other sources, you may need to crop part of the picture to hide parts you do not want or to make it fit in the available space. You can crop two or fours sides at one time to help speed up the process of cropping. In this exercise, you use Help to learn more about cropping and then you practice the new techniques to crop a picture.

   1. Launch Publisher, close the Catalog, and hide the wizard.

   2. Draw a picture frame approximately 4" wide by 6" high.

   3. Insert the picture titled "wedding" from the CD-ROM. Use a corner resizing handle to increase the size of the picture to approximately 4" by 6". Use the rulers to help size the picture.

   4. Open Help and search for information on cropping pictures. Find the topic on how to crop a picture from two sides.

   5. Using the technique described in Help, crop the picture to narrow the focus to the couple shown in the gazebo. Try the technique using a side handle and then using a top or bottom handle. Undo your changes and repeat the process using a corner handle.

   6. Crop the left side so that only the ribbons show. Crop the bottom to hide the lattice. Your picture should look like the one in Figure 2.29.

   7. Increase the size of the figure again, and position it in the top center of the page as shown in Figure 2.29.

   8. Add the Romance design for a background.

   9. Save the file and name it **Wedding**. Close the file.

Figure 2.29

Pictures can be cropped from two or four sides at once.

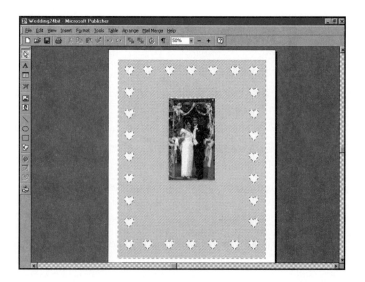

[?] 4. Using Other Drawing Tools

You moved to a new place and are having a house-warming party. You need a map to send to your family and friends so that they can find your new place. In addition to the drawing tools on the Objects toolbar, many other tools can be used to create drawings of your own design. These drawing tools provide additional options to help you express an idea, create an image, or describe a process. In this Challenge exercise, you explore the other drawing tools and a map.

1. Launch Publisher and open a new blank publication.

2. Use Help to learn how to draw a picture using Microsoft Draw.

3. Use the shapes and tools on the AutoShapes toolbar and the Drawing toolbar to draw a map to your home or apartment.

    (*Hint:* When Microsoft Draw is open, the drawing frame is displayed and the AutoShapes toolbar is floating on the screen. The Drawing toolbar moves to the bottom of the window. A number of the drawing commands are now found under the Draw menu on the Drawing Toolbar.)

4. Add a fill color to the shape that represents your home. Include directional arrows to indicate one-way streets if necessary.

5. Print your map and Save the publication as `Map to My House`. Close the file.

[?] 5. Exploring Clip Art Gallery

Thousands of clip art images available, including some pictures. In this exercise, you work with the Clip Art Gallery and explore the different categories, searching techniques, and images that can be used.

1. Open Publisher and open a blank publication.

2. Choose Insert, Picture, Clip Art from the menu.

3. Choose the background category and select a background you like. Resize it to fill the available space.

4. Draw a clip art frame in the upper half of the page. Use the Search for clips box, and type a keyword for an object that could be rotated.

5. After you insert the figure, right-click on the clip art and choose Help on This Picture from the shortcut menu. Review the topic Rotate or flip a picture, and then close Help.

6. Return to the image and use (Alt) to rotate the figure approximately 30 degrees.

7. Add another clip art frame. This time add one of the photographs.

8. Print your results. Save the file as `Clip Art` and close it.

Discovery Zone

Discovery Zone exercises help you gain advanced knowledge of project topics and/or application of skills. These exercises focus on enhancing your problem-solving skills. Numbered steps are not provided, but you are given hints, reminders, screen shots, and/or references to help you reach your goal for each exercise.

In these exercises you create new files.

[?] I. Saving an Image of Your Own to Use in a Publication

It is fun to personalize a card or invitation by adding your own photos. Several methods are available to do this. You can use a scanner to scan in photographs you have taken. Many film developing companies now offer the option of having pictures saved on a disk. If you have access to a digital camera, you can capture pictures directly to a disk.

Goal: Turn a photograph of your own into a picture file and add the picture to a publication.

With your instructor, family, or friends, explore the options available to you for creating picture files. Find out what services your local film developing outlet provides. Open Help and learn how to add a picture directly from a scanner. Use any method available to you to create your own picture file.

Open Publisher and add the picture file you created to a blank publication. Modify the image by cropping or resizing it. Save the file as `My Picture`.

[?] 2. Creating Your Own Template

You can design your own template in Publisher to give your business or personal publications a unique look. This can include your own background, logo, images, and layout.

Goal: Create a template using the graphic tools you learned about in this project.

Open Help, read about templates, and learn how to create a template.

Open a blank publication. Use clip art, pictures, and drawing tools to create a design you would want to use for your own business. Use at least three different elements. Save the file as a template with the name `My Template`. Print the results.

Project 3

Working with Text

Objectives

In this project, you learn how to

- ➤ **Replace Placeholder Text**
- ➤ **Edit Existing Text**
- ➤ **Use AutoFlow**
- ➤ **Reference Connected Frames on Different Pages**
- ➤ **Add Text Frames**
- ➤ **Create Bulleted and Numbered Lists**
- ➤ **Change Font Characteristics**
- ➤ **Change Paragraph Formatting**

Key terms introduced in this project include

- AutoFlow
- bulleted list
- drop cap
- numbered list

Why Would I Do This?

The most important element in nearly every publication is the text. Text is used in headlines to alert the reader to the topic being covered. In the most common text frames, the text provides the details about the topic of the publication. Text frames are also used to display lists of information, with each item in the list set off with numbers or bullets.

You can format text in Publisher text frames in much the same way you format text using a word processor. You can format individual characters by adding such features as boldface, underline, and italics. You can also format paragraphs, changing paragraph spacing, line spacing, and first line indents.

In this project, you replace placeholder text added when you create a publication using a wizard. You edit text, import text created using a word processor, and add text frames. You also format characters and paragraphs.

Visual Summary

When you have completed this lesson, you will have created and modified text in a two-page newsletter in several ways, including the addition of numbered and bulleted lists, new text frames, and continuation messages in documents that span multiple pages.

ARMSTRONG POOL, SPA, AND SAUNA

THE WATER'S EDGE

VOLUME 5, NUMBER 2

JUNE 30, 2001

Planning for the Winter Season

With the temperatures in the 90s and the air conditioners running full blast, it is kind of difficult to shift gears and think about our winter program. Here it is July, however, and the first shipments of saunas are only a month away, as are our first large spa shipments of the season. Let's lower the temperature about 60° and take a quick look at what's coming this fall.

Our fall program begins when our customers get ready to close their pools for the winter. We will be carrying three different lines of pool covers this year—polypropylene, vinyl, and a new nylon-reinforced vinyl. We will once again advertise these using the "Good, Better, Best" campaign.

The pool chemical areas in each store will be de-emphasized as the spa and sauna displays are expanded. Our first spa/sauna tent sale will be held on Thanksgiving weekend this year. This is a little later in the season than we've held this sale the last few years, but we're hoping people will consider these big-ticket items as Christmas presents for the whole family!

One of our new marketing strategies for spas this year will be

(Continued on page 2)

Caption describing picture or graphic.

Winter Sales Goals

- 1,500 portable spas
- 500 built-in spas
- 2,000 pool covers
- 200 wet saunas
- 50 dry saunas
- 100 above ground swimming pools
- 50 inground swimming pools

Top Salespeople
May

1. Bill McMahon
2. George Nelson
3. Ann Cantelon
4. Charity Hawken
5. Tom Johnson

Taylor Store Finally Ready to Open

We are happy to announce that the Taylor store, next to the fire station, will finally open its doors on August 1. After many zoning problems, that resulted in the addition of a sprinkling system and replacement of the 4' fence with a 6' fence, we have finally gotten approval from the building inspector to open.

Charity Hawken, currently the assistant manager of the Novi store, will manage the new store. Bill Cantelon has been hired away from Vanguard Pools and will serve as assistant manager.

Continuation message

Bulleted list

Numbered list

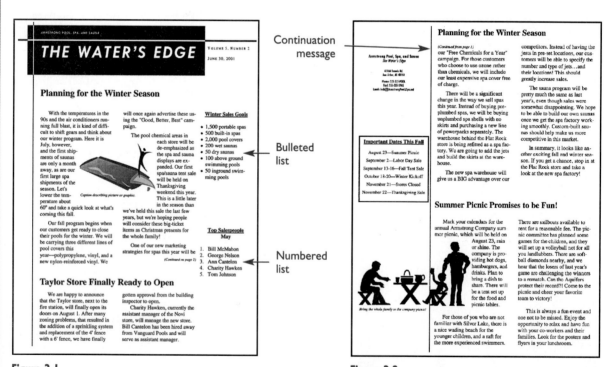

Figure 3.1
Text frames and lists have been added to the front page of the newsletter.

Planning for the Winter Season

(Continued from page 1)
our "Free Chemicals for a Year" campaign. For those customers who choose to use ozone rather than chemicals, we will include our least expensive spa cover free of charge.

There will be a significant change in the way we sell spas this year. Instead of buying preplumbed spas, we will be buying unplumbed spa shells with no skirts and purchasing a new line of powerpacks separately. The warehouse behind the Flat Rock store is being refitted as a spa factory. We are going to add the jets and build the skirts at the warehouse.

The new spa warehouse will give us a BIG advantage over our competitors. Instead of having the jests in pre-set locations, our customers will be able to specify the number and type of jets...and their locations! This should greatly increase sales.

The sauna program will be pretty much the same as last year's, even though sales were somewhat disappointing. We hope to be able to build our own saunas once we get the spa factory working smoothly. Custom-built saunas should help make us more competitive in this market.

In summary, it looks like another exciting fall and winter season. If you get a chance, stop in at the Flat Rock store and take a look at the new spa factory!

Armstrong Pool, Spa, and Sauna
The Water's Edge

Important Dates This Fall

August 23—Summer Picnic
September 2—Labor Day Sale
September 13-16—Fall Tent Sale
October 18-20—Winter Kickoff
November 21—Stores Closed
November 22—Thanksgiving Sale

Summer Picnic Promises to be Fun!

Mark your calendars for the annual Armstrong Company summer picnic, which will be held on August 23, rain or shine. The company is providing hot dogs, hamburgers, and drinks. Plan to bring a dish to share. There will be a tent set up for the food and picnic tables.

For those of you who are not familiar with Silver Lake, there is a nice wading beach for the younger children, and a raft for the more experienced swimmers.

There are sailboats available to rent for a reasonable fee. The picnic committee has planned some games for the children, and they will set up a volleyball net for all you landlubbers. There are softball diamonds nearby, and we hear that the losers of last year's game are challenging the winners to a rematch. Can the Aquifers protect their record?! Come to the picnic and cheer your favorite team to victory!

This is always a fun event and one not to be missed. Enjoy the opportunity to relax and have fun with your co-workers and their families. Look for the posters and flyers in your lunchroom.

Bring the whole family to the company picnic!

Figure 3.2
Placeholder text has been replaced, and a continuation message has been added.

Lesson I: Replacing Placeholder Text

When you use a wizard to create a publication, as you did in Project 1, "Getting Started with Publisher," placeholders are created to hold text and images. Placeholder text looks like real text but is actually just an image of text. When you click on it, you select the entire placeholder. Once the placeholder is selected, you can replace it by typing in new text, by pasting text from the Clipboard, or by importing text from another location.

In this lesson, you type over a title placeholder and then insert an article created in Microsoft Word.

To Replace Placeholder Text

1 **Find and open the Pub-0301 file on your CD-ROM. Choose File, Save As from the menu and save the file as** `Summer Newsletter`**.**
Save the file on your floppy disk or whichever storage device you are using.

> **X** A dialog box may appear telling you that the printer this publication was designed for cannot be found. Click OK—you will select the correct printer when you print the publication.

+ **2** **Click the Secondary Story Headline; then click the Zoom In button on the Standard toolbar until the publication is shown at 100%.**
The selected text frame remains centered in the work area (see Figure 3.3). Notice that all of the placeholder text has been selected.

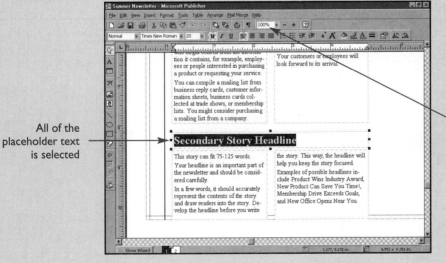

All of the placeholder text is selected

The publication is displayed at 100%

Figure 3.3
The placeholder has been selected, and the publication is displayed at full size.

3 **Type** `Taylor Store Finally Ready to Open`**.**
Notice that the placeholder text is deleted as soon as you type the first letter.

4 **Click on the placeholder text in the article underneath the title you just typed.**
The placeholder text for the article is selected.

5 **Select Insert, Text File from the menu.**
The Insert Text dialog box is displayed.

continues ▶

To Replace Placeholder Text (continued)

 Find and select the Taylor Store Opening article on your CD-ROM, and then click OK.

The Word article replaces the placeholder text (see Figure 3.4).

> ✖ A dialog box may appear telling you that there is too much text to fit in the existing frame, asking if you want to use AutoFlow. Click No to close the dialog box. There is no more text—this message always appears when the end of the text reaches the last line of a text frame. A Text in Overflow indicator displays at the end of the frame.

Figure 3.4
A document created in Microsoft Word has replaced the placeholder text.

The title has been typed in

A Word document has been inserted

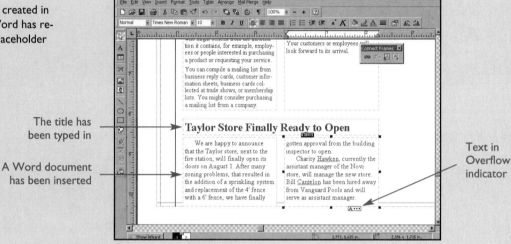

Text in Overflow indicator

 Click the Save button to save your work.

Leave the publication open for the next lesson.

> ⚠ **Font and Paragraph Formatting**
> When you insert text created in another program, the font and paragraph characteristics of the original document are maintained. For example, the text you just inserted used a 12-point font size and the paragraphs were indented $1/4$". The original placeholder text is 11 points with no paragraph indenting.

Lesson 2: Editing Existing Text

When you work on a publication that you previously created, you will often want to make changes to the text. Editing text in Publisher is exactly the same as editing text in a word processing program such as Microsoft Word.

In this lesson, you edit text that was typed into the sample file.

To Edit Existing Text

1 **Scroll up until you can see the banner at the top of the first page.**
The volume and date information should be displayed to the right of the banner.

2 **Click to the right of the date, hold down the mouse button, and drag to the left until the entire date is highlighted.**
You could also press (←Backspace) several times to remove the date. Your screen should look like Figure 3.5.

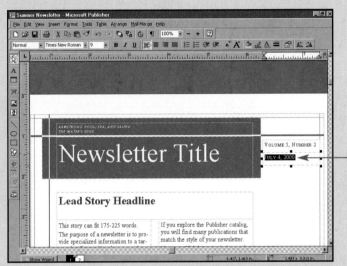

Figure 3.5
The text to be edited is selected.

Selected text

 Selecting Text
Some shortcuts are available for selecting text. To select a single word, move the mouse pointer over the word and double-click. To select a paragraph, move the pointer anywhere over the paragraph and triple-click.

---

3 **Type June 30, 2001.**
The new text replaces the selected text.

4 **Use the page navigation controls to move to the second page of the publication; then scroll down until you can see the title and article about the company picnic.**

5 **Double-click on the word Fall in the article title.**
The word is highlighted.

6 **Type Summer.**
The new word replaces the old one (see Figure 3.6). Notice that the font characteristics (18-point, bold) remain the same.

7 **Click the Save button to save your work.**
Leave the publication open for the next lesson.

continues ▶

To Edit Existing Text   (continued)

Figure 3.6
The title has been
changed.

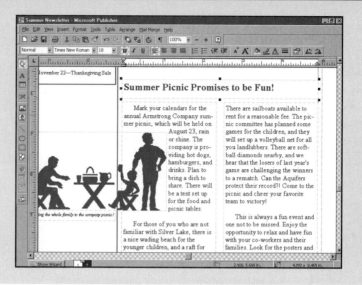

Lesson 3: Using AutoFlow

In Lesson 1, you inserted text from a Microsoft Word document. The text in that document fit nicely in the space provided by the placeholder. This will not happen very often; it is much more common to have the inserted document require more space than the placeholder provides. When this happens, one of your options is to use a feature called **AutoFlow.** This feature enables you to automatically place the remaining text in an empty text frame on another page.

In this lesson, you insert a Microsoft Word document and use the AutoFlow feature to place the overflow text.

To Use AutoFlow

1 **Move to the second page of the newsletter, if necessary, and click anywhere in the Back Page Story placeholder.**
All of the placeholder text is selected (see Figure 3.7). The Connect Frames toolbar should also appear somewhere on the screen.

 The Connect Frames toolbar may be docked on one of the edges of the screen. If you do not see it, choose <u>T</u>ools, Connect <u>T</u>ext Frames from the menu. It is generally a good idea to keep this toolbar available when you work with text frames.

2 **Press** <kbd>Del</kbd>.
All of the placeholder text is deleted, although the text frame is not removed. You need an empty text frame to use the AutoFlow feature.

3 **Use the page navigation controls to return to page 1; then click on the lead story text frame.**
All the lead story text is selected.

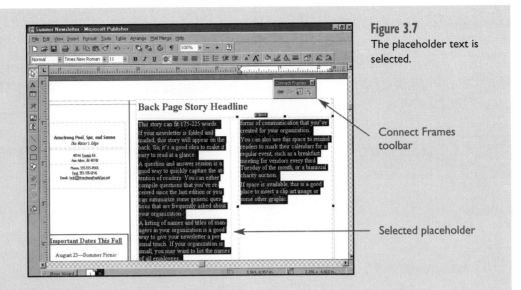

Figure 3.7
The placeholder text is
selected.

Connect Frames
toolbar

Selected placeholder

4 **Choose Insert, Text File from the menu. Find and select the Winter
Season Article file from your CD-ROM and click OK.**
The Microsoft Word file is imported into the newsletter, and a dialog box lets
you know that the document is too big for the text frame (see Figure 3.8). It
asks if you want to use the AutoFlow feature.

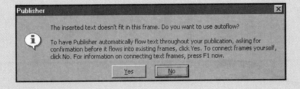

Figure 3.8
A dialog box asks if you
want to use the AutoFlow
feature.

5 **Click Yes.**
The program looks for the next empty text frame. If it finds one, it asks if you
want to place the overflow text in this frame (see Figure 3.9) If you have several
empty text frames, you can click No until you find the one you want to use.

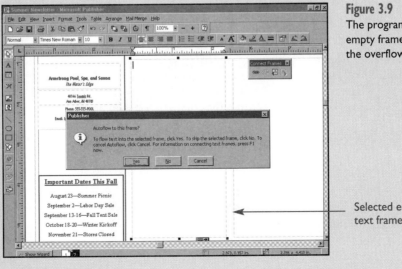

Figure 3.9
The program has found an
empty frame to use for
the overflow text.

Selected empty
text frame

continues ▶

To Use AutoFlow   (continued)

Choosing Not to Use the AutoFlow Feature
You can choose not to use the AutoFlow feature when you insert text. If you do not flow the rest of the text into an empty text frame, you can do it later by clicking in the text frame that contains too much text. Click the Connect Text Frames button in the Connect Frames toolbar and then click in any empty text frame to pour in the overflow text.

6 Click Yes.
The rest of the text flows into the two columns of the empty text frame, and the last column is selected.

7 Click the Go to Previous Frame button in the Connect Frames toolbar.
The first column of the text frame is now selected (see Figure 3.10). You can also use the Go to Previous Frame button attached to the top of the text frame.

Figure 3.10
The Go to Previous Frame button takes you to the previous column.

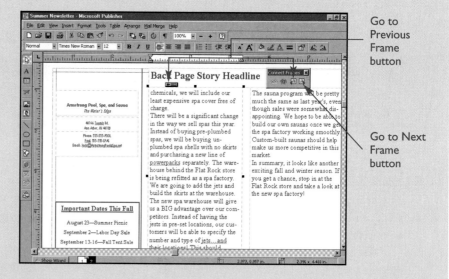

8 Click the Go to Previous Frame button again.
You are now taken to the second column of the article on the first page.

9 Scroll up, select the Lead Story Headline placeholder, and change it to Planning for the Winter Season.

10 Use the page navigation control to move to page 2, select the Back Page Story Headline, and change it to Planning for the Winter Season.

11 Click the Save button to save your work.
Leave the publication open for the next lesson.

Lesson 4: Referencing Connected Frames on Different Pages

In Lesson 3, you inserted text on the front page of the newsletter and continued it on an-other page. Any time you separate different parts of the same article, it is a good idea to let the reader know where the article is continued or where it came from. Publisher offers you a great feature that enables you to do this easily.

In this lesson, you change the frame properties of the continued article to let the reader navigate the article easily.

To Reference Connected Frames on Different Pages

1 **On page 2 of the newsletter, select the left column of the Planning for the Winter Season article.**
You can click anywhere in the column to select it.

2 **Right-click on the selected column; then choose Change Frame, Text Frame Properties from the shortcut menu.**
The Text Frame Properties dialog box is displayed (see Figure 3.11).

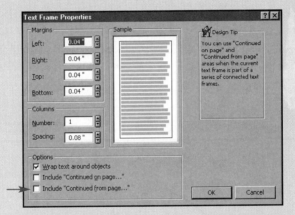

The Include "Continued from page..." check box

Figure 3.11
The Text Frame Properties dialog box en-ables you to direct the reader to other parts of an article.

3 **Select the Include "Continued from page..." option and click OK.**
The (Continued from page 1) message is displayed at the top of the column (see Figure 3.12).

4 **Click the Go to Previous Frame button.**
The second column of the first-page portion of the article is selected.

5 **Right-click on the selected column; then choose Change Frame, Text Frame Properties from the shortcut menu.**
The Text Frame Properties dialog box is displayed.

6 **Select the Include "Continued on page..." option and click OK.**
The (Continued on page 2) message is displayed at the bottom of the column (see Figure 3.13).

7 **Click the Save button to save your work.**
Leave the publication open for the next lesson.

continues ▶

To Reference Connected Frames on Different Pages (continued)

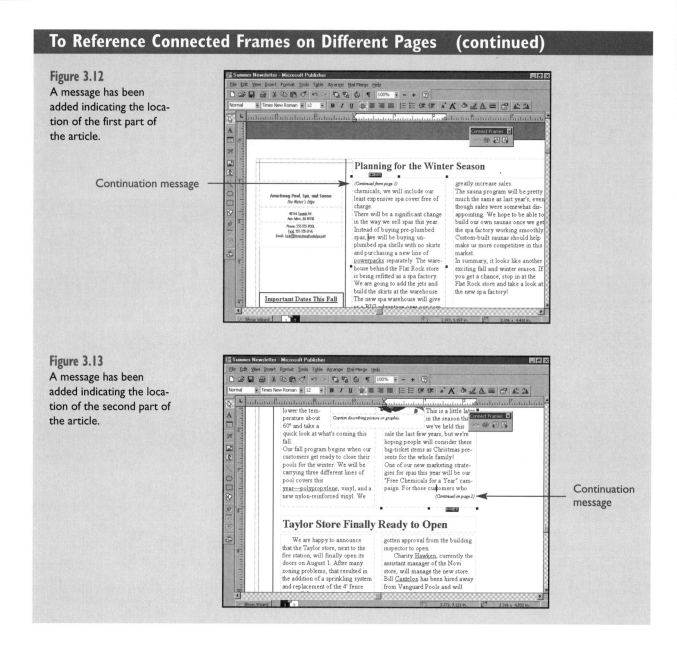

Figure 3.12
A message has been added indicating the location of the first part of the article.

Continuation message

Figure 3.13
A message has been added indicating the location of the second part of the article.

Continuation message

Lesson 5: Adding Text Frames

If there are not enough text frames after you have created a publication using a wizard or if you are starting a publication from scratch, you need to know how to create new text frames. You can create text frames to hold articles, schedules, or lists.

In this lesson, you create two text frames to which you will add a bulleted list and a numbered list in Lesson 6.

To Add Text Frames

➊ **On page 1 of the newsletter, use the Zoom Out button until the publication is displayed at 50%.**
Look in the Zoom box on the toolbar to see the relative size of the document.

A **2** **Click the Text Frame Tool button in the Objects toolbar.**

The pointer turns to cross hairs.

3 **Move the pointer to the right of the top edge of the top article, click, and drag down about 2½" and to the right edge of the document.**

A frame box is displayed, with the pointer in the lower-right corner (see Figure 3.14). Use the vertical ruler to help you determine the right height.

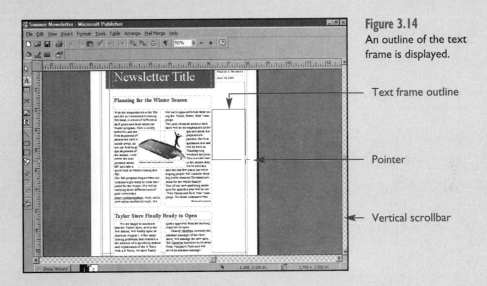

Figure 3.14
An outline of the text frame is displayed.

Text frame outline

Pointer

Vertical scrollbar

4 **Release the mouse button.**

The text frame is created, and the insertion point appears in the upper-left corner of the frame.

+ **5** **Click the Zoom In button until the publication is shown at 75%; then type Winter Sales Goals and press ↵Enter twice.**

Your new text frame should look like Figure 3.15.

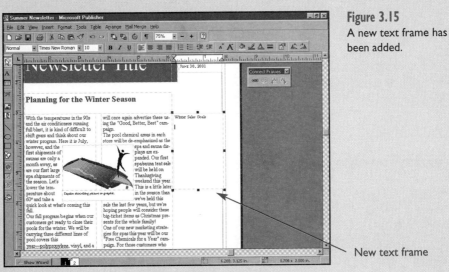

Figure 3.15
A new text frame has been added.

New text frame

continues ▶

To Add Text Frames (continued)

6 Use the Zoom Out button until the publication is displayed at 50%.

7 Click the Text Frame Tool on the Formatting toolbar; then create another text frame the same size as the first one and place it about 1" below the first text frame.

8 Click the Zoom In button until the publication is shown at 75%; then type Top Salespeople and press ↵Enter. Type May and press ↵Enter twice.

You should now have two new text frames (see Figure 3.16).

Figure 3.16
A second text frame has been added.

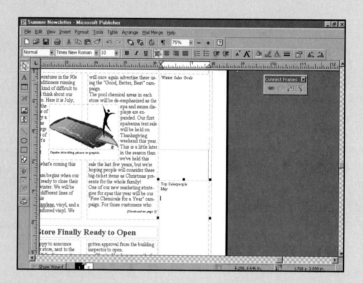

9 Click the Save button to save your work.

Leave the publication open for the next lesson.

Lesson 6: Creating Bulleted and Numbered Lists

When you display information, you can use one of two types of lists supported by Publisher. The first type is a **numbered list,** which is best used to display information that is in some set order, such as sequential instructions. The second type is a **bulleted list,** which is used to display information that is in no particular order.

In this lesson, you create both a numbered list to show the ranking of the top salespeople and a bulleted list to show company sales goals for the winter season.

To Create Bulleted and Numbered Lists

1 Make sure the insertion point is in the second line after the word **May** in title of the last text frame you created.

2 Click the Zoom In button until the publication is shown at 100%; then click the Numbering button on the toolbar.

Notice that a number is automatically inserted (see Figure 3.17). The spacing will be the same for every number so that the list will line up perfectly.

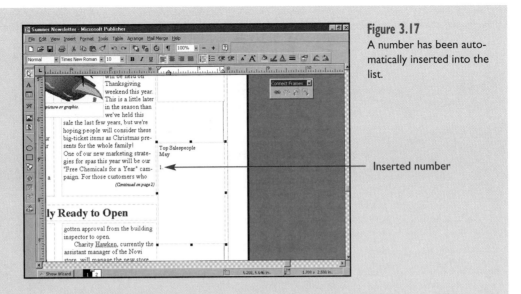

Figure 3.17
A number has been auto-
matically inserted into the
list.

Inserted number

3 **Type** `Bill McMahon` **and press** `↵Enter`.
A second number is automatically inserted, and a fixed-size space is inserted
after the number.

4 **Complete the list by adding** `George Nelson, Ann Cantelon, Charity`
`Hawken,` **and** `Tom Johnson.`
Your list should now contain five names (see Figure 3.18).

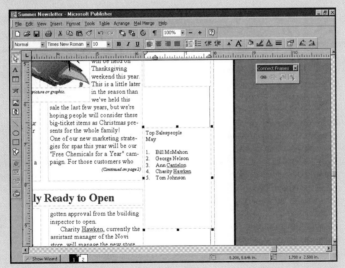

Figure 3.18
The numbered list has five
entries.

5 **Click in the second line after the Winter Sales Goals title in the first
text frame you created.**

6 **Click the Bullets button.**
A bullet is displayed in the same manner a number was displayed for the numbered list.

continues ▶

To Create Bulleted and Numbered Lists (continued)

7 **Enter the following information, pressing** ⏎Enter **after each entry:**

```
1,500 portable spas

500 built-in spas

2,000 pool covers

200 wet saunas

50 dry saunas

100 above-ground swimming pools

50 inground swimming pools
```

Notice that with the longer entries, the second line wraps around to line up with the first line, leaving the bullets in a column by themselves (see Figure 3.19).

Figure 3.19
The text entries in the bulleted list line up automatically.

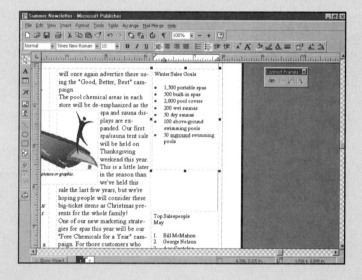

 8 **Click the Save button to save your work.**
Leave the publication open for the next lesson.

(i) Changing Numbers and Bullets
If you do not like the look of the standard bullet, you can change it to any symbol available with any font on your computer. To do this, select all of the bulleted points, then choose Format, Indents and Lists from the menu. Click the New Bullet button and select the font and bullet shape you want. You can also use the same menu option to change the numbered list from numbers to letters or to different numbering styles if you desire.

Spelling Errors

Some of the words you type into the publication may have a wavy red line below them. This means that the words are not found in the Microsoft dictionary. If these lines do not appear, the automatic spell checker may have been turned off. To turn it back on, select <u>T</u>ools, <u>S</u>pelling, Spelling <u>O</u>ptions from the menu; then click the Check <u>s</u>pelling as you type check box. You will learn how to correct spelling errors and add new entries to your dictionary in Project 6, "Working with Publisher Tools."

Lesson 7: Changing Font Characteristics

You can change the font characteristics in any text frame in the same way you would change them in a word processor. You can change the formatting of a word or group of words, or you can change the font characteristics in the entire text frame.

In this lesson, you change the font characteristics in the two text frames you created earlier in this project.

To Change Font Characteristics

1 **Place the insertion point in the Winter Sales Goals text frame; then choose <u>E</u>dit, <u>H</u>ighlight Entire Story from the menu.**
All of the text in the text frame is highlighted.

2 **Click the arrow on the right of the Font Size box and select 12.**
The font size of all of the text in the text frame is increased (see Figure 3.20).

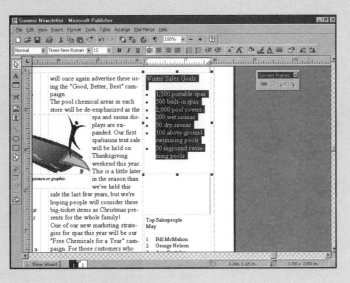

Figure 3.20
The font size of the entire text box has been increased.

3 **Repeat the first two steps to increase the font size of the Top Salespeople text frame to 12 points.**

continues ▶

To Change Font Characteristics (continued)

4 Highlight the title of the **Winter Sales Goals text frame and then click the Center, Bold, and Underline buttons.**

The title is now distinctive from the rest of the text in the text frame.

5 Repeat the procedure in step 4 to change the look of the two-line title in the **Top Salespeople text frame.**

6 Highlight the word May in the same title and click the Underline button to turn the underline off. Click anywhere in the text box to deselect the word.

Your two new text frames should look like Figure 3.21.

Figure 3.21
The title text in both of the new text frames has been changed.

Bold, underlined, and centered text

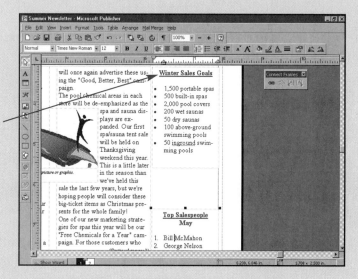

7 As a finishing touch to your newsletter, go to the banner at the top of the first page, highlight the phrase **The Water's Edge, and click the Cut button.**

The message is removed but stored in the Windows temporary memory location called the Clipboard. If you had pressed Del, the message would have been removed and not stored.

8 Highlight the newsletter title and click the **Paste button.**

The text you just cut now replaces the placeholder text for the title, using the same font style as the original placeholder text.

9 Click the Save button to save your work.

Leave the publication open for the next lesson.

 Font Size

Font size refers to the height of a font. It is measured in $1/72$" intervals. A 12-point font is $1/6$" high, whereas a 36-point font is $1/2$" high.

Lesson 8: Changing Paragraph Formatting

You have already changed paragraph formatting in Lesson 7 when you centered text in the titles of the new text frames. If you are familiar with Microsoft Word, you have probably used the Format, Paragraph menu option. This option is not available in Publisher—each formatting option has its own menu choice.

In this lesson, you add space between paragraphs and indent first lines in the lead article. You also make some formatting changes to the lists you created.

To Change Paragraph Formatting

1 **Place the insertion point in the Planning for the Winter Season article; then choose Edit, Highlight Entire Story from the menu.**
All of the text for this article is selected, including the text of the second page.

2 **Choose Format, Line Spacing from the menu.**
The Line Spacing dialog box is displayed (see Figure 3.22). This dialog box enables you to increase or decrease the spacing between lines and also enables you to change the spacing between paragraphs.

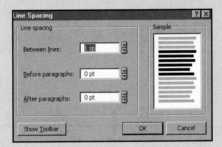

Figure 3.22
The Line Spacing dialog box enables you to change line spacing or increase the spacing between paragraphs.

3 **Change the After paragraphs spacing to 6 pt and then click OK.**
You may have to highlight the Font Size box and type 6 if that option is not available. The space between the paragraphs is increased.

4 **Choose Format, Indents and Lists from the menu.**
The Indents and Lists dialog box is displayed (see Figure 3.23). This dialog box enables you to indent the first lines of paragraphs, change alignment, and work with bulleted and numbered lists.

5 **Highlight the existing entry in the First line box, type .25, then click OK. Click anywhere in the article to deselect the text.**
The first line of each paragraph is now indented ¼" (see Figure 3.24).

6 **Highlight just the bulleted text in the Winter Sales Goals text frame.**
Do not select the title or blank line below the title.

7 **Choose Format, Indents and Lists from the menu.**
Notice that a whole new group of options are available in the Indents and Lists dialog box (see Figure 3.24). If you had selected the numbered list, the Numbered List options would be displayed.

continues ▶

To Change Paragraph Formatting (continued)

Figure 3.23
The Indents and Lists dialog box enables you to change paragraph indents or alignment.

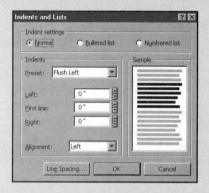

Figure 3.24
The first line of each paragraph is indented, and there is increased space between paragraphs.

First line indent

Increased spacing after paragraphs

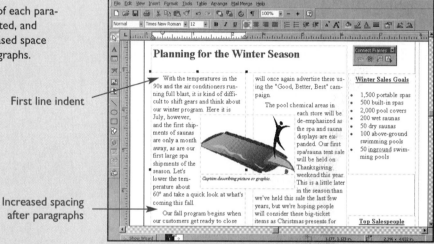

Figure 3.25
The Indents and Lists dialog box displays different options depending on what type of text is selected.

8 **Click the down arrow once on the Indent list by box.**
The number in the Indent box changes to .15".

9 **Click OK.**
The indent changes to .15". Notice that the bulleted list text is closer to the bullets than it was.

10 **Select File, Print from the menu. Select the correct printer, if necessary, and then click OK.**
The newsletter is printed.

11 **Click the Save button, close the publication, and close Publisher.**

Summary

In this project, you worked with text frames. You replaced placeholder text by typing over it and by inserting text created in other programs. You imported text and used the AutoFlow feature to continue the article in another text frame; you then added text to direct the reader to the rest of the article. You added text frames and created both a bulleted list and a numbered list. Finally, you made changes to the text and paragraph formatting before printing the newsletter.

You will probably need to connect text frames if you use Publisher often. Go to the Publisher Help index and type **connect**. Read through the options; then scroll to the bottom of the box and run the Connecting text frames tutorial.

Checking Concepts and Terms

True/False

For each of the following statements, check *T* or *F* to indicate whether the statement is true or false.

__T __F **1.** You can edit placeholder text the same way you edit text that you have typed in. [L1]

__T __F **2.** Editing text in a Publisher frame is the same as editing text in a Microsoft Word document. [L1]

__T __F **3.** You can select all of the text in a paragraph by double-clicking on the paragraph. [L2]

__T __F **4.** You need an empty text frame if you want to use the AutoFlow feature. [L3]

__T __F **5.** If an article appears on more than one page, it is always a good idea to use continuation messages to let the reader know where the article came from or where it is continued. [L4]

__T __F **6.** Text frames can be used to hold articles, bulleted lists, or numbered lists. [L5]

__T __F **7.** You can use letters instead of numbers in a numbered list. [L6]

__T __F **8.** You can use many different symbols for bullets in a bulleted list. [L6]

__T __F **9.** In a bulleted list, if the text wraps to a second line, the left edge of the text in the second line is lined up with the left edge of the bullet. [L6]

__T __F **10.** The Line Spacing dialog box enables you to change line spacing and paragraph spacing. [L8]

Multiple Choice

Circle the letter of the correct answer for each of the following questions.

1. You can replace placeholder text by _____. [L1]

   a. typing in new text

   b. pasting text from the Clipboard

   c. inserting text from a file created using another program

   d. all of the above

2. Use the _____ menu option to bring in text from another file. [L1]

   a. File

   b. Edit

   c. Insert

   d. Tools

3. When you bring in text from another document that is too big to fit in the current text frame, you can use the _____ feature to place the overflow text in another text frame. [L3]

   a. Connect

   b. OverFlow

   c. AutoCorrect

   d. AutoFlow

4. Which of the following enables you to flow text to another text frame at any time? [L3]

   a. the Connect Text Frames button in the Connect Frames toolbar

   b. the Overflow button on the bottom of the text frame

   c. the Insert menu option

   d. none of the above—you need to do this when you first insert the article

5. You need to change the _____ of a frame to automatically reference the location of other parts of an article (such as "continued on page 2"). [L4]

   a. connecting links

   b. text frame properties

   c. indents and lists

   d. Design Gallery object

6. How do you create a new text frame? [L5]

   a. Select Insert, Object from the menu; then select Text Frame from the Object Type menu.

   b. Click the Text Frame Tool button, move the pointer to an open area, click and drag down and to the right, and then release the mouse button.

   c. Hold down (Alt), move the pointer to an open area, click and drag down and to the right, and then release the mouse button.

   d. none of the above

7. Which of the following statements about lists is true? [L6]

   a. Numbered lists should be used to display information that has no particular order.

   b. Bulleted lists should be used to display ordered information.

   c. Numbered lists should be used to display ordered information.

   d. Numbered lists and bulleted lists can be used interchangeably.

8. The first step in changing the font characteristics in an entire story is to choose _____. [L7]

   a. Edit, Select All from the menu

   b. Change Frame, Text Frame Properties from the shortcut menu

   c. Whole Page from the shortcut menu

   d. Edit, Highlight Entire Story from the menu

9. An 18-point font is about how tall? [L7]

   a. 0.18"

   b. $\frac{1}{4}$"

   c. $\frac{1}{2}$"

   d. $\frac{1}{16}$"

10. The Indents and Lists dialog box enables you to format _____. [L8]

    a. paragraphs

    b. bulleted lists

    c. numbered lists

    d. all of the above

Screen ID

Label each element of the Access screen shown in Figure 3.26.

Figure 3.26

A. Numbered list

B. Zoom In button

C. Text Frame Tool button

D. Zoom Out button

E. Bulleted list

F. Center button

G. Page navigation controls

H. Go to Next Frame button

I. Bold button

J. Go to Previous Frame button

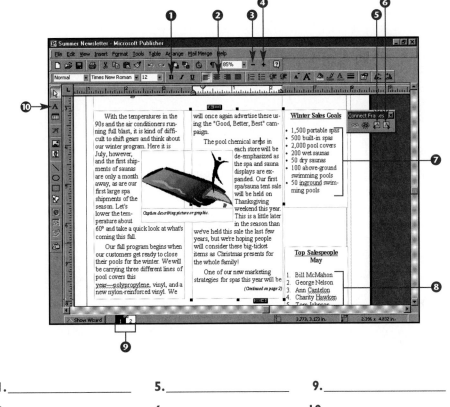

1._____	5._____	9._____
2._____	6._____	10._____
3._____	7._____	
4._____	8._____	

Discussion Questions

1. You formatted text by adding boldface and underline characteristics. You can also italicize text and even change its color. Is it possible to use too many formatting features on text?

2. In Lessons 3 and 4, you inserted text that was too big for the existing text frame, so you sent the overflow text to an empty text frame on the second page. Would you use this feature if you were using Publisher to create a multiple-page Web site? If so, how would you let the reader know where to go to see the rest of the article? If not, how would you solve the text overflow problem?

3. You can type text directly into text frames in Publisher. Why would the Insert Text feature be important? Why might you need to know how to bring in text from different sources, especially if you were editing a newsletter?

4. It is possible to connect unconnected text frames, as well as to disconnect connected text frames. Can you think of any circumstances when you might want to use either of these features?

5. You have now had some experience working with Publisher and should be getting a feel for creating publications. From your experience, what do you consider to be the best font size for a newsletter? How many columns are the most readable? Is it important to include graphics? Why or why not? What are some other general principles for newsletter formatting that you think are guidelines that you can use in the future?

Skill Drill

Skill Drill exercises reinforce project skills. Each skill reinforced is the same, or nearly the same, as a skill presented in this project. Each exercise includes a brief narrative introduction, followed by detailed instructions in a step-by-step format.

The following exercises once again deal with the Helping Hands organization. You will develop a newsletter intended for Helping Hands volunteers, mapping the upcoming events for the year.

1. Replacing Placeholder Text

In this exercise, you use the Catalog to pick out the Greeting Card template and then you run the Greeting Card wizard to set the card up.

To replace placeholder text in a title and an article, complete the following steps:

1. Find and open the Pub-0302 file on your CD-ROM. Choose File, Save As from the menu and save the file as **Helping Hands Newsletter**.

2. Click the Secondary Story Headline and use the Zoom In button to increase the size to 75%.

3. Type **More Volunteers Needed!** as the new title.

4. Click the bulleted list placeholder text on the left side of page 1 and type the following events:

   Fix It Week

   Helping Hands Walkathon

   Shelter Phone-a-thon

   Air Show

   Children's Clinic Dinner

5. Click anywhere in the article below the More Volunteers Needed! title that you just changed.

6. Choose Insert, Text File from the menu; find and select the Volunteers document on your CD-ROM; and then click OK.

7. Click the Save button to save your work. Leave the publication open for the next exercise.

2. Editing Existing Text

Looking at your newsletter, you decide that a couple of the titles need sprucing up. The title for the top article is repeated on the second page, so you will have to change that one twice.

To edit existing text, complete the following steps:

1. Select the title above the bulleted list you just edited. This is not placeholder text, so you will need to click at one end or the other and drag across the title.

2. Type **Events for 2001:** in place of the old title.

3. Select the Upcoming Events title for the lead article.

4. Type **Busy Year Ahead!** in place of the old title.

5. Highlight and select the new title you just typed in.

6. Click the Copy button on the toolbar.

7. Use the page navigation controls to move to page 2.

8. Select the Upcoming Events title near the middle of the back page. Notice that the article below it is empty.

9. Click the Paste button to replace the old title with the new one.

10. Place the insertion point to the right of the word fundraiser in the message on the left side of page 2 and add an **s** to change the word to fundraisers.

11. Click the Save button to save your work. Leave the publication open for the next exercise.

3. Using the AutoFlow Feature

You have a very long article that is the centerpiece of the newsletter. It gives details of some of the major fund-raising activities for the coming year. It is too long to fit in the existing text frame on the first page, so you will need to use the AutoFlow feature to send some of the overflow text to a text frame on the second page.

To use the AutoFlow feature and guide readers to the rest of the article, complete the following steps:

1. Use the page navigation controls to move to page 1.

2. Click anywhere in the top article on the page to select the placeholder text.

3. Choose Insert, Text File from the menu; find and select the Helping Hands Upcoming Events document on your CD-ROM; and then click OK.

4. When prompted to use AutoFlow, click Yes.

5. When the program asks if you want to AutoFlow to the empty text frame on the second page, click Yes.

6. Click the Save button to save your work. Leave the publication open for the next exercise.

4. Adding a Text Frame with a Numbered List

The local middle school has helped out greatly by having a canned food drive. The various classes participated in what turned out to be keen competition. You are going to send certificates to all of the classes, but it would also be a nice gesture to publish the names of the top classes in the newsletter. This is an ideal use for a numbered list.

To add a text frame and a numbered list, complete the following steps:

1. Click the page navigation control to move to page 1. If you cannot see the bottom of the More Volunteers Needed! article, scroll down.

2. Click the Text Frame Tool button on the Objects toolbar.

3. Move the pointer to the left edge of the page, aligning it evenly with the top of the title of the bottom article.

4. Click and drag down to the 10" mark and to the right to the 2" mark. Release the mouse button.

5. Type **East Middle School** and press (←Enter). Type **Canned Food Drive** and press (←Enter). Type **Winners** and press (←Enter) twice.

6. Click the Numbering button on the toolbar.

7. Type the following:

    Ms. Murray (6th)
    Ms. Armstrong (7th)
    Mr. Turner (8th)
    Mr. Long (6th)
    Ms. Denny (7th)

8. Click the Save button to save your work. Leave the publication open for the next exercise.

5. Changing Font Characteristics

Some of the text that you inserted has retained the font characteristics of the original document. To make the newsletter consistent, you will need to change the font type and the font size of several text frames.

To change font characteristics, complete the following steps:

1. Choose Edit, Highlight Entire Story from the menu to select all of the text in the text frame you just created.

2. Change the font to Comic Sans MS.

3. Select all of the text in the More Volunteers Needed! story and use the Font drop-down arrow to change the font to Comic Sans MS. Use the Font Size drop-down arrow to change the font size to 11 point.

4. Use the same procedure you used in step 3 to change the font type and size in the Busy Year Ahead! article.

5. Select the three-line title in the text frame you created in exercise 4. Click the Bold button and then click the Center button.

6. Click the Save button to save your work. Leave the publication open for the next exercise.

6. Changing Paragraph Formatting

Finally, a few formatting options will help give the newsletter a finished look. These options include paragraph indents and the spacing between the numbers and text in the numbered list.

To change paragraph formatting, complete the following steps:

1. Choose Edit, Highlight Entire Story from the menu to select all of the text in the More Volunteers Needed! text frame.

2. Choose Format, Indents and Lists from the menu.

3. Change the First line indent to 0.3" and click OK.

4. Select just the numbered list portion of the text frame you just added.

5. Choose Format, Indents and Lists from the menu again.

6. Change the Indent list by box to 0.15" and click OK. Your front page should look like Figure 3.27.

7. Close the publication, and close Publisher.

Figure 3.27
The front page of the newsletter is finished.

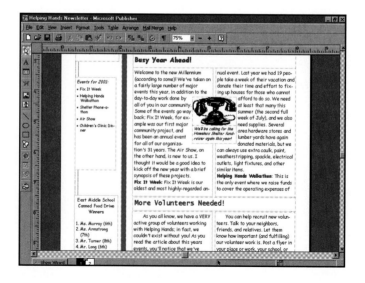

Challenge

Challenge exercises expand on or are somewhat related to skills presented in the lessons. Each exercise provides a brief narrative introduction, followed by instructions in a numbered step format that are not as detailed as those in the Skill Drill section.

In the following exercises, you work with a newsletter created for a (fictitious) Cornwall Historical Heritage Society (CHHS). This issue of the newsletter focuses on a small area on the northwest coast of Cornwall that is closely associated with the Arthurian legends. You will use this newsletter to try some new things, such as importing a file other than one created in Microsoft Word, adding a decorative drop cap, changing the look of a list and a text frame, using tabs, and pouring text into an empty text frame.

All of the exercises can be done independently. Figures 3.28 and 3.29 show the results of doing all of the exercises. Refer to them after doing each exercise to make sure your work is correct.

1. Importing Text from a Text File

Throughout the lessons and Skill Drill section of this project, you have imported text created using Microsoft Word. In this exercise, you will bring in text created and saved in text (.txt) format, a common method of saving documents. Text files can be read into virtually any word processor or desktop publishing program, but they can contain only a very limited amount of formatting.

1. Open Pub-0303 and save it as **CHHS Newsletter**.
2. Select the placeholder text in the text frame under the Tintagel Castle headline on the first page of the newsletter.
3. Choose Insert, Text File from the menu.
4. Choose Plain Text from the Files of type box at the bottom of the Insert Text dialog box. This will display only files with a .txt extension.
5. Select the Tintagel.txt file and click OK. (You may not be able to see the file extension, which is why you selected Plain Text in the previous step.)
6. Highlight all of the text and change the font size to 12 point. If the entire article is not displayed, increase the length of the first column (grab the middle handle and drag down) by one line.
7. Save your work and leave the publication open for the next exercise.

2. Adding a Drop Cap to a Text Frame

Many formatting options are available in Publisher, but one of them makes your publication look much more professional (if used sparingly)—the drop cap. A **drop cap** is an enlarged first letter or letters in an article. It can be set off from the paragraph or embedded in the text. It is commonly used in magazines. If you did the first exercise, skip step 1.

1. Open Pub-0303 and save it as **CHHS Newsletter**.
2. Highlight the letter "T" that begins the article on Tintagel that you just imported. (*Note:* If you did not do the first exercise, highlight the letter "T" that begins the bottom article on the page.)
3. Choose Format, Drop Cap from the menu.

4. Select the third option down in the second column and click OK. Because the drop cap takes up room in the text, you may have to lengthen the first column so that you can read all of the text.

5. Save your work and leave the publication open for the next exercise.

[?] 3. Using Tabs to Line Up Decimal Points

Tabs are used in Publisher in much the same was as they are used in Microsoft Word. In this exercise, you will use a decimal tab to line up decimal points in a list of visitors to popular sites.

1. Go to page 2 of the newsletter. (If you have not done either of the first two exercises, open Pub-0303 and save it as `CHHS Newsletter` first.)

2. Create a text frame on the left side of the page. It should be about $1\frac{1}{2}$" wide and 2" long.

3. Change the font size to 11 point before you start typing.

4. Use the available Help to learn how to select a decimal tab and place it in the horizontal ruler at the top of the screen. Place a decimal tab $1\frac{1}{4}$" from the left side of the text frame.

5. Add a title that says `Tourists (thousands)`; then add a blank line after the title.

6. Enter the following information:

```
Tintagel Castle   43.2
Land's End        38.7
Jamaica Inn       24.8
Gwennap Pit       21.4
Truro Cathedral   15.7
Advent Church      8.3
Dozmary Pool       2.0
```

7. Make the title bold. When you are finished, save your work.

4. Adding Borders to a Text Frame

You can change many of the characteristics of the text frame itself. This includes the outside border and the background color or shading. In this exercise, you add a border to a small text frame.

1. If you have not done any of the first three exercises, open Pub-0303 and save it as `CHHS Newsletter`.

2. Select the address box at the upper-left corner of page 2.

3. Find and click the Line/Border Style button on the toolbar.

4. Look through the various border options; then find and use the Twisted Lines BorderArt border.

5. Adding this wide border will automatically shrink the size of the text in the text frame. Increase the size of the text frame to increase the text to a readable size (check it at 100%).

6. Save your work and leave the publication open for the next exercise.

[?] 5. Pouring Text into an Empty Text Frame

The article at the bottom of the first page, "Touring King Arthur's Country," is much longer than it appears. Click on the second column and notice the Text in Overflow indicator. Now go to the second page. You will see that the same title appears at the top of the page.

In this exercise, you will need to use the available Help to learn how to flow the overflow text from the article on the first page into the text frame on the second page. Adjust the column lengths so that the they are even. When you are finished, save your work, print the newsletter, and close Publisher.

Drop cap →

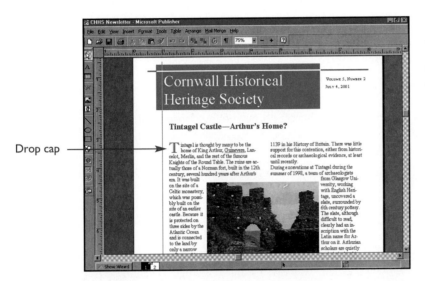

Figure 3.28
A text file has been imported and formatted, and a drop cap has been added.

New border →

Decimal tabs →

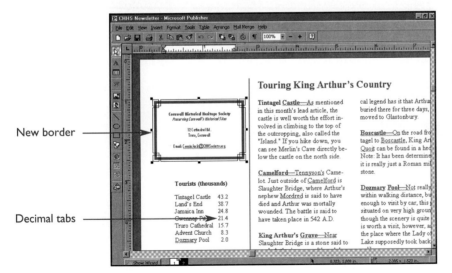

Figure 3.29
A border has been placed around a text frame, and a decimal tab has been added to a list.

Discovery Zone

Discovery Zone exercises help you gain advanced knowledge of project topics and/or application of skills. These exercises focus on enhancing your problem-solving skills. Numbered steps are not provided, but you are given hints, reminders, screen shots, and/or references to help you reach your goal for each exercise.

These exercises use a modified version of the Cornwall Historical Heritage Society newsletter you worked with in the Challenge exercises. In this case, a single-column format was used. Examine both pages to get a feel for the different looks you can use in a newsletter. You will add page numbers to this publication, and you will make extensive changes to a numbered list.

[?] I. Adding Page Numbers to a Newsletter

Many newsletters are 4, 8, or even 16 pages long. They are always in multiples of two, and usually in multiples of four. This makes it easy to print four pages on one sheet of 11" × 17" paper; then you just fold it in half. When you create newsletters longer than two pages, it is always a good idea to add page numbers. To begin this exercise, open Pub-0304 and rename it **CHHS Newsletter 2**.

Goal: Add page numbers to the CHHS Newsletter 2.

The page numbers should:

- appear on each page.
- be centered on the bottom of the page.

Hint: This exercise can all be done using one Help window, if you find the right one!

Save your work. Print out page 2 only to see if your page numbers are working.

2. Changing a Numbered List to a Lettered List

Lists, as you have seen earlier, can be set off with bullets or numbers. You can modify the look of the bullets and change the numbers to letters if you desire. You can also change other list formats. If you did not do the first Discovery Zone exercise, open Pub-0304 and rename it `CHHS Newsletter 2`.

Goal: Change the numbered list to a lettered list, then modify the list formatting.

You will be using the numbered list on the left side of the second page. Your list should:

- use capital letters instead of numbers.
- be followed by a right parenthesis) rather than a period.
- have a 0.20" indent.
- have 1.5 spaces between the lines.

Your list should look like Figure 3.30. Save your work; then print the second page of your newsletter. Close Publisher.

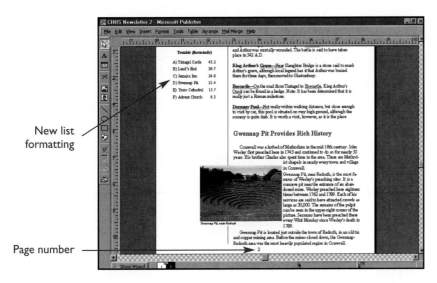

New list formatting

Page number

Figure 3.30
The formatted lettered list and the page number are displayed.

Project 4

Working with Frames

Objectives

In this project, you learn how to

➤ **Group Frames as One Object**

➤ **Ungroup and Rearrange Text and Picture Frames**

➤ **Edit a Grouped Object**

➤ **Resize and Move Grouped Objects**

➤ **Wrap Text Around Frames**

➤ **Change the Appearance of the Text Frame**

➤ **Add a Decorative Border to a Page**

Key terms introduced in this project include

- border
- color schemes
- ungroup

Why Would I Do This?

One of the strongest features of a desktop publishing program is its capability to blend graphic images with text on the same page. To do that effectively, the program defines the boundary of each image with a picture frame, which is a rectangle that may be used to select, resize, or move the image. Picture frames and text frames can be combined to form a group that can be moved and resized together. This feature is especially useful for adding captions to pictures.

For example, if you have a picture in a picture frame and its caption in a text frame, you can move them to a new location in one step if they are grouped together. In some cases, you can produce complex effects by overlapping and layering several text and picture frames. Once these frames have been positioned correctly, it is useful to group them together so that they can be moved and resized as a group without losing the positions that they have relative to each other.

Visual Summary

When you have completed this project, you will have created a flyer that contains a picture and a caption that have been grouped together. The text frame has been formatted to wrap around the picture and its caption.

Figure 4.1
A picture and its caption are grouped together, and the text is wrapped around them.

The text is wrapped around the picture and its caption

Custom border

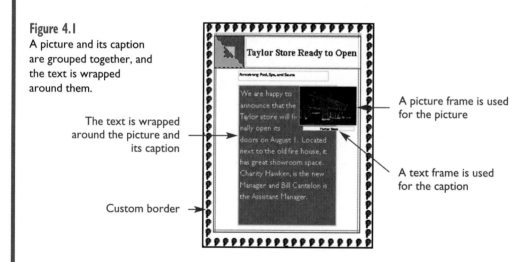

A picture frame is used for the picture

A text frame is used for the caption

Lesson 1: Grouping Frames as One Object

In many cases, you want to treat several frames as one item because they are related. A picture and its caption are a good example to two frames that belong together. Grouping the frames together does this.

In this lesson, you select the frame that contains the graphic that you have chosen to use and the frame that contains the caption. You then group them together.

To Group Frames as One Object

1 **Launch Publisher and Open the Pub-0401 publication file. Save the file to your disk as Flyer-Business.**

The one-page flyer is displayed.

2 **Move the mouse pointer to a location above and to the left of the picture caption. Click and draw a box that completely encloses the caption and the picture, as shown in Figure 4.2.**

The frames containing both the caption and the picture must be inside the box if they are to be selected together.

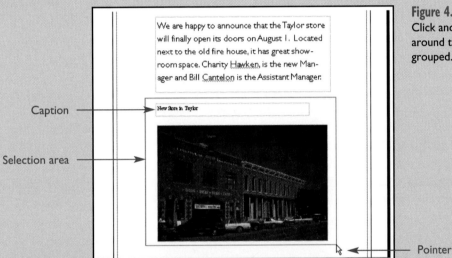

Caption

Selection area

Pointer

Figure 4.2
Click and draw a box around the objects to be grouped.

3 **Release the mouse button.**

Selection handles are displayed around both objects. The Group Objects button is displayed at the bottom of the group of selected objects (see Figure 4.3). The Group Objects button is used to group all of the currently selected objects into a single object.

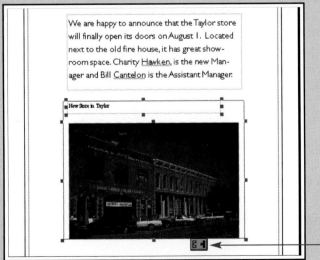

Group Objects button

Figure 4.3
When two or more objects are selected at the same time, the Group Objects button is displayed.

continues ▶

To Group Frames as One Object (continued)

4 **Click the Group Objects button.**
The two objects are grouped together. A single frame with selection handles surrounds both objects. The Group Objects button turns into the Ungroup Objects button that can be used to ungroup the objects, if necessary. You will learn how to use the Ungroup Objects button in the next lesson. Leave the objects onscreen for use in the next lesson.

Lesson 2: Ungrouping and Rearranging Text and Picture Frames

If you do not like the arrangement of the objects in a group, you can **ungroup** them (that is, remove the grouping characteristic so that you can work with the objects individually), move the objects relative to each other, and then group them again.

In this lesson, you use the Ungroup Objects button to separate the caption and picture into separate objects. You move the caption to a new location that is centered below the picture and then group the objects again.

To Ungroup and Rearrange Text and Picture Frames

1 **Confirm that the grouped objects are still selected (you will see selection handles around the caption and picture) and hover the mouse pointer over the Ungroup Objects button.**
You can use the Ungroup Objects button to separate the objects so that they are no longer part of a group.

2 **Click the Ungroup Objects button.**
Separate selection handles appear around the caption and the picture to indicate that they are separate objects, and the Ungroup Objects button changes back to the Group Objects button.

3 **Click on an empty area of the page to deselect both frames.**

4 **Place the pointer over the caption frame until it turns into the Move pointer.**
The Move pointer looks like a small truck and indicates that you can click and drag the frame to another location.

 Move Pointer
If you do not move the Move pointer, a ScreenTip displaying additional information will appear. If the Move pointer is placed on a picture frame, the ScreenTip displays the message "Picture Frame: Double-click to change." If you place the Move pointer on a text frame, the ScreenTip displays the message "Text Frame." Similar ScreenTip messages are used to describe table frames and WordArt frames.

⑤ Click and drag the caption frame to a new position below the picture. Center the text frame (not the actual text) below the picture and release the mouse button (see Figure 4.4).

Even though the text frame is centered below the picture, the text itself may be aligned at the left of the frame resulting in an off-center appearance. The text will be repositioned in the next lesson.

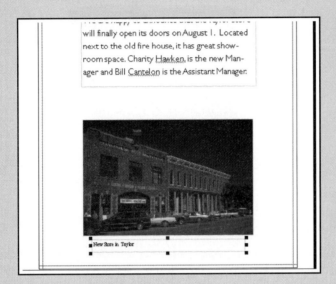

Figure 4.4
The caption frame has been repositioned below the picture.

Selecting Frames
You can select several frames that are near each other by dragging a box around them with the mouse pointer. If that is not convenient or if other objects are nearby that you do not want to select, press ⬆Shift and click the objects one at a time to select them.

⑥ Click on an empty area of the page to deselect the caption. Click and drag a box around the caption and the picture to select them.

⑦ Click the Group Objects button. The picture and caption are grouped together in their new configuration (see Figure 4.5). Leave the publication open for use in the next lesson.

continues ▶

To Ungroup and Rearrange Text and Picture Frames (continued)

Figure 4.5
The picture and its caption have been regrouped in a new configuration.

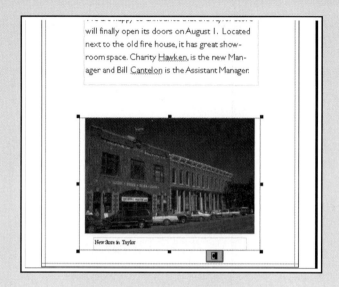

Lesson 3: Editing a Grouped Object

Most other desktop publishing programs require that you ungroup objects before you can edit any of them. Microsoft Publisher enables you to edit the objects as individuals or as a group. If you have several frames grouped together, this is a useful feature because it saves you the trouble of ungrouping, selecting, and regrouping each time you want to make a change to the text in one of the frames.

In this lesson, you edit the text of the caption, change its font size, and center it within its frame while it is still grouped with the picture.

To Edit a Grouped Object

66% ▼ **1** **Click the down arrow next to the Zoom box and change the zoom to 100%. Use the horizontal and vertical scrollbars to display the entire picture and caption.**
The caption is left-aligned within the text frame. Even though the text frame itself is centered beneath the picture, it appears that the text is not centered. This can be corrected by centering the text within the text frame. The caption would also be easier to read if it were boldface.

2 **Click the caption to select its frame.**
Notice that the selection handles indicate that a single frame exists for the grouped picture and caption, but a thin, red line around the caption frame indicates that it is selected for editing. The insertion point is placed in the text and can be used to edit the text (see Figure 4.6).

3 **Edit the text so that the new caption reads Taylor Store.**

 4 **Click and drag across the caption text to select it and click the Bold button.**
The caption is emphasized with boldface.

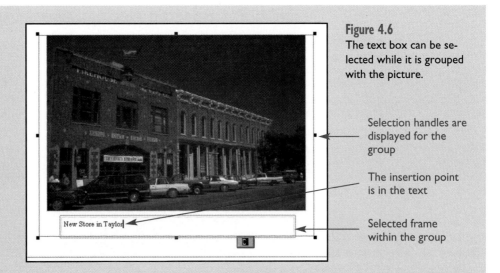

Figure 4.6
The text box can be selected while it is grouped with the picture.

Selection handles are displayed for the group

The insertion point is in the text

Selected frame within the group

5 Click the **Center** button to center the caption text under the picture.

6 Click the down arrow in the Font Size box and change the font size to 12 point. Click outside the caption box to deselect it.
The caption is centered under the picture and emphasized with bolding and a large font size (see Figure 4.7).

Figure 4.7
The caption has been edited and its formatting changed while it is grouped with the picture.

7 Click the **Save** button and save the changes you have made. Leave the publication open for use in the next lesson.

Lesson 4: Resizing and Moving Grouped Objects

One of the main advantages of grouping objects is that they can be moved and resized as a group. If picture frames are grouped with text frames and the group is resized, the frames are resized together but the contents of the frames are affected in different ways. The pictures are stretched or shrunk to fit the new frame size, but the font size of the text does not change. If the new frame is not large enough to hold the text, given the text's font size, it will not shrink the size of the text. Instead, an overflow button will appear on the smaller text box if it is selected.

In this lesson, you reduce the size of the picture and its caption and move it to a location near the top of the flyer.

To Resize and Move Grouped Objects

❶ Click on the picture to select the group.
The selection handles surrounding the group indicate that it is selected.

❷ Move the pointer to the selection handle in the lower-left corner of the group.
The pointer turns into the Resize pointer, a small, two-headed arrow that is displayed when the pointer is in position to change the size of the frame (see Figure 4.8).

Figure 4.8
Use selection handles to resize the entire group.

Taylor Store

Resizing Groups
If you use the corner selection handles, the picture will be resized proportionally. If you use one of the selection handles on the side of the group to resize the group, the picture will be distorted. For example, if you drag the side handle, the picture will change its width but not its height. If you hold the Ctrl key when you drag one of the handles, the opposite side of the frame moves in or out while the center of frame does not move. For example, if you want to make a group of objects smaller and keep the center of the group in the same place, you would hold down the Ctrl key when you resize the group.

3 **Click and drag the selection handle up and to the right to decrease the size of the group to half of its former height and width.**

The picture and text frames are resized. Notice that the caption font remains at 12 point. The size of the text is not affected by reducing the size of the text frame (see Figure 4.9).

Picture is resized to fit the smaller frame

The text frame is reduced but the font size is not

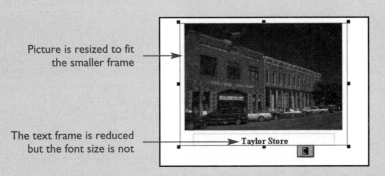

Figure 4.9
Resize the group by using the selection handles.

X   **Working with Reduced Text Frames**
If the resized text frame is too small to contain the text, you might need to ungroup the frames, adjust the size of the text frame, and then regroup. You can also reduce the font size to make the text fit in the text frame.

4 **Click the drop-down arrow next to the Zoom box and select Whole Page from the list.**

When you are moving frames, it is a good idea to view the entire page so that you can see how the frames relate to each other. The flyer might look better if the picture was next to the text that describes it.

5 **Move the pointer onto the grouped picture and caption.**

The pointer turns into the Move pointer.

6 **Click and drag the grouped picture and caption to a position on the right side of the flyer, overlapping the text.**

Your screen should look like Figure 4.10. Leave the publication open for the next lesson.

The picture obscures part of the text

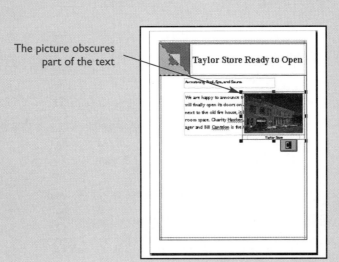

Figure 4.10
The grouped picture and caption overlap the text frame.

Lesson 5: Wrapping Text Around Frames

If the picture is smaller than an adjoining text frame, you can make the text flow around the picture to make the picture a more intimate part of the text. If the picture relates to a particular portion of the text, it is better if the picture can be close to the sentences that relate to it. Publisher makes this possible by wrapping the text around the picture frame.

In this lesson, you change the properties of the text frame to wrap the text around any object that overlaps the text frame.

To Wrap Text Around Frames

① **Click on the text box to select it.**
The selection handles are displayed. Notice that the text frame extends behind the picture.

② **Choose F̲ormat, Text Frame Prop̲erties from the menu.**
The Text Frame Properties dialog box is displayed.

③ **Click the W̲rap text around objects option and click OK.**
The text is rearranged in the portion of the text frame that is not behind the picture. Notice that the Text in Overflow indicator appears. This lets you know that the frame is not large enough to display all of the text while the picture is overlapping it and taking up space (see Figure 4.11). In some cases, a yellow caution text balloon will appear with additional information. It will go away if you continue working.

Figure 4.11
The Text in Overflow indicator shows the text frame needs to be resized.

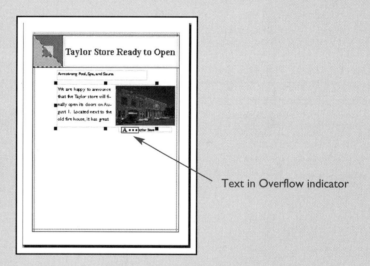

Text in Overflow indicator

④ **Click and drag the bottom selection handle downward to increase the size of the text box (see Figure 4.12). Release it and confirm that the Text in Overflow indicator is no longer displayed. Increase the size of the frame again if necessary until the Text in Overflow indicator is not displayed.**
All of the text is displayed in the larger text frame.

⑤ **Click the Save button to save your work.**
Leave the publication open for the next lesson.

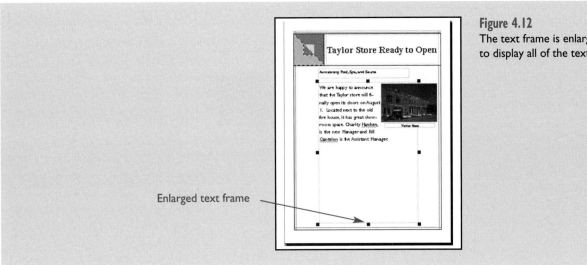

Figure 4.12
The text frame is enlarged
to display all of the text.

Enlarged text frame

Lesson 6: Changing the Appearance of the Text Frame

In some cases, you may want to emphatically separate the contents of a frame from the adjacent objects or draw attention to the contents of the frame. You can do this by using a wider line for the frame border or using a different fill color. The **border** is the edge of the frame, and it can have a range of appearances. It can be a transparent line that is invisible, or it can be a thick line in a contrasting color. You can even use small images in a repeating pattern for a border. The border serves the same function as a picture frame, and it is just as important. The type of border you choose should complement the contents of the frame. The background color of the frame can also be changed to enhance the difference between the contents of the frame, the border, and the surrounding objects.

In this lesson, you change the format of the text frame border from none to a wide line. You also change the fill color and the font color.

To Change the Appearance of the Text Frame

1 **Confirm that the text box is still selected from the previous lesson.**
The selection handles are displayed around the text frame to indicate that it has been selected.

2 **Click the Line/Border Style button to display a short menu of width and style options.**

3 **Click the widest of the three lines that are displayed.**
The border of the text box is replaced by a wide line (see Figure 4.13).

4 **Click the Line Color button and select Accent 3 from the menu of options. (Accent 3 is the fourth from the left.)**
The color of the border line is changed to the third accent color.

continues ▶

To Change the Appearance of the Text Frame   (continued)

Figure 4.13
Many line widths are available to be used as frame borders.

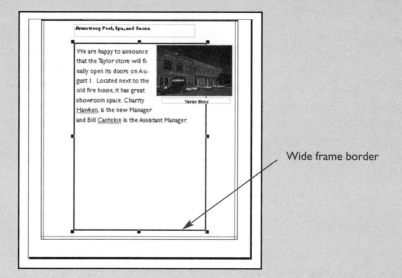

Wide frame border

 Using Accent Colors and Color Schemes
When you display a menu of line colors, a ScreenTip displays an accent number rather than a color. The actual color changes depending on which color scheme is applied to the publication. Publisher has many sets of colors, called *color schemes*, that are designed to work together to provide pleasing combinations. Once a color scheme is chosen, fill colors and line colors may be selected from the preselected accent colors.

5 **Click the Fill Color button to display a menu of fill color options.**
A menu of options is displayed.

6 **Click the Accent 1 option (the second option).**
The fill color of the text frame changes to the accent color.

7 **Click and drag across the text in the text box to select it. Click the Font Color button and choose Accent 5.**

8 **Click the down arrow next to the Font Size box and select 28 from the list. Click the Bold button and then deselect the text by clicking outside of the text area.**
Your publication should now look like Figure 4.14.

9 **Click the Save button to save your work.**
Leave the publication open for use in the next lesson.

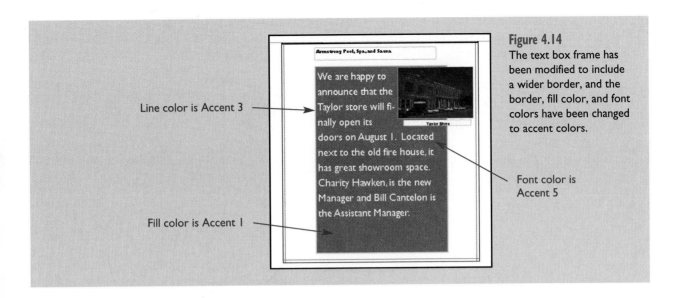

Figure 4.14
The text box frame has been modified to include a wider border, and the border, fill color, and font colors have been changed to accent colors.

Line color is Accent 3

Font color is Accent 5

Fill color is Accent 1

Lesson 7: Adding a Decorative Border to a Page

A decorative border around the page can indicate the general theme of the publication and can make the publication more attractive. For example, if the publication is a flyer that is announcing a birthday party, a decorative border consisting of party hats or confetti would be appropriate.

In this lesson, you drag a rectangle around the whole page and then select a decorative border from a menu of predesigned borders.

To Add a Decorative Border to a Page

1 **Click the Rectangle Tool on the objects toolbar. The pointer turns into cross hairs (the precision select pointer). Move the pointer to the upper-left corner of the page and then click and drag a rectangle that encloses the page.**
A rectangle surrounding the page is displayed with selection handles (see Figure 4.15).

2 **Select Format, Line/Border Style, More Styles from the menu.**
The Border Style dialog box is displayed.

3 **Click the BorderArt tab.**
Available borders are displayed.

4 **Select the Balloons...Hot Air option and click OK.**
The page is surrounded by a border of small hot air balloons (see Figure 4.16).

5 **Close the publication and save the changes. Close Publisher.**

continues ▶

To Add a Decorative Border to a Page   (continued)

Figure 4.15
The entire page has been selected.

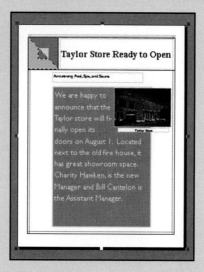

Figure 4.16
A border has been added to the page.

Summary

In this project, the text and picture frames were grouped and ungrouped. The text in a text frame was edited while it was grouped with the picture. The two frames were moved and resized while they were grouped together, and then a different text frame was formatted to wrap text around the group when the group was moved onto the text frame. The text frame was formatted to change the border, fill color, and font color. Finally, a border was placed around the entire page.

You can supplement your knowledge of using and formatting frames by using the Office Assistant and typing `How do I format picture frames`. Pay particular attention to the topic that focuses on lining up frames.

Checking Concepts and Terms ✓

True/False

For each of the following statements, check *T* or *F* to indicate whether the statement is true or false.

__T __F **1.** You can select several objects by dragging a box around them. [L1]

__T __F **2.** If you want to select two frames that are not near each other so that you can group them, you can do so by holding down Ctrl and clicking on each object. [L2]

__T __F **3.** The Group Objects button changes into the Ungroup Objects button after it is clicked. [L1]

__T __F **4.** If you want to edit the text in a text frame that is grouped with another frame, you must ungroup the two frames before you can make any changes to the text. [L3]

__T __F **5.** If you place a picture frame over a text frame and then wrap the text around the picture, the text frame will automatically resize, if necessary, to make room for the text that was displaced by the picture. [L5]

__T __F **6.** The thickness of a frame border can be changed. [L6]

__T __F **7.** If you resize a text frame and make it smaller, the text within the box is automatically reduced in point size to fit the frame. [L4]

__T __F **8.** You can use the Fill Color button to change the fill color of a text frame. [L6]

__T __F **9.** If two frames are grouped together, a single rectangle with one set of selection handles surrounds them when the group is selected. [L1]

__T __F **10.** If you resize a group using the corner selection handle, the picture is resized proportionally. [L4]

Multiple Choice

Circle the letter of the correct answer for each of the following questions.

1. The button that is used to combine two or more frames into a single group is the _____ button. [L1]

   a. Format Frames

   b. Ungroup Objects

   c. Merge

   d. Group Objects

2. If two frames are grouped together and you select one of the frames, the selected frame is enclosed by _____. [L3]

   a. a thin black line with selection handles

   b. a thin black line with sizing handles

   c. a thin red line

   d. a marquee

3. When two objects are grouped together using the appropriate button, that button changes into the _____ button. [L3]

   a. Reformat Frames

   b. Ungroup Objects

   c. Split Window

   d. Group Objects

4. If a text box contains text that is 12 points in size and you reduce the size of a text box to half of its original height and width, text will be _____ points in size. [L4]

   a. 4

   b. 6

   c. 8

   d. 12

5. If you place a picture on top of part of a text frame and then wrap the text around the picture and the text will not fit in the frame, the text frame will _____. [L5]

a. display a Text in Overflow indicator

b. automatically lengthen to accommodate the text

c. automatically widen to accommodate the text

d. display a marquee to draw attention to the problem

6. When editing a text object that is grouped with another object, you may not _____. [L3]

a. change the border line width

b. move the text object relative to the other object

c. change the fill color

d. change the font size or color

7. To add a border to the entire page, you start by _____. [L7]

a. choosing Format, Borders and Shading from the menu

b. selecting the page frame

c. choosing Insert, Page Frame from the menu

d. drawing a rectangle around the page using the Rectangle tool

8. You can select frames to be grouped by holding down _____ and clicking each frame. [L2]

a. ◆Shift

b. Ctrl

c. Alt

d. Tab↹

9. If you decrease the size of a group of frames using the selection handle on the side of the group, _____. [L4]

a. the picture will be distorted and the font size of the text will be reduced

b. the picture will be distorted and the font size of the text will not be reduced

c. the picture will not be distorted and the font size of the text will be reduced

d. the picture will not be distorted and the font size of the text will not be reduced

10. When you are choosing a new accent color for a fill color or a line, the ScreenTip displays _____. [L6]

a. the name of the color

b. the accent number for that color scheme

c. the name of the publication

d. none of the above

Screen ID

Label each element of the Publisher screen shown in Figure 4.17.

Figure 4.17

A. Text that wraps around a picture

B. Border around the page

C. Rectangle tool

D. Fill Color button

E. Frame border

F. Mouse pointer on a selection handle

G. Line Color button

H. Selection handle

I. Line Border/Style button

J. Font Color button

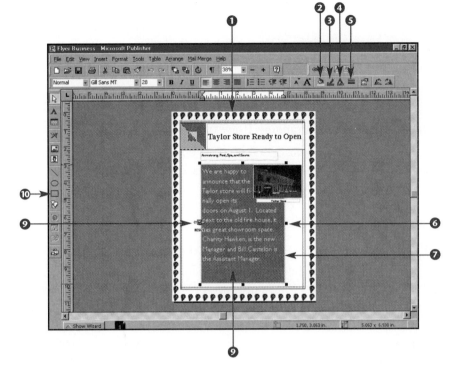

1. _____   5. _____   9. _____

2. _____   6. _____   10. _____

3. _____   7. _____

4. _____   8. _____

Discussion Questions

1. This project used a picture and its caption as an example of two frames that would be grouped together. What are some other examples of frames that would appropriately be grouped together?

2. What are the advantages of editing an individual object that is grouped with other objects? Why might ungrouping cause problems?

3. Under what circumstances might you change the fill color of a text frame? Where have you seen this done? Does it draw your attention, or do you find it distracting? Why?

4. In this project, you changed frame borders and backgrounds, changed font colors, and added page borders. Do you think it is possible to add too many enhancements to a page? What would too many enhancements do?

5. When the picture frame forced some of the wrapped text out of the text box, did you think that the program gave you sufficient warning of this problem? If not, how would you change the program. If so, describe what it does that successfully drew your attention to the problem.

Skill Drill

Skill Drill exercises reinforce project skills. Each skill reinforced is the same, or nearly the same, as a skill presented in this project. Each exercise includes a brief narrative introduction, followed by detailed instructions in a step-by-step format.

In the following exercises, you will modify a flyer for a nonprofit group using the same skills you learned in this project.

I. Ungrouping and Rearranging Objects

A flyer for a nonprofit organization has been laid out, and you are told to make room for some additional text that should be placed in a prominent location in the flyer. In this series of exercises, you rearrange the objects in the flyer to make room for the additional text. First, you will ungroup the picture and its caption and move the caption below the picture.

To ungroup and rearrange the objects in the flyer, complete the following steps:

1. Launch Publisher and choose to open an existing file. Open Pub-0402 and save the publication on your disk as `Flyer-Nonprofit`.

2. Click on the picture to select the group and click the Ungroup Objects button.

3. Click on an empty area to deselect the objects. Select the picture and move it upward. Place the caption below the picture as shown (see Figure 4.18).

4. Select the picture and its caption. Click the Group Objects button to group them together.

5. If you plan to do the next exercise, leave the publication open and skip the first step. Otherwise, close the publication.

Figure 4.18
The objects have been ungrouped and re-arranged.

2. Editing the Text in the Text Frame While It Is Grouped

This exercise can build upon the previous exercise, or you may open the file indicated in step 1 and modify it instead. Both methods producer the file Flyer-Nonprofit.

Before you resize the picture and its caption, you will edit the caption and reduce its font size. Fortunately, you do not have to ungroup the objects to make changes to the caption in the text frame.

To edit the text in the caption while it is grouped, complete the following steps:

1. Launch Publisher and choose to open an existing file. Open Pub-0402 and save the publication on your disk as Flyer-Nonprofit.

2. Move the pointer to the right of the last word in the caption but still within the frame.

3. Click once to select the frame and place the insertion point to the right of the last letter in the caption.

4. Use the (+Backspace) key to delete the last word in the caption and replace it with Park!.

5. Select all of the text in the caption and change its font size to 12 point.

6. If you plan to do the next exercise, leave the publication open and skip the first step. Otherwise, close the publication.

3. Selecting and Grouping Objects

The map at the lower-left corner of the flyer consists of several individual objects. They may be moved and resized together if they are first grouped. Grouping them will give you the option to make the map smaller, if necessary to make more room for the anticipated additional text. Group the elements of the map so that it may be moved as a unit.

To select and group objects, complete the following steps:

1. Launch Publisher and choose to open an existing file. Open Pub-0402 and save the publication on your disk as Flyer-Nonprofit.

2. Click and drag a box around all the elements of the map to select them all.

3. Click the Group Objects button that appears below the frames.

4. If you plan to do the next exercise, leave the publication open and skip the first step. Otherwise, close the publication.

4. Resizing and Moving Grouped Frames and Wrapping Text Around Them

You can make more room in the middle of the flyer by resizing the picture and moving it and its caption to the upper-right corner of the flyer. In this exercise, you resize the picture and its caption as a group; you then move the group so that it overlaps the text frame above it.

To resize and move grouped frames and wrap text around them, complete the following steps:

1. Launch Publisher and choose to open an existing file. Open Pub-0402 and save the publication on your disk as Flyer-Nonprofit.

2. Click and drag one of the picture's corner selection handles to make the picture about one-third of its current height and width.

3. Drag the picture with its caption to the upper-right corner of the flyer. Do not place it in the extreme upper-right corner. Leave space for a decorative border around the flyer.

4. Click the text frame with the information about the fundraiser to select it. Choose Format, Text Frame Properties from the menu.

5. Click the Wrap text around objects option and click OK.

6. Drag the bottom selection handle to enlarge the text box so that the Text in Overflow indicator is no longer displayed.

7. Select the text and click the Align Left button.

8. Click the Fill Color button and select Accent 4 from the Scheme colors. If you plan to do the next exercise, leave the publication open and skip the first step.

5. Adding a Decorative Border to the Page

In this exercise, you will add a border to the page.

To add a decorative border to the page, complete the following steps:

1. Launch Publisher and choose to open an existing file. Open Pub-0402 and save the publication on your disk as `Flyer-Nonprofit`.

2. Click the Rectangle tool on the objects toolbar. Click and draw a rectangle around the perimeter of the page on top of the outermost guideline.

3. Select Format, Line/Border Style, More Styles from the menu. Click the BorderArt tab

4. Select the Trees option and click OK. The flyer should look like the one shown in Figure 4.19.

Figure 4.19
The flyer has been formatted as described in exercises 1 through 5.

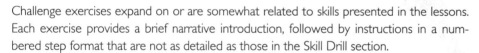

Challenge

Challenge exercises expand on or are somewhat related to skills presented in the lessons. Each exercise provides a brief narrative introduction, followed by instructions in a numbered step format that are not as detailed as those in the Skill Drill section.

In the exercises that follow, you will be modifying a flyer that is appropriate for announcing a party. Each exercise describes a modification to the flyer. They do not depend on each other, and the finished flyer may display all or any one of the modifications described in this section. The figure that accompanies the Challenge exercises displays the results of doing all of the exercises.

1. Resizing a Group Using the Side Selection Handles

In this exercise, you intentionally distort a picture by resizing it using the side handles.

1. Open the file Pub-0403 and save it on your disk as `Flyer-exercise`.

2. Select the second grouped picture and caption.

3. Click and drag the selection handle on the bottom side downward to make the picture seem tall and thin (see Figure 4.20)

Figure 4.20
Dragging a side selection handle distorts the picture but not the caption.

4. Add a second page to the publication. Create your own flyer in which you paste a clip art image into the flyer twice and distort the second one to make some humorous point. Save the publication.

5. If you plan to do the next exercise, leave the publication open and skip the first step.

2. Using Clip Art Images in a Border

The program includes a variety of boundary patterns, but you can use images from the ClipArt Gallery to make a border as well.

1. Open the file Pub-0403 and save it on your disk as `Flyer-exercise`.

2. Click the Rectangle Tool button and drag a rectangle around the perimeter of the page.

3. Select Format, Line/Border Style, More Styles from the menu. Click the BorderArt tab, if necessary.

4. Click the Create Custom button.

5. Confirm that the Use Clip Gallery to choose the picture option is selected and click the Choose Picture button.

6. Search for clips on the topic of exercise. Select a clip art picture that you think is appropriate for the topic and click the Insert Clip button.

7. Click OK to close the dialog box and then click OK again to close the Border Style dialog box.

8. If you plan to do the next exercise, leave the publication open and skip the first step.

3. Customizing the Lines Used as a Border

If the border of the frame is a line, you can choose to remove it from one or more sides. In this exercise, you place a line border around the large text frame and then remove the lines on the top and right side of the frame.

1. Open the file Pub-0403 and save it on your disk as `Flyer-exercise`.

2. Select the large text frame and click the Line/Border Style Button.

3. Click the More Styles option and click the Line Border tab, if necessary.

4. Click the 8 pt option to place an 8-point line border around the frame.

5. Click on the left of the sample frame in the Select a side box to select it.

5. Click the None box in the Choose a thickness area. The left border line is removed.

7. Select the right side of the box and remove the border line from the right side.

8. Click the OK button. The large text box displays an 8-point border at the top and bottom of the frame. Enlarge the frame to show all of the text as shown in Figure 4.21. Save the publication and then close it.

Figure 4.21
The border lines on the sides of the frames may be edited separately or removed.

4. Placing Text on a Picture

If the color of the picture is fairly uniform, you might want the text to display on top of the picture. In this exercise, you bring the text box to the front, pick a font color that is visible on the picture, and change the fill color of the text box so that the text is also visible in the text box.

1. Open the file Pub-0404 and save it on your disk as `Flyer-goal`.

2. Move the caption text box onto the picture near the top.

3. Select the caption text box and change its fill color to No Fill.

4. Select all the text in the caption text box and change the font color to white.

5. Resize the caption box so that it is the same size as the picture.

6. Change the Line/Border style to none.

7. Select both the caption and the picture by dragging a selection area that encloses the picture and caption. Group the two together. Save the publication.

8. If you plan to do the next exercise, leave the publication open and skip the first step.

5. Using Automatic Copyfitting to Prevent Text Overflow

When you place a picture on a text frame that is formatted to wrap text around pictures, the text will flow around the picture. If there is not enough room in the text frame, the Text in Overflow indicator displays at the bottom of the text frame. In some cases, this indicator may be off the screen and you may not notice it. An alternative is to change the property of the text frame to make it change the font size to fit the available space.

In this exercise, you change the property of the large text frame to use automatic copyfitting.

1. Open the file Pub-0404 and save it on your disk as `Flyer-goal`.
2. Click the large text frame to select it. Notice that the text size is 24 point.
3. Choose Format, AutoFit Text, Shrink Text on Overflow from the menu.
4. Move the picture upward so that it overlaps the last two rows of text. Notice that the text flows around the picture but that it also decreases in size to remain inside its text frame.
5. Click on the text frame. Notice that the text size is now less than 24 points (see Figure 4.22)
6. Close the publication and save your changes.

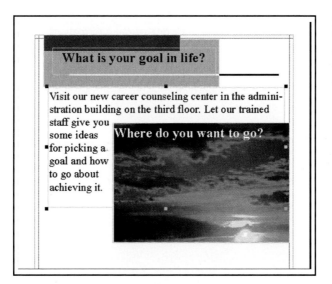

Figure 4.22
The AutoFit feature reduces the size of the text when it wraps around another object.

Discovery Zone

Discovery Zone exercises help you gain advanced knowledge of project topics and/or application of skills. These exercises focus on enhancing your problem-solving skills. Numbered steps are not provided, but you are given hints, reminders, screen shots, and/or references to help you reach your goal for each exercise.

[?] 1. Creating Custom Border Art

Publisher can take a simple picture that contains a design and create a border where that picture is replicated around the perimeter of the page.

To begin this exercise, open Pub-0405 and save it to your disk as `Personal Flyer`.

Goal: Create a flyer with a custom border.

Use Publisher Help to look up information on how to create a custom border.

Draw a rectangle around the perimeter of this flyer and apply a custom border. Change the <u>B</u>order size option to 20 pts and deselect the <u>U</u>se Default Size option. Choose a picture that is not part of the Clip gallery. Use the picture Pub-0406.gif, which is stored with your other student files.

Dozens of other pictures suitable for borders may be provided as background images. If your copy of Office is installed on the computer you are using (network installations are different), look for them in the following location: C:\Program Files\Microsoft Office\ Clipart\Publisher\Backgrounds. Then select a different background image for your border from these files.

2. Creating a Flyer to Announce an Event of Your Choice

Create a flyer to announce an event of your choice that includes the features described in this project.

Goal: Create a flyer that has a picture grouped with a caption. The picture/caption group overlaps a text box, and the text within the box wraps around the picture. The flyer also has a border around the perimeter that uses a picture or clip art.

Launch Publisher and use the wizard to create a flyer. Pick one of the informational flyers in the wizard and accept all of the wizard's default settings. Save the flyer as `Personal Flyer2`.

Delete the picture placeholder and insert your own picture. Add your own text to the text box. Rearrange the picture and text box so that they overlap and the text in the text frame wraps around the picture.

Finish the flyer by adding a border around the flyer that uses BorderArt.

Project 5

Using Tables, Charts, and Mail Merge

Objectives

In this project, you learn how to

➤ **Add a Table to a Publication**

➤ **Add Rows and Columns to a Table**

➤ **Resize and Format a Table**

➤ **Add an Object from Another Source**

➤ **Resize and Move Excel Chart**

➤ **Change Chart Elements**

➤ **Create an Address List**

➤ **Merge an Address List with a Publication**

➤ **Run Mail Merge**

Key terms introduced in this project include

- cell
- column selector
- data source
- field

- Mail Merge
- Object Linking and Embedding (OLE)
- row selector

Why Would I Do This?

You can create many different types of publications with Publisher, from simple flyers to polished brochures. Each publication is selected to convey information to a particular audience with a specific goal in mind. You may need to share information, sell a product or idea, create a promotional piece, or encourage participation or support. Just as each type of publication is selected with a specific audience and goal in mind, you also want to choose techniques that are best suited for presenting different types of information.

Publisher has some special features that can be used to convey information and deliver your publication to its intended audience. Sometimes information that you want to include in a publication is a comparison of data or a listing that is identified by groups or categories. This type of information is best displayed in a table or a chart. In Publisher, you can create a table much as you would in a word processing program. You can also include graphs in a publication by inserting a chart from Excel or another charting program. Charts are just one example of many objects that you can insert into a publication.

You will want to mail some of the pieces that you create directly to your audience. You can do this in Publisher by including a mailing address area. This feature is available on newsletters, brochures, and other types of publications. By selecting the mailing label option, you can create a self-contained mailer and avoid the expense and time required to stuff and address envelopes.

In this project, you learn how to work with tables in Publisher and how to add a chart object from Excel. You also create a mailing list and learn how to use the **Mail Merge** feature, which is a program that merges an address list with a publication or other document to create a personalized, addressed publication. To learn how to use these special features, you will finish creating a brochure that has been designed to mail to customers. The layout of the brochure has already been selected, the content has been written, and pictures have been added. To finish the brochure, you will add a table showing prices, import a chart from Excel, create an address list, and merge the list with the brochure.

Visual Summary

When you have completed this project, you will have created a brochure that promotes spas and saunas for the upcoming season; this brochure will be mailed to customers.

Figure 5.1
The inside of the brochure shows a table of sample prices and a chart showing increased popularity of spas and saunas.

A chart from Excel has been added

A table has been added

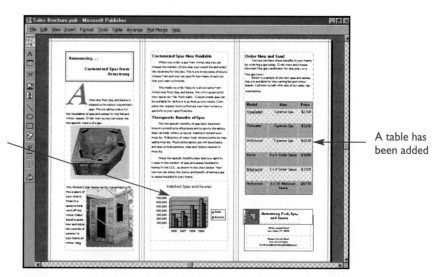

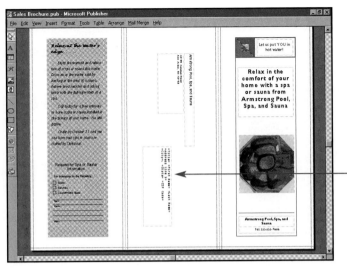

Figure 5.2
The outside of the brochure contains a mailing label for sending the brochure to your customers.

Address list is merged in mailing label area

Lesson 1: Adding a Table to the Publication

Some information that you may want to include is best displayed in a column and row format. Tables are ideally suited for this purpose and can be used in Publisher. If you have worked with tables in a word processing program, you will find this process to be very similar.

In this lesson, you open an existing publication and rename it as Sales Brochure. This is the fall/winter sales piece that is being created to mail to existing pool customers. The marketing department wants to promote spas and saunas to existing customers who have bought pools from Armstrong Pool, Spa, and Sauna. Research indicates that a customer who has purchased a pool is more likely to buy a spa or sauna. This year, the company is able to customize spas to a customer's specifications and that service is highlighted in the brochure.

In this lesson, you add a table that shows comparative prices for spas and saunas.

To Add a Table to a Publication

1 **Open the Pub-0501 file and save the file on your disk as Sales Brochure.**
The sales brochure is displayed with its new name (see Figure 5.3). The brochure is two pages long. Page 1 serves as the outside cover, with an area reserved for a mailing address on the middle panel. The inside of the brochure (page 2) has most of the content.

2 **Click the Page Navigation button for page 2 to display the second page of the brochure.**
The text on the right-hand panel urges the customer to take action by calling to order a spa or sauna. Below it, you will add a table and enter prices for the more popular spas and saunas.

continues ▶

To Add a Table to a Publication   (continued)

Figure 5.3
The outside of the
brochure includes a front
cover and a mailing area.

Panel used for mailing address

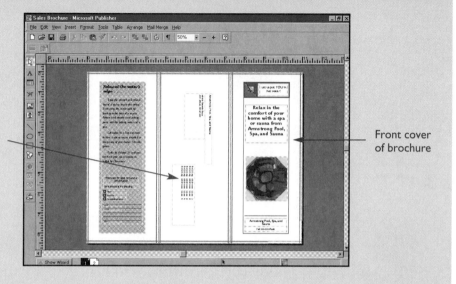

Front cover
of brochure

![icon] ❸ **Click the Table Frame Tool on the Objects toolbar and position
your mouse pointer in the third panel under the text box, as shown
in Figure 5.4.**
The mouse pointer changes to cross hairs. Next you will click and drag to
open a table frame.

Figure 5.4
To add a table, first select
the Table Frame tool.

Table Frame tool →

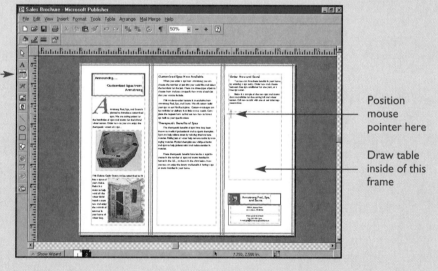

Position
mouse
pointer here

Draw table
inside of this
frame

❹ **Click and drag down and to the right to open a table frame inside of
the frame outline that shows on the brochure.**
When you release the mouse, the Create Table dialog box opens (see Figure
5.5). The number of rows or columns showing in the dialog box will vary depending on how large you made your table frame.

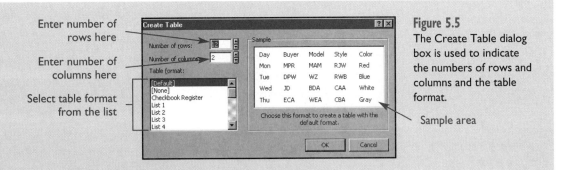

Enter number of rows here

Enter number of columns here

Select table format from the list

Figure 5.5
The Create Table dialog box is used to indicate the numbers of rows and columns and the table format.

Sample area

5 **Type 6 in the Number of rows box.**
You plan to include prices for three saunas and three spas.

6 **Make sure 2 is displayed in the Number of columns box and [Default] is selected in the Table format box.**
The table will list the name of the spa or sauna and its price. You can click on the different formats listed to see the available options. The selected style displays in the same box on the right (see Figure 5.6).

7 **Click OK. Increase the zoom to 100%.**
A table grid is displayed in the space where you drew the table frame (see Figure 5.6). The insertion point is shown in the first cell of the table. A *cell* is the intersection of a row and column and is where you enter the data for the table. A *column selector* is shown at the top of each column, and a *row selector* is shown at the left side of each row. They are used to select entire columns or rows. When you point to this area, the ScreenTip displays "Select Cells."

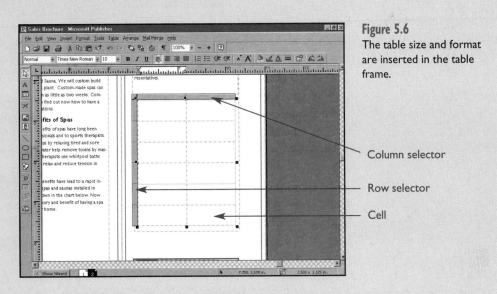

Figure 5.6
The table size and format are inserted in the table frame.

Column selector

Row selector

Cell

8 **With the insertion point in the first cell, type AquaSplash and press Tab⇆.**
The first spa name is entered, and the insertion point moves to the next empty cell.

continues ▶

To Add a Table to a Publication   (continued)

9 **Type $2,500 and press** Tab⇆.
The price is entered in the second cell, and the insertion point moves to the next row.

10 **Use the same technique to enter the rest of the data as shown in the following list.**

Tidewater $3,000

Hollywood $4,200

Sierra $3,000

Ridgemont $3,500

Hollywood $4,750

After the data have been entered, the table should look like the one in Figure 5.7.

Figure 5.7
The data is entered in the table.

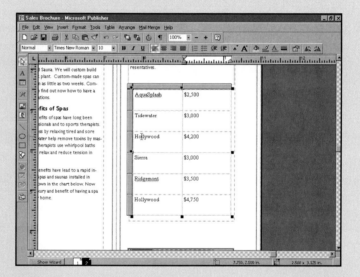

If you press ⏎Enter, the insertion point moves to the next line in the cell, not to the next cell. If this happens, press ⬅Backspace and then press Tab⇆ to move to the next cell.

11 **Save your work and leave the file open for the next lesson.**

 Moving Around in a Table
The same techniques that are used to move around in a table in Word can be used here. Press ⬆Shift+Tab⇆ to move back one cell. Use ⬆ to move up a row and ⬇ to move down a row within the table. If you make a mistake, simply click in the cell, select the text you want to change, and type the correct information.

Selecting the Entire Table
You may want to select an entire table to make a formatting change. You can choose Table, Select, Table from the menu; click and drag across the entire table; or click the Select Cells button in the upper-left corner of the table where the column selectors and row selectors meet. To deselect the table, simply click in a single cell.

Lesson 2: Adding Rows and Columns to a Table

When you create a table, you may need to add more information and increase the number of rows or columns in the table. In our example, you realize that the name does not give the customer any information about the type of spa or sauna. You also decide that titles for the columns would be useful.

In this lesson, you add a middle column and enter a brief description for each item. Then you add a row at the top for the column headings.

To Add Rows and Columns to a Table

1 **Click the column selector at the top of the first column.**
The first column is highlighted.

2 **Choose Table, Insert Columns from the menu.**
A column is inserted to the right of the first column. The table is now too wide for the space on the page. This will be corrected in Lesson 3, so do not be concerned about it at this time.

3 **Click in the top cell in the new column and type 3-person Spa.**
The description for the AquaSplash spa is entered (see Figure 5.8).

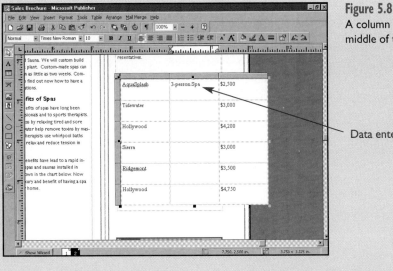

Figure 5.8
A column is added in the middle of the table.

Data entered here

continues ▶

To Add Rows and Columns to a Table   (continued)

4 **Press ⬇ to move to the next empty cell and type** 5-person Spa. **Use the ⬇ key to move to each of the remaining cells and enter the following information:**

7-person Spa

4 x 6 Cedar Sauna

5 x 8 Cedar Sauna

6 x 10 Redwood Sauna

Your table should look like the one in Figure 5.9 after the descriptions are added. Next you will add a row at the top of the table.

Figure 5.9
Descriptions are added
for each spa and sauna.

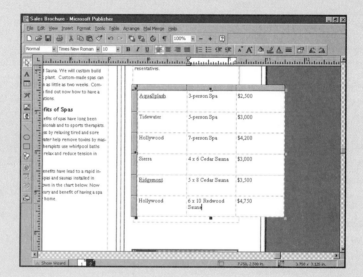

5 **Click the Select Cells button in the upper-left corner of the table to select the entire table.**
The mouse pointer should be shaped like a pointing finger. When you click, the entire table is highlighted.

6 **Choose Table, Insert Rows or Columns from the menu.**
The Insert dialog box opens (see Figure 5.10). Because the entire table has been selected, the program needs more information about what you want to do. You use this dialog box to specify whether you want to insert a row or a column and where you want it to be placed.

Figure 5.10
The Insert dialog box is
used to specify the number of columns or rows
you want to add and
where to place either.

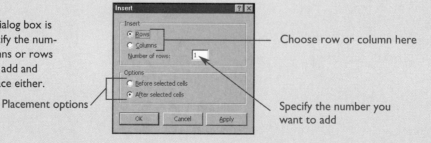

Choose row or column here

Placement options

Specify the number you
want to add

When You Have to Use the Insert Dialog Box
If you want to add a row at the top of a table or a column at the left side of the table, you must use the Insert dialog box. If you select one row or one column and then choose <u>I</u>nsert, <u>R</u>ow, or <u>I</u>nsert, <u>C</u>olumn, the program will place the new row below the selected one, and the new column to the right of the selected one. To give you control over where the row or column will be placed, you must use the Insert dialog box.

7 **Make sure the <u>R</u>ows option is selected, and 1 is displayed in the <u>N</u>umber of rows box. Select the <u>B</u>efore selected cells option.**
Once you have selected your options, you can choose <u>A</u>pply to see how it will look. To effect the change permanently, you need to click OK.

8 **Click OK to make the changes to the table.**
A new row is added to the top of the table.

9 **Click in the new cell in the upper-left corner and type Model, press Tab⇆, type Size, press Tab⇆, and type Price.**
All of the data you want in the table is now entered (see Figure 5.11).

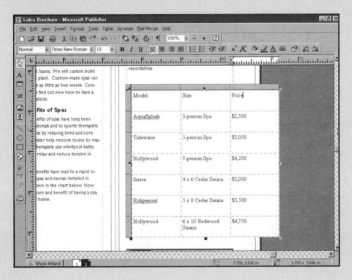

Figure 5.11
The column headings are added to the table.

10 **Save your work and leave the file open for use in the next lesson.**

Lesson 3: Resizing and Formatting a Table

When working with a table in Publisher, you may need to resize the table frame so that the information will fit in the desired space. The rows or columns may be too big or small and therefore may need to be adjusted. In our example, a row and a column were added, which increased the overall space used by the table. Therefore, the size of the table needs to be reduced so that it fits within the available space on the brochure. The price column is wider than necessary, and the column heading row is taller than necessary for the information.

The default format that was used when the table was created is essentially devoid of much style. You can use the Table AutoFormat option to select a different style. You can also make adjustments to a style by changing the font, border, or background characteristics.

In this lesson, you reduce the size of the table, and resize the rows and columns to better suit the data that was entered. You also apply a new format using the AutoFormat feature, and then make some modifications and final adjustments to the format and the table size.

To Resize and Format a Table

1 **Position the mouse pointer over the resize handle in the middle of the right side of the table frame.**
The Table Frame ScreenTip is displayed in addition to the resize icon (see Figure 5.12).

Figure 5.12
Use the resize handles to adjust the size of the table frame.

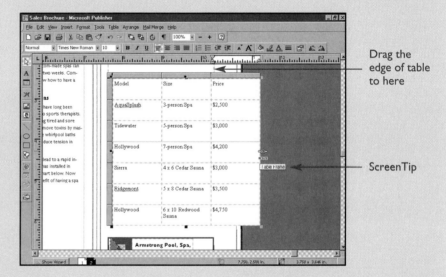

Drag the edge of table to here

ScreenTip

2 **Click and drag to the left until the right edge of the table is aligned with the right edge of the larger text frame.**
Now the table frame is within the frame for this panel.

3 **Click the Select Cells button in the upper-left corner of the table to select the entire table.**

4 **Choose Table, AutoFormat from the menu, and select List 3.**
A preview of the selected format displays in the Sample area.

5 **Click the Options button and deselect the Text formatting and Borders check boxes.**
The effect of removing these options is displayed in the Sample area (see Figure 5.13).

6 **Click OK. With the table still highlighted, click the down arrow next to the Font box and choose Gill Sans MT from the list box.**
The table format style is applied, and the font is changed. The font style selected matches the font that is used in the rest of the brochure.

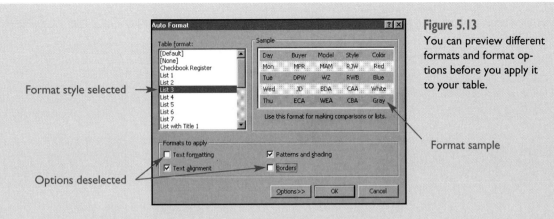

Format style selected →

Options deselected →

Format sample

7 **With the table still highlighted, click the Line/Border Style button and choose the second line that is displayed.**

The table is surrounded by a 2-point border.

8 **Click the Line Color button and select the second color—Accent I (Medium Blue).**

The line around the table is changed to blue, which matches the color scheme used in the brochure.

9 **Click the row selector next to the first row that contains the column headings; then click the Bold button.**

Emphasis is added to the column headings to make them standout from the rest of the text in the table.

10 **Click and drag across the prices in the last column. Do not include the column heading.**

Currency is typically displayed right-aligned where a decimal is implied.

11 **Click the Align Right button to align the prices on the right side of the cells.**

12 **Click in any cell to deselect the prices; then position the mouse pointer on the dividing line between the first two row selectors.**

The mouse icon changes to an Adjust pointer and a ScreenTip displays "Adjust Height of Selected Rows" (see Figure 5.14).

13 **Click and drag up to reduce the height of the first row so that it is just tall enough for the text in the first row.**

This row does not need to be the same size as the data rows.

14 **Position the mouse pointer on the dividing line between the last two column selectors.**

The mouse icon changes to an Adjust pointer, and a ScreenTip displays "Adjust Width of Selected Columns." The price column can be reduced and the middle column expanded.

15 **Hold down ⬆Shift and then click and drag the Adjust pointer to the right so that the last column is just wide enough for the prices.**

The Size column is expanded, and the Price column is reduced.

continues ▶

To Resize and Format a Table (continued)

Figure 5.14

The Adjust pointer can be used to change one or many rows or columns.

Click here to adjust the first row

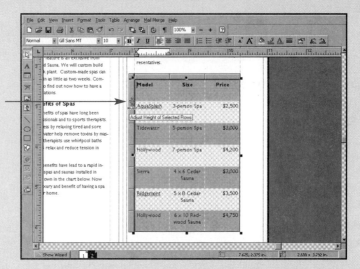

ℹ **Resizing Columns and Rows**

When you hold down ⇧Shift as you resize a column or row, the size of the table does not change. Once you have created the size you want for a table, use this technique to adjust the columns and rows within that table frame.

---

16 Click in an open area to see the results of your changes. Save your work and leave the file open for the next lesson.

The resized and formatted table should look like the one in Figure 5.15.

Figure 5.15

The table is formatted, and the rows and columns are adjusted to fit the data.

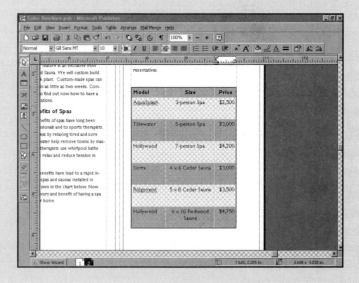

Using the Bold Button

Normally, clicking the Bold button applies bold to the selected text. The Bold button is like a toggle switch; it changes the current condition of selected text. If you selected a group of cells and the text in the first selected cell is bold, clicking the Bold button removes bold from all the selected cells. If you wanted to reapply bold to all of the text, you would click the Bold button again.

Lesson 4: Adding an Object from Another Source

Sometimes you will want to include information that you have created in other applications or from other sources. Rather than trying to recreate the information in Publisher, it is often easier to insert the object. One example of when this is useful is if you want to include a chart or graph that gives a visual picture of financial or numeric information. This is the kind of information that usually is included in annual reports to shareholders or financial reports to supporters. The **Object Linking and Embedding (OLE)** feature that is part of other Microsoft Office applications can also be used with Publisher. OLE enables you to share information between applications. The main difference between linking and embedding is where the data is stored. With a linked file, the original data is store in the source file and is linked to the destination file. If changes are made to the source file, the changes are also reflected in the destination file. An embedded object does not maintain this link. Any changes to the source file are not reflected in the destination file, and any changes in the object after it is embedded does not affect the original source file.

Publisher does not have its own charting program, so this is a good example of when you would need to include information that can be created only in another software.

In this lesson, you insert a chart from Excel in the lower half of the center panel of the Sales Brochure. The chart shows the growth of sales of spas and saunas in homes in the United States in the last several years. When the chart is first inserted, it is much too large. In the next lesson, you will work with changing the chart to fit into the publication.

To Add an Object from Another Source

1 Change the Zoom to Whole Page so that you can see the entire second page of the brochure.
A chart showing the growth of sales of saunas and spas in U.S. homes will be added to the open area at the bottom of the middle panel.

2 If necessary, click the gray area outside of the brochure so that nothing is selected; then choose Insert, Object from the menu.
After a slight delay, the Insert Object dialog box opens. You have two choices in this box. You can create a new object using one of the object types shown in the list box, or you can choose Create from File and select an existing file to insert (see Figure 5.16).

3 Click the Create from File option button.
The Object Type box is replaced by a File box and a Browse button.

continues ▶

To Add an Object from Another Source (continued)

Figure 5.16
The Insert Object dialog box is used to create a new file or find an existing file.

Select this option

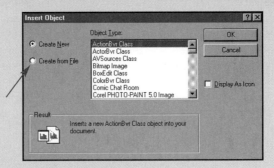

4 **Click the Browse button.**
The Browse dialog box opens (see Figure 5.17). This is similar to the Open and Save dialog boxes. It gives you access to the files on your computer and on your network.

Figure 5.17
The Browse dialog box is used to locate the file you want to insert.

Available files shown here

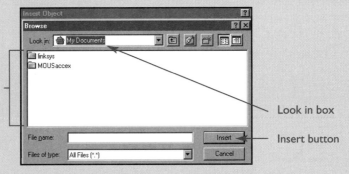

Look in box

Insert button

5 **Use the Look in box to locate the folder for this project; then select the Excel file titled Sales Growth.**
The files for this project are located on the CD-ROM that came with your book. They may also be found on a network drive or your hard drive, if you extracted the files to a folder on your computer.

6 **Click Insert.**
The Insert Object dialog box displays the path to the file you want to use in the File box.

7 **Click OK.**
The chart is inserted and placed on top of the brochure (see Figure 5.18).

 Inserting Excel Charts
Charts in Excel can be saved on their own page, as is the case with the Sales Growth chart. A chart can also be saved as part of the spreadsheet that contains the data. If you insert a chart that is on the same page as the data, the spreadsheet showing the data is also inserted.

8 **Save your work and leave the file open for the next lesson.**

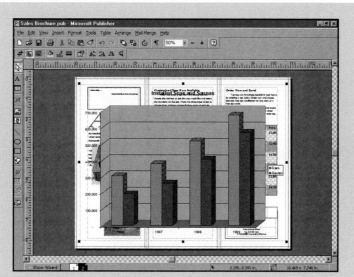

Figure 5.18
The chart covers the en-
tire brochure when it is
first inserted.

 Creating Excel Charts to Use with OLE
If you create a chart that you plan to link or embed in another document or application, the sheet that contains the chart should be the first sheet tab in the
workbook. When you choose Insert, Object, the program automatically selects
the first sheet in the workbook. If that sheet contains the spreadsheet, rather
than the chart, the spreadsheet data will be inserted.

Lesson 5: Editing an Excel Chart

When you insert objects, you usually have to adjust the size or shape. In addition, you
may need to change parts of the object to make it readable in your publication. What
needs to be changed will depend on the object that has been inserted and the method
that was used. To make changes to the chart, you need to change to an editing mode.
This process opens the toolbars that are used in the source application.

In this example, the chart needs to be reduced in size so that it fits in the available space.
The printed information then needs to be enlarged so that it is readable.

To Resize and Move an Excel Chart

1 **Click the resize handle in the upper-right corner and drag toward
the middle of the chart until the right side of the chart is aligned
with the right side of the text frame in the middle panel.**
The chart is reduced in size and aligned on the right side with the text frame.

2 **Click the resize handle in the upper-left corner and drag toward the
middle of the chart until the left side of the chart is aligned with the
left side of the text frame in the middle panel.**
The chart is reduced in size again and displays at the bottom of the middle
panel (see Figure 5.19).

continues ▶

To Resize and Move an Excel Chart   (continued)

Figure 5.19
The chart size is reduced.

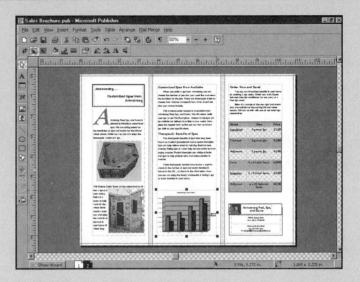

3 Use the pointer when it displays as a Move icon to reposition the chart as needed in the bottom of the middle panel under the text.

4 Change the zoom to 100%.
The words and figures surrounding the chart are too small to read, so some adjustments are needed.

Because the numbers and captions in the chart are too small to read, they need to be modified. Changing font size in a chart is similar to changing font size in other applications. To edit the chart, you first need to change to an editing mode. Then you select the element you want to modify and use the appropriate toolbar buttons to make your changes. In the next section, you learn how to edit parts of the Excel chart.

To Change Chart Elements

1 Choose **Edit, Microsoft Excel Worksheet Object, Edit** from the menu.
A diagonal-line border appears around the chart, and the toolbars displayed change to the Excel toolbars. As you move the mouse pointer around the chart, you will see different ScreenTips that identify parts of the chart. You will use these cues to help change different elements of the chart.

2 Hover the pointer over the chart title until you see the **Chart Title ScreenTip** and then click the chart title to select it.
The chart title is selected, and the Excel Formatting toolbar is activated (see Figure 5.20). According to the toolbar, the font size is 16 point. This is the font size of the original chart if you were to view it in Excel. It is not an accurate representation of the font size you see displayed on your screen after the chart has been resized.

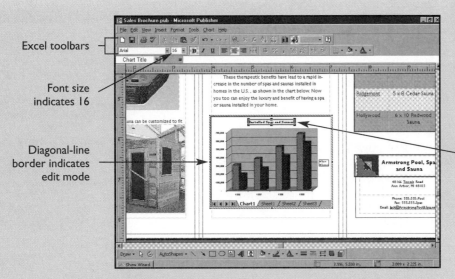

Excel toolbars

Font size
indicates 16

Diagonal-line
border indicates
edit mode

Chart title is selected

Figure 5.20
The chart is in editing
mode, and the Excel
Formatting toolbar is
activated.

3 **Click in another part of the brochure to exit from the edit mode;
then reselect the chart.**
Before the editing program correctly recognizes the font sizes in the resized
chart, it must be activated, closed, and then reopened.

4 **Choose Edit, Microsoft Excel Worksheet Object, Edit from the
menu.**
The chart returns to an edit mode, and the Excel toolbars are displayed (see
Figure 5.21). Excel remembers that the chart title was selected, and the font
size is now accurately shown in the Font Size box on the toolbar.

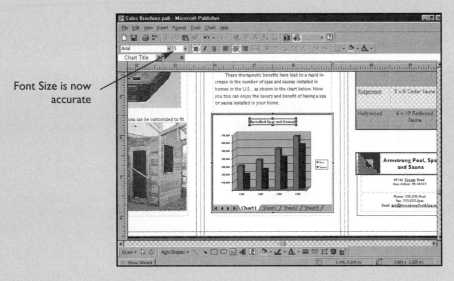

Font Size is now
accurate

Figure 5.21
The chart title is selected,
and the Font Size box ac-
curately reflects a 5-point
font size.

5 **Use the down arrow next to the Font Size box and change the size
to 10 points.**
The chart title font size is increased, and the chart size is adjusted to fit in the
available space (see Figure 5.22). Now that Excel recognizes the resized chart,
it is easy to change other parts. Next you change font size for the Legend,
Category Axis, and Value Axis.

continues ▶

To Change Chart Elements (continued)

Figure 5.22
The chart title is increased in size so that it is now readable.

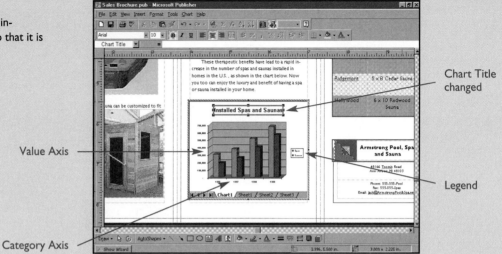

Chart Title changed

Value Axis

Legend

Category Axis

 6 Click the Legend and change the font size to 8 point.
The font for the legend is changed.

> When you click, it is important that you are pointing to precisely the area of the chart you want to change. If the mouse pointer moves to another element when you click, you will have selected another part of the chart. If this happens, move the mouse pointer until you see the correct ScreenTip, then click again.

 7 Click the Category Axis at the bottom of the chart, and change the font size to 8 point.
The font size used for the years at the bottom of the chart changes.

8 Click the Value Axis at the left of the chart and change the font size to 8 point.
The font size used for the numbers at the left of the chart changes.

9 Click in the white area under the chart to leave the editing mode.
The edited chart should look like the one in Figure 5.23.

> If you do not show the same range of numbers along the Value Axis on the left side of your chart, your chart is a different size from the one shown in the figure. Use the resize handle at the bottom middle of the chart object and click and drag to increase or decrease the size of the chart as needed.

10 Save your changes and leave the file open for the next lesson.

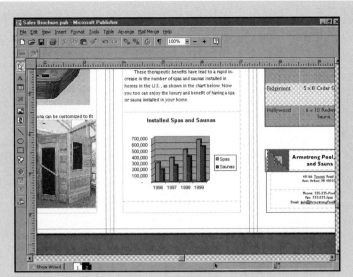

Figure 5.23
The numbers and the
words for the chart are
now legible.

Editing Objects
You can also change to the editing mode by double-clicking the object. On the
Edit menu, the object that is shown on the menu list reflects the object you have
selected. For example, if the object is from Microsoft Word or Microsoft
PowerPoint, the edit menu option will show the application name—Edit
Microsoft Word Object or Edit Microsoft PowerPoint Object.

Lesson 6: Creating an Address List

Each publication you create is designed with a specific goal in mind and is intended for a
particular audience. One of the decisions you must make about your publication is how
you plan to distribute the information. A publication can be posted in a public place, be
available for customers to pick up, or be mailed. If you are creating something that will be
mailed, one of the options is to include a mailing label area on your publication. If you
have included a mailing area, you can create an address list, known as a **data source,** and
merge the names and addresses with the publication to create a preaddressed publication.
The brochure that you have been working with was designed for mailing to existing pool
customers as a way of promoting cross sales of spas and saunas.

In this lesson, you create an address list that will be used to mail the brochure to your
customer list.

To Create an Address List

**1 Click the page navigation control for page 1 to view the outside of
the brochure.**
The middle panel of the brochure was reserved for a mailing label and already
contains the return address for Armstrong Pool, Spa, and Sauna. The mailing
label area in the middle is where the customer's address will appear. The first
step in the process is to create an address list.

continues ▶

To Create an Address List (continued)

2 **Choose Mail Merge, Create Publisher Address List from the menu.**
The New Address List dialog box opens (see Figure 5.24). This dialog box contains fields for the information that is typical for an address label. *Field* is a term used to identify a category of information such as name or address. You can customize the list of fields by clicking the Customize button and adding or deleting fields. You can also just use some of the fields that are shown without customizing the list.

Figure 5.24
The New Address List dialog box is used to create a data source for the Mail Merge process.

Field names

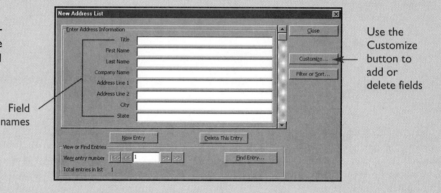

Use the Customize button to add or delete fields

X If the Mail Merge program has not been used previously, you will see a message box asking if you want to install it now. You will need to get the original installation discs to install this feature, or you will need to install it from your network. Talk to your instructor if you need assistance.

3 **Type Mr. in the Title field box and press Tab⇆.**
The title for the first entry is displayed, and the insertion point moves to the next field box.

4 **Type Henry, press Tab⇆, and then type Jones in the Last Name field box and press Tab⇆ twice.**
The first and last names are entered, and the insertion point moves to Address Line 1.

5 **Add the following information for the rest of this entry.**

Address Line 1	2655 Melody Lane
City	Birmingham
State	MI
ZIP Code	48240

When you have completed entering the data, the entry should look like the one in Figure 5.25.

6 **Click the New Entry button to clear the fields and begin a new entry. Type the next three entries as shown in Table 5.1.**

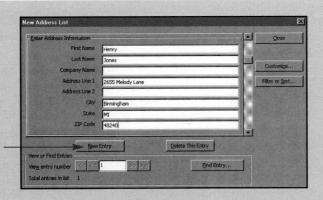

Click here to begin
a new entry

Figure 5.25
The first entry is
recorded.

Table 5.1   Additional Names and Addresses

Title	Ms.	Dr.	Rev.
First Name	Martha	Mary	Joshua
Last Name	Tuttle	Albert	Smith
Address Line 1	Avenue D	569 High St	2250 Marsh Lane
City	Rochester	Troy	Highland Park
State	MI	MI	MI
ZIP Code	48670	48330	48290

Notice that the total number of entries shows 4 after all of the names and addresses have been typed.

7 **When you have typed all the entries, click the Close button.**
A Save As dialog box displays. The program automatically assumes that you want to save the address list you have just created.

8 **Change the Save in box to the disk and folder location that you are using. Type Address List in the File name box.**
Save the address list just like you would any other file you create (see Figure 5.26).

Figure 5.26
The Save As dialog box opens so that you can save your address list for your publication.

Indicates type of file
that is created

continues ▶

To Create an Address List   (continued)

 Address Lists Are Really Access Files
An address list you create in Publisher is actually saved as an Access database file. The Save as type box indicates it is a Microsoft Publisher Address list, but the file extension—.mdb, and the file symbol that is used to identify the file, are both Access file indicators. If you locate the file using Windows Explorer or My Computer and double-click the file name to open it, it will launch Access and open the file as an Access database.

9 Click Save.
The address list is saved. Leave the file open for the next lesson

 Other Terms for Entries
In Publisher, the term *entry* is used to refer to the information about each person that is entered in an Address List. In other applications, other terms are used for entries. For example, in Microsoft Outlook, a list of names and address is known as a *contact list,* and each entry is a *contact.* In Microsoft Access and in Microsoft Word, entries are known as *records.*

Lesson 7: Merging a Mailing List with a Publication

In Lesson 6, you created a data source file using Microsoft Publisher. You could, however, use a mailing list from some other source, such as Access, Excel, or Word. Once you have created a data source for the mailing, you can merge the mailing list with the publication. If you did not reserve a space for the mailing address, you would first have to add a text box to be used to insert the address field names. In our example, a mailing area was created as part of the design of the brochure. You will insert placeholders in the address area for each of the fields you want to use from the address list file. In Project 1, "Getting Started with Publisher," you were introduced to the term placeholder as a temporary object placed in a frame by a wizard that is replaced with text or other objects by the user. When using Mail Merge, you insert *placeholders* for the field names to identify each category of information that will be needed to address a publication. These field name placeholders are replaced by specific data when the merge program is run.

In this lesson, you use Mail Merge to merge the data source—the Address List file—with the brochure.

To Merge an Address List with a Publication

1 Click the text box in the middle panel that is designated for the mailing address and change the zoom to 100% if necessary.
When you click in this text box, the box is selected and the five lines that are reserved for the mailing label are highlighted.

2 **Choose Mail Merge, Open Data Source from the menu.**

The Open Data Source dialog box is displayed (see Figure 5.27). You can use an Outlook contact list or merge data from another type of file. The third option is to create a new file in Publisher, which you did in the previous lesson.

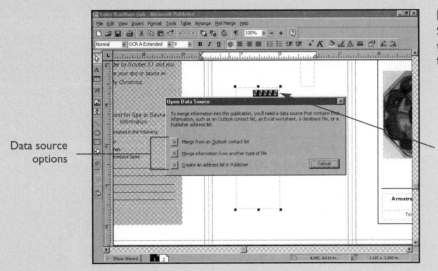

Data source
options

Selected text box

Figure 5.27
Select the middle option to locate the data source file you want to use.

3 **Click the button next to the** Merge information from another type of file **option.**

The Open Data Source dialog box is displayed. Use this to find the file you created in Lesson 6 entitled Address List.

4 **Change the Look in box to the file and folder location where you saved the Address List file. Click the Address List file to select it and then click Open.**

The Insert Fields dialog box is displayed (see Figure 5.28). This dialog box is used to insert each field you want to include. The process is to select a field and then click Insert. You add spaces, new lines, and any other necessary punctuation by using the keyboard.

Figure 5.28
The Insert Fields dialog box is used to select the fields you want to include in your address.

5 **Click the title bar of the Insert Fields dialog box and drag the box to the right so that you can see the address label area underneath.**

If you move the Insert Fields box off of the address label area, you will be able to see what you are doing.

continues ▶

To Merge an Address List with a Publication   (continued)

6 **Click Title and then click Insert.**

A placeholder for the title field is added, and all of the highlighted address lines are removed.

7 **Press** Spacebar **to insert a space; then click First Name and click Insert.**

A space is added followed by a placeholder for the first name field (see Figure 5.29).

Figure 5.29
The first two field place-holders are added to the mailing label area.

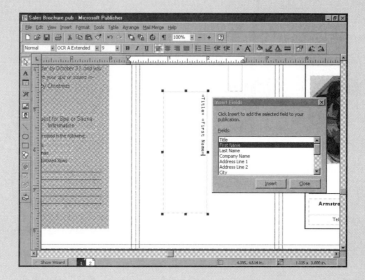

8 **Press** Spacebar **to insert a space; then click Last Name and click Insert.**

A space is added, followed by a placeholder for the last name field. The street address needs to be placed on the next line.

9 **Press** ↵Enter **to move to the next line, then click Address Line 1 and click Insert.**

The placeholder for the street address is placed on the next line.

10 **Press** ↵Enter **to move to the next line; then click City and click Insert.**

The placeholder for the city field is placed on the next line.

11 **Type a comma and a space. Scroll down in the Insert Fields dialog box so that you can see the next two fields.**

A comma and a space are added to the address before you enter the place-holder for the State field.

12 **Click State, click Insert, and then add a space and click ZIP Code and click Insert.**

The last two placeholders are added to the mailing label area. The completed mailing label on your brochure should look like the one in Figure 5.30.

13 **Click Close to close the Insert Fields dialog box. Save your changes and leave the file open for the next lesson.**

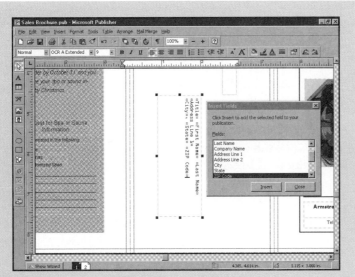

Figure 5.30
Placeholders are used in the mailing area to reserve a place for each of the fields you need to mail your publication

 Add Placeholders
You can also add the placeholders to the mailing label area by double-clicking the field name in the Insert Fields dialog box. If you add something in the wrong place or forget a punctuation mark or a space, simply click the Undo button to reverse the last action and then try again.

Lesson 8: Running Mail Merge

The first step in the Mail Merge process is to create a data source, or address list. The second step is to insert placeholders in the publication for the fields in your data source. The last step in the Mail Merge process is to merge the data from the address list with the publication so that it can be printed.

In this lesson, you merge the actual data with the brochure and then print a sample brochure.

To Run Mail Merge

1 **Choose Mail Merge, Merge from the menu.**
The Preview Data dialog box opens. The right-facing arrow moves the data to the next entry. The left-facing arrow moves the data to the previous entry.

2 **Click the title bar of the Preview Data dialog box and drag the box off of the mailing address so that you can see the data that now appears in the mailing label area.**
The mailing label displays the first entry from the address list you created in Lesson 6 (see Figure 5.31).

continues ▶

To Run Mail Merge   (continued)

Figure 5.31
The address list is merged
with the publication.

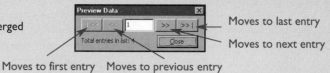

Moves to last entry
Moves to next entry

Moves to first entry   Moves to previous entry

>> **3** **Click the Next Entry button on the Preview Data dialog box to see
the next entry.**

The second entry is displayed in the mailing label area. The Preview Data dialog box displays 2 to indicate the number of the entry that is showing.

4 **Choose File, Print Merge from the menu.**

The Print Merge dialog box opens (see Figure 5.32). This is the same as a Print
dialog box with a few modifications. One of the options in this dialog box is to
print specific entries or to print a test. Also notice that there is a check box
to not print empty lines.

Figure 5.32
The Print Merge dialog
box can be used to select
the entries you want to
print.

Specifies range
of entries

Eliminates empty lines

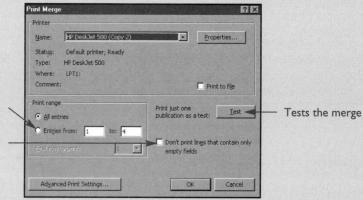

Tests the merge

5 **Type 2 in the Entries from and to boxes; then click Test.**

The two pages of the brochure are printed. The mailing address for Ms.
Martha Tuttle is inserted on the brochure.

6 **Close the Print Merge dialog box and close the Preview Data dialog
box.**

The name and address placeholders are again displayed in the mailing label
area.

7 **Save your changes and close the file.**

If you are finished working, close Publisher and shut down your computer.

Summary

In this project, you learned how to create a table in Publisher. You entered data, added a row and column, and resized and formatted the table. You then learned how to insert objects, specifically an Excel chart. You changed to the editing mode so that you could make changes to the chart. Last, you learned how to create an address list in Publisher, merge a data source with a publication, and then run the Mail Merge program so that you could print a preaddressed publication.

The procedure that was used for inserting an object in this project is known as embedding. You can also link to objects. Look at the Help topic `What is OLE (Objecting Linking and Embedding)?` to understand the differences between these two approaches. There are also useful tutorials and ideas about the Mail Merge process that can be found in Help.

Checking Concepts and Terms

True/False

For each of the following statements, check *T* or *F* to indicate whether the statement is true or false.

__T __F **1.** To insert an object, you must first select the frame where you want the object to be placed. [L4]

__T __F **2.** To resize a table column without changing the width of the table, hold down ⬆Shift while you click and drag the Adjust icon. [L3]

__T __F **3.** To add a table to a publication, choose Table, Insert from the menu. [L1]

__T __F **4.** To insert a row at the top of table, right-click the first row and choose insert row from the shortcut menu. [L2]

__T __F **5.** If you want to display information in a graph or chart, you can create it in Publisher. [L4]

__T __F **6.** To edit an embedded object, you select the object and go to the Edit menu to activate the editing program for that type of object. [L5]

__T __F **7.** You can use the Outlook contact list as a data source for a Mail Merge to a publication. [L7]

__T __F **8.** To select an entire table, click the Select Cells button in the upper-left corner of the table. [L1]

__T __F **9.** When you edit an Excel chart that is embedded in Publisher, you are using Excel tools to change the chart. [L5]

__T __F **10.** When you run Mail Merge, you can check your results by printing a test publication. [L8]

Multiple Choice

Circle the letter of the correct answer for each of the following questions.

1. What is the first step in adding a table to a Publication? [L1]
   a. Choose Table, Create from the menu.
   b. Draw a table frame in the desired location.
   c. Click the Table button and specify the number of rows and columns.
   d. Choose Insert, Table from the menu.

2. If you select a column in a table and choose Table, Insert Column, where is the new column placed? [L2]
   a. to the right of the selected column
   b. to the left of the selected column
   c. before the first column in the table
   d. after the last column in the table

3. How do you select an entire table? [L1]
   a. Click the Select Cells button in the upper-left corner of the table.
   b. Choose Table, Select, Table from the menu.
   c. Click and drag across all of the cells in the table.
   d. all of the above

4. How do you change the font for an element in an embedded Excel chart? [L5]
   a. Highlight the element you want to change and use the Publisher toolbar buttons to change the font.
   b. Open Excel, make the changes in Excel, and then update the embedded chart.
   c. Change to the editing mode, select the element you want to change, and use the Excel toolbars buttons that are available.
   d. none of the above

5. What are the three main steps in doing a Mail Merge? [L8]
   a. creating a data source, inserting field placeholders in the publication, and running Mail Merge
   b. creating the publication, typing the addresses, and printing the results
   c. opening a Publisher address list, inserting field placeholders in the publication, and saving the file
   d. finding the names and addresses, deciding who to send the publication to, and getting a roll of stamps

6. How would you create a chart in Publisher? [L4]
   a. Click the Insert Chart button and use the Microsoft Graphing tool to create the chart.
   b. Insert a chart as an object from Excel.
   c. You cannot use charts in Publisher.
   d. Choose Tools, Chart from the menu.

7. An address list created by using Publisher is saved as what kind of file? [L6]
   a. an Access database file
   b. a Publisher file
   c. it is saved as an embedded part of the publication you have created
   d. a Word table file

8. If you create a chart in Excel that you plan to embed in a publication, where must the chart be located? [L4]
   a. on its own sheet
   b. on the same sheet as the data used to create the chart
   c. in a file that is saved as an OLE file
   d. as the last sheet in the Excel file

9. How do you move back one cell to the left in a table? [L1]
   a. Press Ctrl+Tab↹
   b. Press Alt+Tab↹
   c. Press ⬆Shift+Tab↹
   d. Press ↩+Tab↹

10. In Publisher, what kind of files can you use as a data source when adding a mailing address to a publication? [L7]
   a. Outlook contact list
   b. Access database file
   c. Word data source file
   d. any of the above file types can be used

Screen ID

Label each element of the Access screen shown in Figure 5.33 and Figure 5.34.

Figure 5.33

A. Selected chart element

B. Selected row

C. Screen Tip

D. Excel toolbar

E. Row selector

F. Click here to select entire table

G. Column selector

H. Indicates edit mode

I. Legend

J. Cell

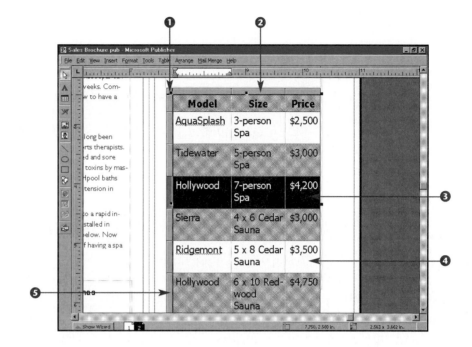

1._____   3._____   5._____

2._____   4._____

Figure 5.34

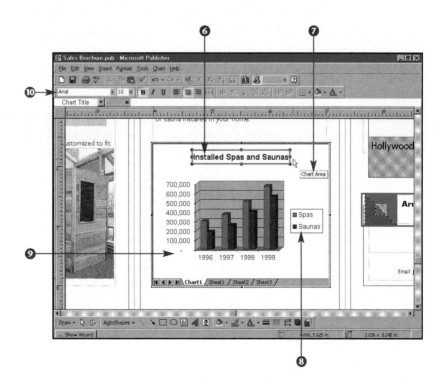

6._____   8._____   10._____

7._____   9._____

Discussion Questions

1. What kinds of publications do you receive in the mail? Which ones use a mailing address printed as part of the publication? When are mailing labels used instead?

2. What issues need to be considered if you want to include a mailing address as part of a publication?

3. In this project, we inserted a chart as an object from another program. What are some examples of other objects that you might want to insert into a publication from some other source? Look through publications you receive to get some ideas.

4. When you create a data source to use with a publication, it generally is used for a mailing label. How else might you use a data source with a publication? How do you react to publications that you receive that have your name included as part of an advertisement? Is this effective?

5. What are some examples of information that is best displayed in a table? What are the advantages and disadvantages of using tables? Are you more or less inclined to examine data in a table?

Skill Drill

Skill Drill exercises reinforce project skills. Each skill reinforced is the same, or nearly the same, as a skill presented in this project. Each exercise includes a brief narrative introduction, followed by detailed instructions in a step-by-step format.

In the following exercises, you will finish an informational brochure that is being created for the Helping Hands organization. The purpose of this brochure is to provide some basic information about the organization to give to potential volunteers and donors. The brochure can be handed out or mailed to people who are interested volunteering for Helping Hands. You will finish the brochure by adding a table, adding a chart, and using the Mail Merge feature to add a mailing label, and data source. The following exercises should be completed in pairs. The first two exercises add and modify a table. The third and fourth exercises add and modify an Excel chart. The last two exercises create an address list, and merge and run the Mail Merge program.

1. Adding a Table

The focus of Helping Hands is to attract volunteers to help with various fund-raising projects. The funds raised are then used to support programs in the community. To highlight the volunteer opportunities that are available this year, you will insert a table listing the name and dates of each event.

1. Open the Pub-0502 Publisher file from the CD-ROM and save it as **HH Brochure**. Move to page 2 of the brochure.

2. Click the Table Frame tool and draw a table in the empty area at the bottom of the right panel.

3. Choose 6 rows and 2 columns in the Create Table dialog box. Make sure the Default Table format is selected and click OK.

4. Change the zoom to 100% and enter the following information in the table:

Table 5.2   Event Dates

Women's Shelter Phone-a-thon	March 17
Walkathon	April 10
Air Show	July 7-8
Fix It Week	July 10-14
Children's Clinic Dinner	September 18
Homeless Shelter Phone-a-thon	October 20

5. Select the entire table and choose T<u>a</u>ble, <u>I</u>nsert Rows or Columns from the menu.

6. Make sure the <u>R</u>ows option is selected and **1** is indicated in the <u>N</u>umber of rows box. Select the <u>B</u>efore selected cells option button and then click OK.

7. Type **Events** in the first cell. Select the first row in the table and choose T<u>a</u>ble, <u>M</u>erge Cells from the menu.

8. Save your changes and leave the file open for the next exercise.

2. Resizing and Formatting a Table

Now that the table has been created and the data have been entered, the table needs to be formatted to match the fonts and formats that have been used in the rest of the brochure. In this exercise, you format the table and then resize the table as needed to fit in the available space.

1. Select the entire table and choose T<u>a</u>ble, Table AutoF<u>o</u>rmat from the menu.

2. Select the Table of Contents 3 format and click OK. Even though this is table is not a table of contents, this style provides some useful formats for our purposes.

3. With the table still selected, change the font to Lucinda Sans Typewriter and change the font size to 12.

4. With the table still selected, click the Line/Border Style button and click More <u>S</u>tyles to open the Border Style dialog box.

6. In the Select a <u>s</u>ide graphic, click the horizontal line in the middle and then click 1 pt. Click OK. A line is added to the table to provide a visual separation for each event.

7. Select the first row in the table and use the Adjust icon to decrease the height of this row so that it is just wide enough for the Title. Repeat this process to decrease the height of the rows for the Walkathon, Air Show, and Fix It Week rows.

8. Select the title row and click the Fill Color button. Select the red color (Accent 1) from the color scheme palette that is displayed.

9. Save your changes. The table in your brochure should look like the one in Figure 5.35.

10. Leave the file open for the next exercise.

3. Inserting an Object

People who contribute to an organization are always interested in how the agency is funded and how the money is spent. In the middle panel of the Helping Hands brochure, you will add a chart that shows the sources of funds and the percentage each funding source is to the whole operation.

To create a query that uses conditions, complete the following steps:

1. In the **HH Brochure**, change to page 2 of the brochure.

2. Change the Zoom to Whole Page if necessary. The chart you are going to insert will be placed in the middle panel, just before "The Helping Dividend" heading. Make sure nothing is selected on the brochure.

3. Choose <u>I</u>nsert, <u>O</u>bject from the menu. Select Create from <u>F</u>ile in the Insert Object dialog box.

4. Click the <u>B</u>rowse button and locate the Sources of Funds.xls file on the CD-ROM. Select the file and click Insert; then click OK.

5. Use the corner Resize icons to resize the chart so that it will fit on one panel of the brochure.

6. Move the chart so that it is in the middle of the middle panel, just before the second heading: "The Helping Dividend."

7. Save your changes and leave the file open for the next exercise.

4. Formatting an Excel Chart

Now that the chart has been inserted into the brochure, you need to change the formatting of the text so that it will be legible.

1. Change the zoom to 100% and make sure the chart is centered on the screen so that you can work with it.

2. With the chart selected, choose Edit, Microsoft Excel Worksheet Object, Edit from the menu. Click the title to select it and notice the size of the font indicated on the toolbar. Clearly, the font size you are looking at is not 14 point in Publisher.

3. Click anywhere else to deselect the chart and close the editing program.

4. Double-click the chart title. The editing mode is re-activated, and this time the true font size is reflected in the font size box on the toolbar. Change the font size to 12 point.

5. Click on any one of the data labels that are displayed around the pie chart. Clicking once selects all of the labels and you a change the font size all at one time. Change the font size to 8 point.

6. Move the mouse pointer around the edge of the pie pieces until you see the Plot Area ScreenTip. Click to select the plot area. A hash-mark box should be displayed around the pie pieces.

7. Click and drag the lower-right resizing handle down and to the right to increase the size of the pie. Make sure you do not increase the size so much that the labels start to divide.

8. If necessary, click and drag the plot area down slightly to better position it in the available space. Your chart should look like the one in Figure 5.35.

9. Deselect the chart to see the final results. Save your changes.

10. Leave the file open to do the next exercise.

Figure 5.35
A table of events is added to the right panel; a chart showing the sources of funds for the Helping Hands organization is added to the middle panel.

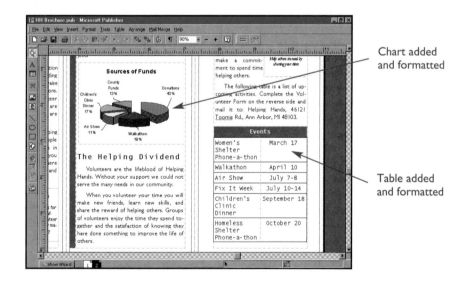

Chart added and formatted

Table added and formatted

5. Creating an Address List

The purpose of this brochure is to provide some information to people who are interested in volunteering for a Helping Hands project. Calls are sometimes received by the agency, and they want to be able to mail information in response to questions. They also send this out annually to people who have volunteered in the past so that they know what the upcoming events will be for this year. The last step in designing this brochure is to create a data source by using the Publisher Address List feature, and then merge the address file with the brochure for mailing.

1. In the **HH Brochure**, change to page 1 of the brochure.

2. Choose **M**ail Merge, **C**reate Publisher Address List from the menu.

3. In the New Address List dialog box, enter the following information.

Table 5.3   Names and Addresses of Brochure Recipients

Title	First Name	Last Name	Address Line 1	Address Line 2	City	State	ZIP Code
Mr.	Earl	McIntyre	122 Maiden Lane	Apt. 201B	Ypsilanti	MI	48197
Mrs.	Henrietta	Green	809 Miller Ave.		Saline	MI	48176
Mr.	David	Botts	304 Wesley		Dexter	MI	48160
Ms.	Martha	Peale	804 Devons		Birmingham	MI	48224

4. After all of the information is entered, click the **C**lose button. Save the file and name it **HH Addresses**.

5. Save your work and leave the file open for the next exercise.

6. Using Mail Merge

After you create or identify a data source, the next step in the Mail Merge process is to insert placeholders in the publication for the field names. Then you run the Mail Merge program and print a test of the final results.

1. On the first page of the Helping Hands brochure, click the mailing address text box to select it.

2. Choose **M**ail Merge, **O**pen Data Source from the menu. Click the arrow next to **M**erge information from another type of file.

3. In the Open Data Source dialog box, locate and select the HH Addresses file that you just created; then click **O**pen.

4. Make sure Title is selected and then click **I**nsert. Add a space and then insert the First Name field; add a space and insert the Last Name field.

5. Press ⏎Enter and insert Address Line 1. Press ⏎Enter again and insert Address Line 2.

6. Press ⏎Enter and add the City, State, and ZIP Code fields with the appropriate spacing and punctuation. Then click the **C**lose button.

7. Choose **M**ail Merge, Merge from the menu. Move to the second entry. Notice how there is an empty line where the second address line would be.

8. Choose **F**ile, **P**rint Merge from the menu.

9. Change the Entries from and to boxes to 2. Click the check box next to Don't print lines that contain only empty fields. Then click the Test button.

10. Close the Print Merge dialog box and then close the Preview box. Save your changes and close the file.

Challenge

Challenge exercises expand on or are somewhat related to skills presented in the lessons. Each exercise provides a brief narrative introduction, followed by instructions in a numbered step format that are not as detailed as those in the Skill Drill section.

You will be using two databases in the Challenge section. The first is the consulting database you created in Project 1, "Getting Started with Publisher." The second is a 5-year database of U.S. tornadoes.

1. Formatting a Bulleted List in a Table

There are many different uses for a table. In some situations, you may want to include bullets or a numbered list in a table layout. In this exercise, you format a table that has been created for a menu for the Mayfield Terrace apartments, which is a senior citizens apartment building. Meals are provided daily, except for Saturday, and a weekly menu is issued for the residents. You will add some additional information to the menu and then format the table to display bullets. Refer to Figure 5.36 for guidance as you complete this exercise.

1. Open Publisher and open Help. Find the topic: Create a numbered or bulleted list in a table cell. Review the information that is provided.
2. Open a Pub-0503 and save it as `Menu`.
3. Add a column on the left side of the table and enter the following in cells that are added:

   `Day`

   `Date`

   `Breakfast`

   `Lunch`

   `Dinner`
4. Adjust the column width to be just wide enough to display the text you entered.
5. Add the dates for the week of March 12 to 17 to the date row. Type `St. Patrick's Day` on the second line in the same cell as March 17.
6. Format the breakfast items with the open arrow bullet style that is shown in Figure 5.36.
7. Format the Monday through Friday lunch menu items with the open diamond bullet that is shown in Figure 5.36.
8. Format the Dinner menu items with the closed diamond bullet that is shown in Figure 5.36. Use this same bullet for the Sunday meal that is listed for lunch.
9. Change the bullet for the dinner on St. Patrick's Day to a shamrock. Use the New Bullet option button to locate a shamrock symbol.
10. Use Table AutoFormat to select the List 4 Table format style.
11. Modify the format by change the alignment for the menu items to flush left. Adjust the first column width if needed. Change the color scheme to use the two shades of peach (Accent 2 and 3) that are on the color palette. Center the information that is displayed for the Sunday dinner cell.
12. The finished menu should look like the one in Figure 5.36. Print the menu. Save the file and then close it.

Figure 5.36
The completed menu is formatted, and bullets are added to the cells.

Day	Sunday	Monday	Tuesday	Wednesday	Thursday	Friday
Date	March 12	March 13	March 14	March 15	March 16	March 17 St. Patrick's Day
Breakfast	⇨ Hot Cereal ⇨ Cold Cereal ⇨ Fruit ⇨ Assorted Juices ⇨ Scrambled eggs and ham ⇨ Coffee, Tea, Milk	⇨ Hot Cereal ⇨ Cold Cereal ⇨ Fruit ⇨ Assorted Juices ⇨ Poached eggs and toast ⇨ Coffee, Tea, Milk	⇨ Hot Cereal ⇨ Cold Cereal ⇨ Fruit ⇨ Assorted Juices ⇨ Pancakes and syrup ⇨ Coffee, Tea, Milk	⇨ Hot Cereal ⇨ Cold Cereal ⇨ Fruit ⇨ Assorted Juices ⇨ Western omelet ⇨ Coffee, Tea, Milk	⇨ Hot Cereal ⇨ Cold Cereal ⇨ Fruit ⇨ Assorted Juices ⇨ French Toast ⇨ Coffee, Tea, Milk	⇨ Hot Cereal ⇨ Cold Cereal ⇨ Fruit ⇨ Assorted Juices ⇨ Danish rolls ⇨ Bagels and cream cheese ⇨ Coffee, Tea, Milk
Lunch	◆ Roast Beef ◆ Potatoes with gravy ◆ Green Beans ◆ Toss Salad ◆ Fruit Pie ◆ Coffee, Tea, Milk	◊ Vegetable beef soup ◊ Crackers ◊ Salad Bar ◊ Assorted sandwiches ◊ Jello ◊ Coffee, Tea, Milk	◊ Creamed carrot soup ◊ Crackers ◊ Salad Bar ◊ Assorted sandwiches ◊ Spice cake ◊ Coffee Tea, Milk	◊ Chicken noodle soup ◊ Crackers ◊ Salad Bar ◊ Assorted sandwiches ◊ Ice cream ◊ Coffee Tea, Milk	◊ Minestrone soup ◊ Crackers ◊ Salad Bar ◊ Assorted sandwiches ◊ Chocolate pudding ◊ Coffee Tea, Milk	◊ Tomato Soup ◊ Crackers ◊ Salad Bar ◊ Grilled cheese sandwiches ◊ Vanilla cake ◊ Coffee Tea, Milk
Dinner	DINNER IS NOT SERVED ON SUNDAYS LUNCH IS SERVED AT 1:00	◆ Tuna Casserole ◆ Steamed carrots ◆ Fruit salad ◆ Dinner rolls ◆ Ice Cream ◆ Coffee, Tea, Milk	◆ Baked chicken ◆ Mash potatoes w/ gravy ◆ Corn ◆ Creamy cold slaw ◆ Dinner rolls ◆ Peach Pie ◆ Coffee, Tea, Milk	◆ Baked Salmon ◆ Rice Pilaf ◆ Vegetable medley ◆ Waldorf salad ◆ Croissants ◆ Lemon meringue pie ◆ Coffee, Tea, Milk	◆ Macaroni & Cheese ◆ Broccoli ◆ Toss salad ◆ Dinner Rolls ◆ Apple Pie ◆ Coffee, Tea, Milk	♣ Corn Beef and Cabbage ♣ Boiled potatoes and carrots ♣ Irish soda biscuits ♣ Old Time Rice Pudding ♣ Coffee, Tea, Milk

2. Inserting a PowerPoint Slide as an Object

The OLE feature of Microsoft Office is designed to help you use information from many sources across applications. In this project, you embedded a Microsoft Excel chart in a brochure. You could also embed objects from other applications such as PowerPoint or Word. In this exercise, you will embed a PowerPoint slide and then use the Show edit option to launch PowerPoint and view the animated slide show.

1. Open Publisher, close the Catalog, and hide the wizard. Choose Insert, Object from the menu.

2. Choose Create from File and use the Browse button to locate the Access Objects.ppt file. Click Insert and then click OK.

3. Choose File, Page Setup and change the orientation to Landscape.

4. Click the object and use the resize icon to increase the dimensions of the object to 6.5" wide by 5" high. Center it on the page.

5. Add a text box that is the same width above the object and type `Objects in an Access Database`. Center the text and change the font size to 28 point.

6. Add a text box in the lower-left corner that is approximately 2" by 1". Type `Data Access Pages`, press `←Enter`, and type `View and Work with Data on the Internet`.

7. Use the Fill Color button and select a deep blue to match the color in the object. Change the font color in this text box to white, the font size to 16 point for the first line, and 14 point for the second line. Center the text.

8. Use the line tool to draw an arrow from the text box to the oval surrounding the boxes on the object. Change the arrow color to red to match the color used in the object. The completed page should look like Figure 5.37.

9. Click the object to select it; and then choose Edit, Microsoft PowerPoint Presentation Object, Show from the menu. PowerPoint opens, and a blue box appears on a white background. Click the mouse repeatedly until each object on the slide has been displayed. When the show is over, PowerPoint will close and the Publisher window will be displayed.

10. Print the page you have created. Save the file as `Access Objects`, and then close it.

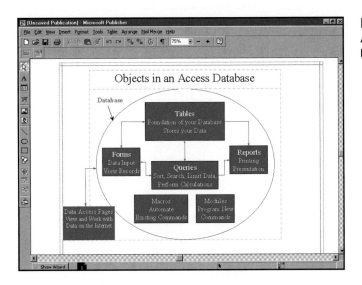

Figure 5.37
A PowerPoint slide is embedded in a publication.

3. Performing a Mail Merge with a Word Address List

When working with a publication, you may want to use a mailing list that has already been created in another type of file, rather than reentering the information by using Publisher. In this exercise, you use a Word file to create a Mail Merge with a newsletter.

1. Open file Pub-0504 file and save it as `Mail Merge`.

2. Select the mailing label area on the second page and increase the zoom to 100%.

3. Choose Mail Merge, Open Data Source, Merge information from another type of file.

4. In the Open Data Source dialog box, change the Files of type box to All Files. Locate and select the Mailing List.doc file and then click Open.

5. Use the techniques you learned in this project to insert the placeholders and punctuation for a proper mailing address. Use all of the fields available.

6. Close the Insert Fields dialog box. Run the Mail Merge program. Find the address with a two-line mailing address and print that one as a test.

7. Save the changes and close the file.

4. Creating Mailing Labels

You can create labels for numerous purposes by choosing one of the label wizard options. You can create labels for computer disks, cassettes, compact discs, videos, binders, and nametags. You can also design a label that can be merged with information from a data source and then merge it to create mailing labels, shipping labels, or return address labels. In this exercise, you create a mailing label and merge it with one of the address files that you have previously created.

1. Start a new publication, scroll down in the Catalog, and choose Labels from the list of wizards. Take a moment to look at the many label options that are available. Then select a mailing label style of your choice from one of the first three categories, mailing address, shipping, or return address.

2. Click Start Wizard and follow the steps in the wizard. Hide the wizard. Notice that the Avery label number for the label you selected is displayed to the right of the label. Once you create the labels, you can print them on this label size.

3. Use the Mail Merge skills you have learned in this project to select a data source and insert placeholders in the mailing label address area. Use one of the address lists you have used previously.

4. Run the merge program and print a sample of the results. It can be printed on plain paper. (*Hint:* Be sure to select Test so that it will print only the first two rows of labels.)

5. Save the file as `Mailing Label`. Close the file.

[?] 5. Working with Tables

You can do many other things with tables in Publisher. In this exercise, you use Help to explore various options. You then create a table, divide cells in a table diagonally, and add a picture. The finished publication should look like the one in Figure 5.38.

1. Open Publisher and look for information in Help about dividing cells diagonally in a table.

2. Create a table that has nine columns and five rows. Select the Checkbook table format. Use the Page Setup dialog box to change the page orientation to Landscape. Resize the table to fill the available space.

3. Type **August** in the first cell in the first row, type **Goals** in the second cell in the first row, then type the days of the week in the remaining seven cells in the first row. Decrease the size of the first row to accommodate the text.

4. Select the cells in all but the first row and the first column. Use the information from Help to add a Divide Up diagonal to these cells.

5. In the second cell in the second row (under Goals), type **Drink 8 glasses of water**. In the same cell, click below the diagonal and type **Exercise 30 minutes**.

6. Select the text about exercising and choose Format, Align Text Vertically, Bottom from the menu. Copy and paste this same information in the remaining cells in the Goal column.

7. Return to Help and look for information about adding a picture to a table.

8. Using the information in Help, add a picture to the first cell in the second row, under August. You can add a picture of your choice or use the redrose.jpg file that came with your student disc. Resize and/or crop the picture as needed to fill the first cell.

9. Change the color scheme of the table if you want.

10. Save the file as **Health Goals**. Print the file and then close it.

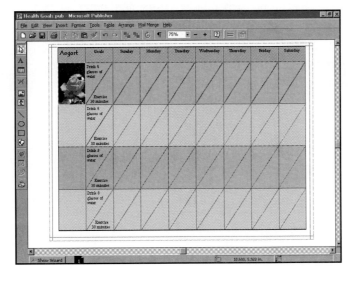

Figure 5.38
Diagonal lines and a picture are added to a table.

Discovery Zone

Discovery Zone exercises help you gain advanced knowledge of project topics and/or application of skills. These exercises focus on enhancing your problem-solving skills. Numbered steps are not provided, but you are given hints, reminders, screen shots, and/or references to help you reach your goal for each exercise.

In the first exercise, you link to a table in a Microsoft Word document. In the second Discovery exercise, you learn how to use the filter feature of the Mail Merge program.

1. Creating a Linked Object from Information in an Existing File

In this project, you have embedded objects from Microsoft Excel and Microsoft PowerPoint. You can also link to an object. Linking to an object means that changes made to the original file will be reflected in your publication.

Open Help and read the information about Object Linking and Embedding (OLE). Look specifically for information about linking to part of a file. Use what you learn from the Help topic to link to a Microsoft Word table in a file titled Lightning Strikes.

Goal: Link a table from a Microsoft Word document to a flyer about the danger of lightning.

The flyer should do the following:

- Use file Pub-0505.pub.
- Display the first table from the Lightning Strikes.doc file. (*Hint:* Leave the Word file open.)
- Use the Paste Link option to add the table to the flyer.
- Show the table under the title that has already been created.
- Display the table so it fills the available space.

Save the flyer as **Lightning Strikes**. After the table is pasted in the flyer, return to the Word document and change the number for golfing to 12, the golfing percentage to 14.5, and the total number to 83.

Return to the Publisher file and click on the table. The figures will be updated in the table in the flyer. Print the flyer and save the changes.

Hint: You will need to save the Word file in a new location because it was opened from a CD-ROM disc. Close both files.

2. Using Filters with Mail Merge

The Mail Merge program in Publisher also has a filter option that enables you to restrict the files that are merged.

Use Help to learn about filtering a data source.

Goal: Create a mailing label that uses the Members.doc file as a source file and filter the data source to include only members in Ypsilanti.

For this exercise, you should do the following:

- Use a mailing label of your choice.
- Use the Members.doc file as the source file.

- Print the labels on plain paper for only those members in Ypsilanti.
- Save the file as Ypsilanti Labels.

Hint 1: Review the fourth Challenge exercise if you need assistance with creating a label.

Hint 2: You have to run the merge before the Filter or Sort option is available on the Mail Merge menu.

Hint 3: There should be three entries.

Working with Publisher Tools

Objectives

In this project, you learn how to

➤ **Check Your Spelling**

➤ **Use Hyphenation in a Text Frame**

➤ **Add a Design Gallery Object**

➤ **Add a Footer to a Publication**

➤ **Check the Design of Your Publication**

➤ **Embed Fonts for Commercial Printing**

➤ **Prepare Images for Color Printing**

➤ **Set Publisher Options**

Key terms introduced in this project include

- CMYK color model
- Design Checker
- Design Gallery Objects
- embed
- footers

- headers
- PostScript
- pull quote
- RGB color model
- service bureau
- TrueType

Why Would I Do This?

When working on any project, having the right tools for the job is crucial. Whether it's having the right hammer to frame a house or the right mixer to blend ingredients for a cake, the proper tools are essential for the success of your task. Microsoft Publisher provides a number of tools to help you design and develop your publication. These tools are mainly found in the Tools menu, although you will also find helpful tools in the Insert and Format menu options and in the Options toolbar.

Publisher tools enable you to prepare your publication for its final destination. You can check your spelling and turn hyphenation on and off. Publisher will also check your design to see whether there will be problems when you print the publication. It checks for overlapping or empty frames and makes sure all of the frames are within the print boundaries on each page.

There are features you can use to add elements to a page. **Headers** and **footers** can be inserted at the top and bottom of each page by inserting them onto the background that lies behind the page. You can also insert preformatted **Design Gallery Objects,** such as mastheads, picture captions, and tables of content, into your publication.

Publisher gives you control over the features that are important if you are going to send your document to a service bureau or commercial printing company. These features include the capability to embed fonts in the publication in case the printer does not have a specific font installed and the option of using a color model that can be read by commercial printers.

Finally, Publisher default options, such as automatic save reminders and several editing features, can be turned on and off. You can even decide what type of special mouse pointers are used when you move, resize, or crop a frame.

Visual Summary

When you have completed this lesson, you will have added a pull quote and a footer that look like the ones shown in Figure 6.1.

Figure 6.1
A pull quote and a footer have been added to a newsletter.

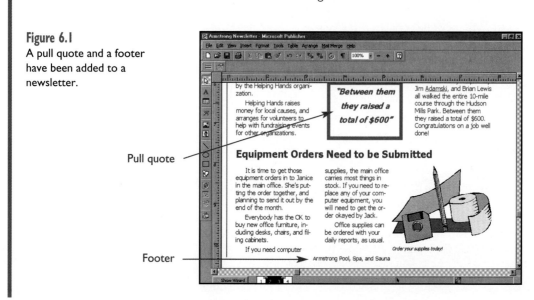

Lesson 1: Checking Your Spelling

Nearly everyone makes mistakes when typing, either by misspelling words or by accidentally hitting the wrong key. Publisher provides an easy way to check the words in your publication against a dictionary stored on the computer. Other Office programs share this dictionary.

When you check your spelling, Publisher identifies all of the words that are not in the dictionary. This does not necessarily mean they are misspelled—they could be technical or uncommon words that have not been added to the dictionary. When an unrecognized word is found, you are given the option of changing it, ignoring it, or adding it to the dictionary.

In this lesson, you check and correct the spelling in an article, and then you add a word to your dictionary.

To Check Your Spelling

1 **Find and open the Pub-0601 file on your CD-ROM. Choose File, Save As from the menu and save the file as Armstrong Newsletter.**
This four page newsletter is an expanded version of the newsletter you used in Project 3, "Working with Text."

2 **Use the navigation buttons to move to page 2.**

3 **Click in the center panel of the middle story; then click the Zoom In button until the article is shown at 100%.**
Your screen should look like Figure 6.2. Notice that several of the words in the article are underlined with a wavy red line. This means that these words are not in the dictionary.

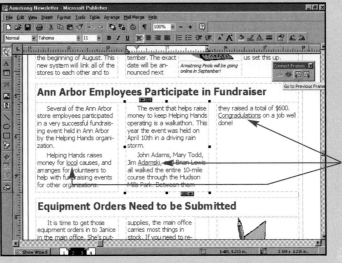

Figure 6.2
A wavy red line indicates a word that is not found in the dictionary.

Unrecognized words

X If the unrecognized words are not underlined in red, choose Tools, Spelling, Show Spelling Errors in the menu.

continues ▶

To Check Your Spelling   (continued)

4 **Choose Edit, Highlight Entire Story from the menu.**
This is not really necessary, but it ensures that you start the spell check from the beginning of the text frame. Otherwise, the check begins at the insertion point location.

5 **Choose Tools, Spelling, Check Spelling from the menu.**
The Check Spelling dialog box displays the first unrecognized word, in this case a misspelled word. At this point, you can type the correct spelling in the Change to box, or you can look in the Suggestions box to see if the correct word is there (see Figure 6.3). The most likely (and in this case, correct) suggestion is displayed in the Change to box.

Figure 6.3
The Check Spelling dialog box displays the unrecognized word and offers suggestions.

Unrecognized word

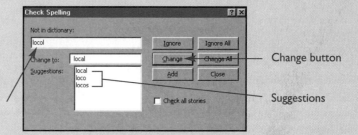

Change button

Suggestions

6 **Click the Change button.**
The word in the Change to box is substituted for the unrecognized word, and the next unrecognized word is displayed. This is a last name, and it is spelled correctly. You can add it to your dictionary if you anticipate using it frequently, or you can ignore the word.

7 **Click the Ignore button.**
The program moves on to the next unrecognized word, which is also misspelled. The correct spelling is the only suggestion.

8 **Click the Change button. Click No when a dialog box asks you if you want to check the rest of your publication; then click OK when the program tells you that the spell check is complete.**

9 **Use the navigation buttons to move to page 4. In the second paragraph of the top article, double-click the word "powerpacks" to select it. Choose Tools, Spelling, Check Spelling from the menu.**
The Check Spelling dialog box is displayed. There is an option to add the word to the dictionary (see Figure 6.4).

Figure 6.4
An unrecognized word can be added to your dictionary.

Add button

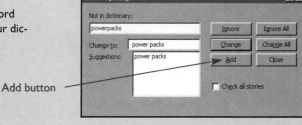

⑩ **Click the <u>A</u>dd button.**
The new word is added to the dictionary.

 ⑪ **Click <u>N</u>o when asked if you want to continue checking the story. Click the Save button to save your work, but leave the publication open for the next lesson.**

Using the Custom Dictionary
When you add a word to the dictionary, it is not added to the main dictionary, but to a supplemental dictionary stored on your computer. In most cases, the file will be found at C:\Windows\Application Data\Microsoft\Proof\Custom.dic. You can open this file in any word processor and add specialized words that you might use often but that are likely not included in a standard dictionary. You can also edit this dictionary in case you added a misspelled word.

Lesson 2: Using Hyphenation in a Text Frame

Hyphenation can be turned on and off for individual text frames. This feature can make some frames look much better, while detracting from the look of others. Hyphenation is generally a wise option if the right edge of a text frame contains large gaps. It is also useful when you are justifying text. It is often a bad idea when using narrower columns, because it can create words ending in hyphens in several successive rows of text. The only way to know how hyphenation will work in a text frame is to try it.

In this lesson, you turn on hyphenation in a text frame.

To Use Hyphenation in a Text Frame

❶ **Use the navigation buttons to move to the first page of the newsletter.**
You should be able to see the bottom of the top article. Notice that there are some large gaps at the ends of lines (see Figure 6.5).

❷ **Click anywhere in the text frame.**

❸ **Choose <u>T</u>ools, <u>L</u>anguage, <u>H</u>yphenation from the menu.**
The Hyphenation dialog box is displayed (see Figure 6.6).

❹ **Click the <u>A</u>utomatically hyphenate this story check box; then click OK.**
The text in the text frame is hyphenated. Notice how much less jagged the right edge of each column is (see Figure 6.7).

 ❺ **Click the Save button to save your work, but leave the publication open for the next lesson.**

continues ▶

To Use Hyphenation in a Text Frame   (continued)

Figure 6.5
This text frame is not hyphenated.

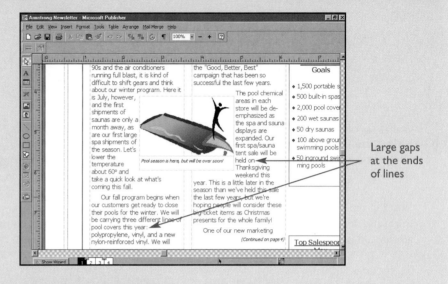

Large gaps at the ends of lines

Figure 6.6
The Hyphenation dialog box enables you to turn hyphenation on and off.

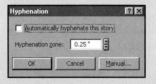

Figure 6.7
The right edge is less jagged after hyphenation.

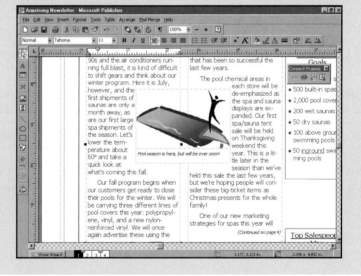

Hyphenation Guidelines
Microsoft offers some simple guidelines for using hyphenation. First, do not hyphenate more than two consecutive lines. Second, never use a hyphen in a title or heading. Finally, never hyphenate the last line in a column—the first word at the top of the next column should be a whole word.

The Hyphenation Zone
The Hyphenation zone in the Hyphenation dialog box enables you to set the minimum distance from the right edge where hyphenation is allowed. The larger you make this number, the fewer hyphens your text will have, but the more jagged the right edge will look. A small number can result in too many hyphenated words.

Lesson 3: Adding a Design Gallery Object

When you set up a publication using the Publication Wizard, you select a preformatted design. Publisher has a feature that enables you to add objects that fit well with the document design you are using. You can add such things as mastheads, order forms, coupons, sidebars, or even a table of contents. One of the objects, the **pull quote,** is used extensively in magazines, newspapers, and newsletters. It is a small box with an important or pertinent quote from the surrounding article.

In this lesson, you add a pull quote in the style of the newsletter you have been working on.

To Add a Design Gallery Object

1 Use the navigation buttons to move to page 2 and click in the article you spell checked.

2 Click the Design Gallery Object button on the Objects toolbar.
The Design Gallery dialog box is displayed (see Figure 6.8).

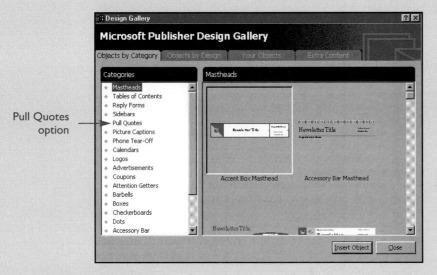

Pull Quotes option →

Figure 6.8
The Design Gallery dialog box enables you to insert several different types of objects into your publication.

3 Select Pull Quotes and then scroll down the Pull Quotes panel and select the Crossed Lines Pull Quote.
This is the design style that has been used for this newsletter (see Figure 6.9).

4 Click the Insert Object button.
The pull quote box is placed in the middle of the screen.

continues ▶

To Add a Design Gallery Object   (continued)

Figure 6.9
You can match the look of the Design Gallery Object with the publication design.

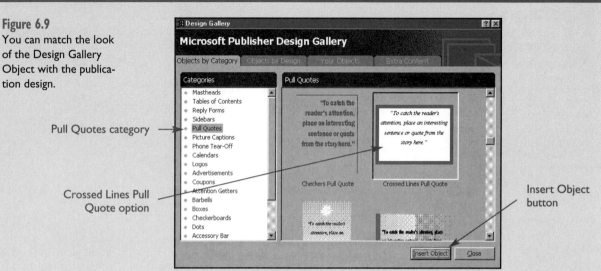

Pull Quotes category

Crossed Lines Pull Quote option

Insert Object button

5 **Move the pointer to the bottom of the pull quote box. When it turns into a Move pointer, click and drag the box to the bottom of the middle column of the article.**
Your pull quote box should now be positioned as shown in Figure 6.10.

Figure 6.10
The pull quote box has been repositioned.

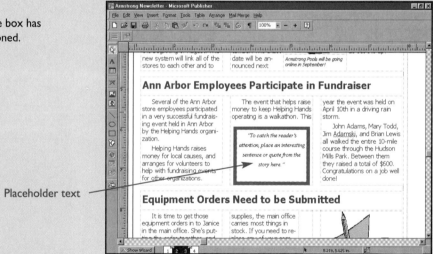

Placeholder text

6 **Click anywhere on the placeholder text. Type** `"Between them they raised a total of $600"`.
Make sure you include the quotation marks. You could also have copied the text from the article and pasted it over the placeholder text.

7 **Choose Edit, Highlight Entire Story from the menu and then click the Font Size button and change the font size to 14 point.**

8 **Click the Bold button to make the text bold.**

☑ ⑨ Click the Italic button to make the text italic; then click outside the pull quote box.
Your pull quote box should look like Figure 6.11.

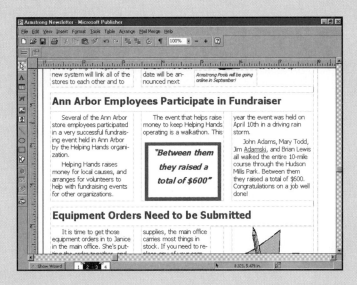

Figure 6.11
The placeholder text in the pull quote box has been replaced and formatted.

🖫 ⑩ Click the Save button to save your work, but leave the publication open for the next lesson.

Adjusting the Frame to Accommodate the Design Gallery Object
When you insert a Design Gallery Object, you may push some of the text in the text frame into overflow. You can do several things to fix this. You can reduce the size of the Design Gallery Object or increase the size of the text frame. You can also select all of the text and reduce the font size. Finally, if your text is in one unconnected text frame, you can let the program make automatic adjustments by selecting Format, AutoFit Text, Best Fit from the menu.

Lesson 4: Adding Headers and Footers to a Publication

In most multiple-page publications, there will be items or information that you want to have appear on every page. These could include page numbers, the date and/or time, a title, or a company logo or slogan. In every Publisher publication, there is a background that can hold information that you want to put on every page. You add text (or graphics) once to the background, and it appears on every page of the publication. In most cases, the recurring information will go at the top of the page (in a header) or the bottom of the page (in a footer).

In this lesson, you put the company name in the footer area of the background.

To Add a Footer to a Publication

1 Use the navigation buttons to move to page 4. Select <u>V</u>iew, <u>G</u>o to Background from the menu.

A blank page is displayed, but it is a little bit too big to see well.

2 Click the Zoom Out button to reduce the size to 75%. Scroll down until you can see the bottom of the background.

3 Click the Text Frame Tool button on the Objects toolbar; then create a text frame at the bottom of the page that is about ¼" high and the width of the work area.

The background page should look like Figure 6.12. Notice that the new text frame is below the page frame.

Figure 6.12
A text frame has been added to the background.

New text frame

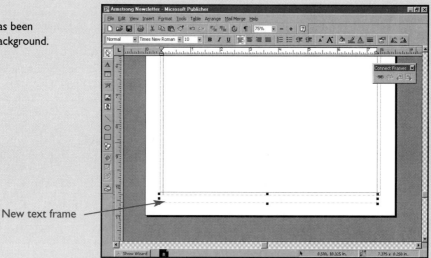

4 Type Armstrong Pool, Spa, and Sauna in the new text box.

5 Click the Center button to center the text.

The text looks small, but remember that it is being shown at only 75% (see Figure 6.13).

Figure 6.13
A footer has been added to the background.

Footer text

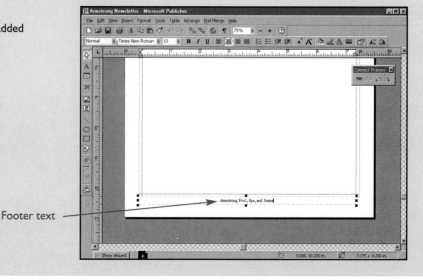

6 Select **E**dit, Select **A**ll from the menu. Click the Font box drop-down arrow and select the Tahoma font.

7 Select **V**iew, G**o** to Foreground from the menu.

The new footer appears at the bottom of the page (see Figure 6.14).

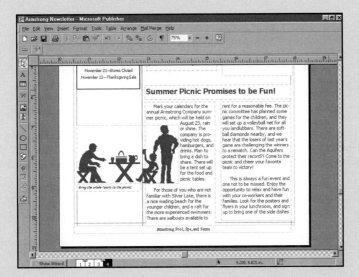

Figure 6.14
The footer is displayed on the page.

8 Use the navigation buttons to move to page 1.

Make sure that the footer is displayed on this page also.

As you scroll through the pages in your newsletter, you will see that one of the frames overlaps the footer. You will need to check for this every time you add anything to the background. In this publication, you will take care of the problem in Lesson 5.

9 Click the Save button to save your work, but leave the publication open for the next lesson.

Lesson 5: Checking the Design of Your Publication

When you have finished working on your publication and believe it is ready to print, there is a **Design Checker** tool that checks for problems in the publication's layout and design. The Design Checker will check for things such as empty frames, text in the overflow area, covered objects, and objects that are all or partially outside of the designated print areas of a page.

In this lesson, you run the Design Checker to find and fix minor problems with your publication.

To Check the Design of Your Publication

1 **Select Tools, Design Checker from the menu.**
The Design Checker dialog box is displayed (see Figure 6.15). This dialog box enables you to specify the pages to check, including the background.

Figure 6.15
The Design Checker dialog box lets you specify which pages to check.

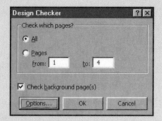

2 **Make sure All pages are selected and then click the Options button in the Design Checker dialog box.**
An Options dialog box is displayed (see Figure 6.16).

Figure 6.16
The Options dialog box enables you to select the types of problems to check.

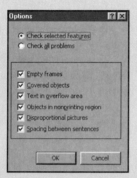

3 **Click the Check all problems button and then click OK twice.**
The Design Checker dialog box gives you the option of fixing the identified problem, ignoring it, or continuing on to the next problem. The design check begins at the insertion point, which should be the footer that you were working on in Lesson 4. In this case, the Design Checker determines that the footer is in the nonprinting region for the printer (see Figure 6.17).

 Some printers enable you to print very close to the edge of a page. If your Design Checker does not identify a nonprinting area, look at Figure 6.17 to see what the message looks like; then move on to the next identified problem in step 5. You will run into the same problem with the picture in steps 8 through 10, as well as in some of the exercises at the end of the project.

4 **Move the pointer above the footer text frame and drag it up about ⅛".**
You do not have to close the dialog box to move the text frame. This should move the text within the print area for most printers.

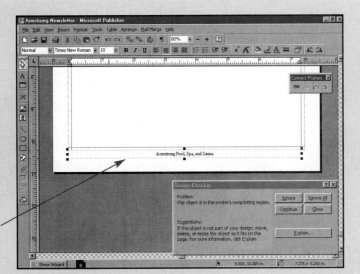

The footer is too close to the edge of the page

Figure 6.17
The Design Checker has determined that the footer is in a nonprinting area.

(i) **Minimum Distance to the Edge of a Page**

The minimum distance to the edge of a page depends on the type of printer you are using. A good rule of thumb is to leave a minimum of $1/4$" between a frame and the edge of the page. Most small offset presses need $1/4$" on the gripper edge (the edge that runs into the press first). Try printing the page to make sure you have left enough room.

---

5 **Click the Continue button in the Design Checker dialog box. If it does not move to the next problem, click the Ignore button.**

The Design Checker has found that the volume information text frame overlaps the date text frame. Because both of these text frames are readable, this is not really a problem.

6 **Click Ignore.**

The date text box is overlapped by the volume text box, again causing no problems.

7 **Click Ignore.**

A blank frame has been found behind the clip art image at the top of the second page (see Figure 6.18).

Delete Frame button

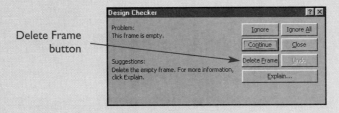

Figure 6.18
An empty frame has been found.

8 **Click the Delete Frame button and then click Continue.**

The picture at the bottom of page 3 is outside of the print area.

9 **Click on the picture and move it up about $1/4$".**

Your screen should look like Figure 6.19.

continues ▶

To Check the Design of Your Publication (continued)

Figure 6.19
The picture has been moved inside the print area.

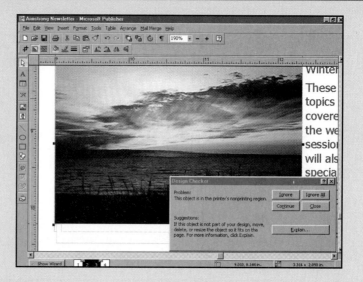

10 **Click Continue.**
The program has found text in the overflow area (see Figure 6.20).

Figure 6.20
There is more text in the text frame overflow area.

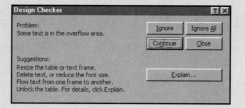

11 **Click the handle in the middle of the bottom of the text frame with the Resize pointer and drag it down $1/4$". Click Continue.**
A dialog box tells you that the design check is complete.

12 **Click OK; then click the Save button to save your work.**

13 **Click the Print button to print the newsletter, but leave the publication open for the next lesson.**

Lesson 6: Embedding Fonts for Commercial Printing

You might want to use a ***service bureau*** to prepare high-quality, high-resolution originals on photographic paper or film. The output can then be taken to a commercial printer for printing. Some commercial printers also offer image-setting services. When you use these services, some extra steps need to be taken to prepare your document.

If your service bureau has Microsoft Publisher available, you can give them your file on disk and they will be able to print it. If they do not have Publisher, you will have to **embed** the fonts in the document. This means saving the font characteristics in your document file. There are two main types of fonts available: **TrueType** and **PostScript.** The only type of fonts you can embed are TrueType fonts, and you can embed only the TrueType fonts for which you have a license. If you use PostScript fonts, the service bureau will need to have those exact fonts installed, or you will have to supply the fonts on a disk.

In this lesson, you determine what fonts and font types are used in your publication, and whether you can embed the fonts. Once that is determined, you change some fonts and embed others.

To Embed Fonts for Commercial Printing

1 Choose Tools, Commercial Printing Tools, Fonts from the menu.
A list of all of the fonts in the document is displayed (see Figure 6.21). The list includes the font name, font type, and license restrictions. If you want to embed the fonts, you will need to change any fonts that have licensing restrictions.

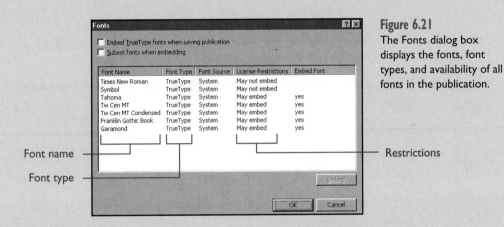

Font name
Font type

Restrictions

Figure 6.21
The Fonts dialog box displays the fonts, font types, and availability of all fonts in the publication.

2 Click OK.
The Font dialog box closes. Now you have to find the restricted fonts (Symbol and Times New Roman) so that you can change them.

continues ▶

To Embed Fonts for Commercial Printing (continued)

 Finding fonts in a document can be difficult. You cannot search for fonts as you can in Microsoft Word. However, you can do several things to speed up the process. First, look through the document to see if you can recognize different fonts. Second, select special symbols, such as long dashes, that might come from a different font. When you select text, the font type shows up in the Font box in the Formatting toolbar.

The unusual fonts will often be used for bullets in bulleted lists. If you cannot find a font (particularly one called Symbol), highlight the bulleted list; choose Format, Indents and Lists from the menu; and then click the New Bullet in the Indents and Lists dialog box. The font name is displayed. If it is one of the restricted fonts, you can change it here.

Finally, if you suspect that two different fonts are used in a text frame, you can click in the frame and then choose Edit, Select All from the menu. If no font name appears in the Font box on the Formatting toolbar, there are at least two fonts used in the frame.

3 **Use the navigation buttons to move to page 2. Move to the top of the page and select all of the text in the volume and number text frame.**

The Font box in the Formatting toolbar will display the font type, which is the restricted Times New Roman font (see Figure 6.22).

Figure 6.22
The font type is displayed in the Font box on the Formatting toolbar.

Font type

Selected text

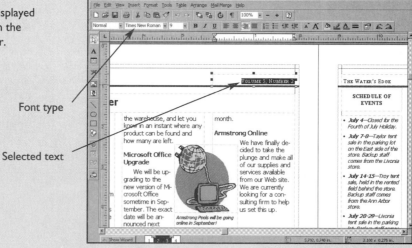

4 **Click the Font drop-down arrow and select the Tahoma font.**

5 **Select all of the text in the slogan, "The Water's Edge," just to the right of the volume and number text frame.**

It is also Times New Roman.

6 **Click the Font drop-down arrow and select the Tahoma font.**

You have now changed all of the text in the Times New Roman font. Now you have to change the Symbol font.

7 **Select all of the text in the Schedule of Events bulleted list; then choose Format, Indents and Lists from the menu.**

The Indents and Lists dialog box is displayed (see Figure 6.23).

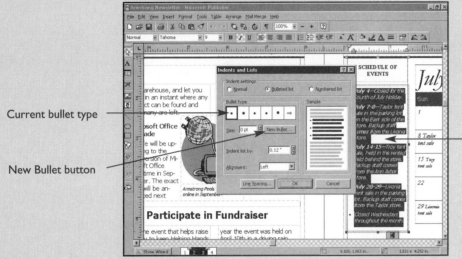

Figure 6.23
The Indents and Lists dialog box enables you to change the shape of a bullet.

Current bullet type

New Bullet button

Selected bulleted list

8 **Click the New Bullet button; then select Tahoma from the Font box and Geometric Shapes from the Subset box.**

Several bullet shapes are displayed (see Figure 6.24).

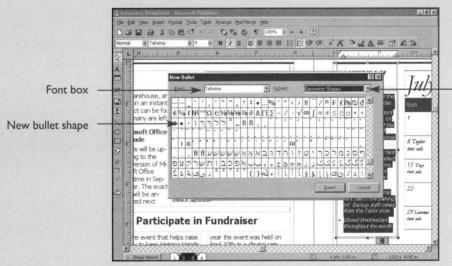

Figure 6.24
You can change the shape of a bullet to any character in the font list.

Font box

New bullet shape

Subset box

9 **Choose the bullet in the second column, click Insert, and then click OK.**

The new Tahoma bullet replaces the Times New Roman bullet. Now it is time to embed the fonts.

10 **Choose Tools, Commercial Printing Tools, Fonts from the menu.**

Notice that the only font with license restrictions is Times New Roman, and no text in the publication is in that font.

continues ▶

To Embed Fonts for Commercial Printing   (continued)

11 Click the Embed **T**rueType fonts when saving publication check box and then click the **S**ubset fonts when embedding check box.
Your Fonts dialog box should look like Figure 6.25.

Figure 6.25
Two embedding options have been selected.

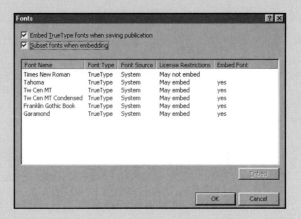

12 Click OK to close the Fonts dialog box. Click the Save button to save your work, but leave the publication open for the next lesson.

Deciding Whether to Embed Fonts
Embedding fonts increases the file size. If you had just embedded the fonts, the file would have increased in size by about a megabyte. By choosing to embed only a subset of the fonts, the file size increased by only about 350 Kb. If you are sure your publication is ready to be printed, use the font subset. If you think the printing firm might have to make some changes, you will want to embed the entire fonts.

Lesson 7: Preparing Images for Color Printing

If you have included color images in your newsletter and want to print them, the way you proceed depends on the method you are going to use for printing. If you are going to print on a color printer in house using Publisher, you are all set. Publisher saves images using the **RGB color model** (red, green, blue), which your color printer will recognize. If you are going to have your publication printed by a commercial printer, however, you will need to use a different procedure to store your document.

When you prepare your publication for commercial process-color (or four-color) printing, you will be separating the colors in your document into cyan, magenta, yellow, and black, which is known as the **CMYK color model**. Commercial printers then mix these colors to create images that look like they were taken with a camera and pasted on the page.

In this lesson, you save the newsletter you have been working on using the CMYK color model.

To Prepare Images for Color Printing

1 Choose Tools, Commercial Printing Tools, Color Printing from the menu.
The Color Printing dialog box is displayed (see Figure 6.26).

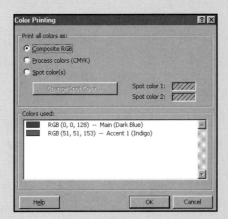

Figure 6.26
The Color Printing dialog box gives you several options for setting up your color printing.

2 Click the Process colors (CMYK) option; then click OK.
The colors are separated.

3 Click the Save button to save your work.
This saves the color separations and slightly increases the file size. You can print the color separations if you have a color printer. You can even print them on a black and white printer to see what is printed on the four parts of each page.

4 Choose File, Print from the menu.
The Print dialog box is displayed.

5 Click the Pages button in the Print range area and choose to print from 3 to 3.

6 Click the Print separations button in the Separations area and make sure All is selected.
Your Print dialog box should look like Figure 6.27.

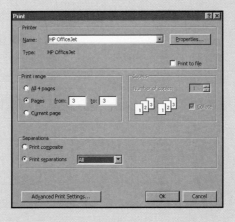

Figure 6.27
Four pages will be printed for a single newsletter page, each one representing one of the four colors.

continues ▶

To Prepare Images for Color Printing   (continued)

7 **Click OK.**

The separations are printed. Notice that because the text is a shade of blue, it appears on three of the four pages. Leave the publication open for the next lesson.

Planning Ahead

If you are planning to use a service bureau to process your publication for commercial printing, it is a good idea to discuss your project with them before you start. They may have recommendations or restrictions on fonts and colors, and they will also be able to help with process-color printing.

Lesson 8: Setting Publisher Options

Publisher gives you control over several of the features of the program in the Tools, Options menu choice. If you are using a slower computer and the font previews in the font box are taking too long to display, you can turn this feature off. You can also turn hyphenation on and off and set the amount of time between reminders to save your work. There are several other very useful features that you can control.

In this lesson, you change some of the Publisher options. (*Note:* If you are doing this in a lab, ask the lab manager for permission to make these changes.)

To Set Publisher Options

1 **Choose Tools, Options from the menu.**

The Options dialog box opens to the General tab (see Figure 6.28).

Figure 6.28
The Options dialog box has four tabs for different categories of options.

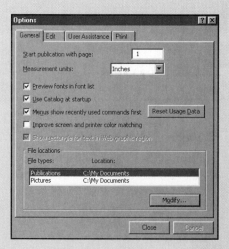

2 **Click the Preview fonts in font list check box to turn it off.**

The fonts will not be previewed when you click the drop-down arrow on the Font box in the Formatting toolbar.

X Throughout this lesson, you may find that someone has already made the change you are supposed to make. Go ahead and change it back.

3 Click the Edit tab in the Options dialog box.
Several editing options are offered.

4 Deselect the When selecting, automatically select entire word check box.

5 Click the User Assistance tab and change the Minutes between reminders to 12 minutes.

6 Click the Close button on the Options dialog box.

7 Click in any text frame and then click the down-arrow on the Font box in the Formatting toolbar.
Notice how fast the fonts appeared, but that the all of the font names now look the same (see Figure 6.29).

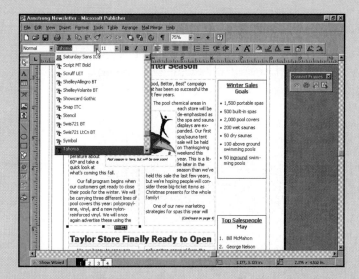

Figure 6.29
The font preview has been turned off.

8 Close your newsletter and close Publisher.

Summary

In this project, you used some of the many tools available in Publisher. You checked your spelling and turned hyphenation on and off. You added a pull quote from the Design Gallery and added a footer to the document background. When you finished your newsletter, you ran the Design Checker to see if there were any flaws in your layout and design. You used some of the tools provided for preparing your publication for professional printing. Finally, you changed some of the program options.

Publisher provides a good introduction to commercial printing. In the Help menu, type `commercial` and search for commercial_printing. Read the "About commercial printing" and "Set up a publication for a printing service" topics for a good introduction to this complex subject.

Checking Concepts and Terms ✓

True/False

For each of the following statements, check *T* or *F* to indicate whether the statement is true or false.

__T __F **1.** Headers and footers are placed in the publication foreground. [Intro]

__T __F **2.** If a word has a wavy red underline under it, it is definitely misspelled. [L1]

__T __F **3.** When you add a word to the dictionary, it is added to a supplemental dictionary that you can edit using a word processor. [L1]

__T __F **4.** The effectiveness of hyphenation can be determined only by trying it and examining the outcome. [L2]

__T __F **5.** The hyphenation zone is the area of the text frame that has automatic hyphenation turned on. [L2]

__T __F **6.** A pull quote is a quotation that is usually found in a margin outside of the text frame. [L3]

__T __F **7.** You can embed only TrueType fonts. [L6]

__T __F **8.** The Tools, Commercial Printing Tools, Fonts menu option displays a list of all of the fonts used in a publication. [L6]

__T __F **9.** Embedding fonts increases the file size. [L6]

__T __F **10.** If you are planning to use a service bureau for your publication, it is a good idea to talk to them before you begin your project. [L7]

Multiple Choice

Circle the letter of the correct answer for each of the following questions.

1. If you want something to appear on every page, you would put it in the _____. [L4]

   a. foreground
   b. background
   c. template
   d. none of the above

2. A wavy red line under a word means that _____. [L1]

   a. the word is definitely misspelled
   b. the word is not in the dictionary stored on the computer
   c. there is a grammar problem with the word
   d. the spacing before or after the word is incorrect

3. When you run the spell checker and the program finds an unrecognized word, you can _____. [L1]

   a. add it to the dictionary
   b. change it
   c. ignore it
   d. all of the above

4. Which of the following is true about using hyphenation? [L2]

   a. You should not use hyphens in more than two consecutive lines.
   b. You should never end a column with a hyphen.
   c. You should not use hyphens in a title or header.
   d. all of the above

5. When you add a Design Gallery Object, you sometimes force text into the overflow area. You can fix that by _____. [L3]

   a. reducing the size of the Design Gallery Object
   b. reducing the size of the font in the text frame
   c. increasing the size of the text frame
   d. all of the above

6. The Design Checker does not check for _____. [L5]

   a. objects that do not look good together
   b. empty frames
   c. text in the overflow area
   d. objects that are outside of the designated print area

7. You should probably place objects no closer than _____ from the edge of a page. [L5]

    a. 1"

    b. $\frac{1}{2}$"

    c. $\frac{1}{4}$"

    d. $\frac{1}{8}$"

8. Which of the following is not true of fonts used in a publication to be sent to a service bureau? [L6]

    a. Using a subset of a font will save file space.

    b. You can embed only PostScript fonts in the publication.

    c. Some fonts have licensing restrictions and cannot be embedded.

    d. If you use PostScript fonts, the service bureau will need to have those fonts installed on their own machines, or you will have to provide them.

9. To find a font in a document, you can _____. [L7]

    a. examine the publication for fonts that look different.

    b. select special symbols and check the Font box.

    c. select all of the text in a text frame and check to see if the Font box is blank.

    d. all of the above

10. When you prepare a publication for four-color printing, you separate the publication into which of the following four colors? [L7]

    a. cyan, magenta, yellow, and black

    b. red, green, blue, and white

    c. red, yellow, green, and blue

    d. white, black, red, and green

Discussion Questions

1. In most cases, the spell checker is on all of the time. This means that your document will usually contain several of the wavy red lines. Do you like to know immediately when a word is not recognized, or would you rather turn that feature off and do your spelling check all at once? Why?

2. When you looked at all of the available Design Gallery Objects, you probably noticed that nearly all of the features added when you create a publication using a wizard could be added separately. What advantage would there be to starting with a blank publication and adding objects as you need them? What advantages are there to using the wizard?

3. When you add headers, footers, or other objects to the background, these objects appear on all of the pages of the publication. Publisher gives you the option of turning the background objects off on individual pages. When might you want to use this feature?

4. You checked the design of your publication when the publication was complete. Would it be a good idea to run this tool several times while you are creating the publication? Why?

5. Working with fonts and graphics that will be used by a service bureau requires a lot of time and knowledge. If you were given an assignment to create a newsletter that would be sent to a service bureau, when would you want to get the service bureau people involved in the process? Why?

Skill Drill

Skill Drill exercises reinforce project skills. Each skill reinforced is the same, or nearly the same, as a skill presented in this project. Each exercise includes a brief narrative introduction, followed by detailed instructions in a step-by-step format.

You have expanded the Helping Hands newsletter to four pages and changed the design. Now that you are nearly finished, you decide to do some final touch-ups and edits to get it ready to print on your company printer.

1. Checking Your Spelling

You notice that several words have red underlines in the bottom story on the second page. These need to be checked and fixed when necessary.

To check your spelling, complete the following steps:

1. Find and open the Pub-0602 file on your CD-ROM. Choose File, Save As from the menu and save the file as **Helping Hands Newsletter - Revised**.

2. Use the navigation buttons to move to page 2. Click at the beginning of the bottom story and then click the Zoom In button until the article is shown at 100%.

3. Choose Tools, Spelling, Check Spelling from the menu.

4. Click the Change button to change "anonomous" to the suggested "anonymous."

5. Click the Ignore button to skip the unrecognized word "Photographics."

6. Click the Change button to change "framd" to the suggested "framed."

7. Click the No button to stop the spell check here. Leave the publication open if you are going to continue to another exercise.

2. Adding Hyphenation

The bottom article on the second page has very ragged right edges because hyphenation has not been turned on. You want to turn hyphenation on to see if it will make a difference.

To add hyphenation, complete the following steps:

1. Place the insertion point in the bottom article of the second page, if necessary.

2. Choose Tools, Language, Hyphenation from the menu.

3. Click the Automatically hyphenate this story check box and then click OK. Notice how much better the story looks.

4. Click the Save button to save your work. Leave the publication open if you are going to continue to another exercise.

3. Adding a Sidebar Using the Design Gallery Tool

The bottom article on the second page could use either a sidebar or a pull quote. Looking at the layout of the page, you decide that a sidebar in the left margin would work best.

To add a sidebar using the Design Gallery tool, complete the following steps:

1. Make sure you are on page 2 of the newsletter. Click the Design Gallery Object button on the Objects toolbar.

2. Select Sidebars from the Categories panel and then scroll down the Sidebars panel and select the Marquee Sidebar, if necessary.

3. Click the Insert Object button.

4. Use the Move pointer to move the sidebar into the margin to the left of the article.

5. Click the placeholder bulleted list and press Del.

6. Click the Bullets button to turn off the bulleted list.

7. Click the placeholder text at the top of the sidebar, then type **The photograph is very relaxing. You can almost hear the waves crashing on the shore.**

8. Select all of the text in the sidebar; then click the drop-down arrow on the Font Size box to change the font size to 12 point.

9. Click the Italic button.

10. Click the handle at the bottom of the sidebar and pull it up until it is just below the text. Move the box about half-way down the article.

11. Leave the publication open if you are going to continue to another exercise.

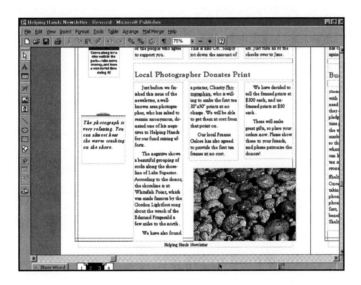

4. Adding a Footer to the Background

It would be a good idea to add the name of the newsletter to the footer. To do this, you will have to work in the background.

To add a footer to the background, complete the following steps:

1. Select View, Go to Background from the menu.

2. Click the Zoom Out button to reduce the size to 75%. Scroll down until you can see the bottom of the background.

3. Click the Text Frame Tool button on the Objects toolbar; then create a text frame at the bottom of the page that is about ¼" high and the width of the work area.

4. Type `Helping Hands Newsletter` in the new text box.

5. Click the Center button on the toolbar to center the footer text.

6. Select View, Go to Foreground from the menu. Make sure the footer appears on the page. The page you have worked on in these exercises should look like Figure 6.30.

7. Save your work. Leave the publication open if you are going to continue to another lesson.

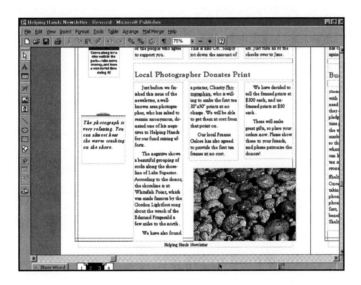

Figure 6.30
The spelling has been corrected, hyphenation has been turned on, and a sidebar and footer have been added to the newsletter.

5. Using the Design Checker

You are nearly ready to print your newsletter. It is time to let Publisher take a look and see if anything appears to be wrong with the publication layout and design. Once again, your results may depend on the printer you are using.

To use the Design Checker, complete the following steps:

1. Select Tools, Design Checker from the menu.

2. Make sure All pages are selected and then click the Options button in the Design Checker dialog box.

3. Click the Check all problems button, if necessary; then click OK twice.

4. Click the Delete Frame button to delete the empty frame; then click Continue. Repeat the procedure for the next empty frame.

5. When you get to the `text in overflow error`, move the dialog box if it is in the way and then use the handle at the bottom of the text frame to

increase the length of the frame. Add a period to the end of the sentence.

6. Click Ignore to ignore the next `text in overflow error` because there is no more text in that text frame.

7. Move the picture of the phone about ½" to the left. Click Continue.

8. Click OK when the Design Check is complete. Save your work. Leave the publication open if you are going to continue to another exercise.

6. Changing Publisher Options

In Lesson 8, you changed some of the default Publisher options. You will now change these options back to their original settings.

To change Publisher options, complete the following steps:

1. Choose <u>T</u>ools, <u>O</u>ptions from the menu.

2. Click the <u>P</u>review fonts in font list button to turn it back on.

3. Click the Edit tab in the Options dialog box. Click the When selecting, automatically select entire <u>w</u>ord check box.

4. Click the User Assistance tab and change the Minutes between reminders back to **15** minutes (or whatever it was when you changed it in Lesson 8).

5. Click the Close button on the Options dialog box.

6. Click in any text frame and then click the down-arrow on the Font box in the Formatting toolbar. Check to see whether the font preview is turned on.

7. Close the publication and close Publisher.

Challenge

Challenge exercises expand on or are somewhat related to skills presented in the lessons. Each exercise provides a brief narrative introduction, followed by instructions in a numbered step format that are not as detailed as those in the Skill Drill section.

In the following exercises, you work with the Cornwall newsletter you used in Project 3. You will use several more Publisher tools and use refinements of some of the tools you used in the lessons. These exercises are not dependent on each other. You can do some or all of them, and in any order. If you are not going to do the first exercise, do step 1 anyway.

1. Using Manual Hyphenation

You do not have to accept the hyphenation suggested by Publisher. You have the option of manually placing hyphens in a text frame.

1. Find and open the Pub-0603 file on your CD-ROM. Choose <u>F</u>ile, Save <u>A</u>s from the menu and save the file as **Cornwall Newsletter**.

2. Move to page 2 and select all of the text in the "Gwennap Pit Provides Rich History" text frame.

3. Select the Hyphenation feature from the menu.

4. Turn off automatic hyphenation and click <u>M</u>anual.

5. Accept the hyphenation of "Methodist," but do not hyphenate "famous."

6. Accept the hyphenation of "abandoned."

7. Save your changes. Leave the publication open if you are going to continue to another exercise.

2. Inserting the Current Date and Page Number in a Footer

In Lesson 2, you added some text to the background of a newsletter. The text then appeared exactly the same on every page. You can also add things that vary from page to page or from draft to draft. You can add the page number that varies by page. You can add the date or time frames that always reflect the current date or time. In this exercise, you add a page number and the current date to the footer area of the newsletter.

1. Go to the newsletter background.

2. Add a text frame on the left side of the footer under the page frame.

3. Use the Insert, Date and Time option from the menu to enter a date in the "February 3, 2000" format.

4. Create another text frame on the right side of the background and choose Insert, Page Numbers from the menu. Right-align the page number. The text frame should be directly to the right of the date and time text frame.

5. Move back to the foreground. If any of the text frames cover up part of the page number, use the shortcut menu on those frames to turn off any fill colors.

6. Save your changes. Leave the publication open if you are going to continue to another exercise.

3. Changing the AutoFormat Features

Publisher automatically makes some changes in your publication as you type. For example, it will replace straight quotes with smart quotes. It will also automatically begin to add bullets or numbers if it appears that you are creating a list. Many people consider some or all of the AutoFormat features to be nuisances.

Use Publisher Help to find out how to turn AutoFormat features on or off. Turn off the automatic bulleted and numbered lists, and turn off the smart quotes option. (*Note:* If someone has already done this on your computer, turn those features on instead.)

4. Preparing for High-Quality Black-and-White Printing

If you are going to take your publication to a commercial printer, there are some steps you need to take even if you are going to use only black and white. Following this procedure will result in higher-resolution output, darker black, and more distinctive grays.

1. Select Tools, Commercial Printing Tools, Color Printing from the menu.

2. Select the Spot color(s) option.

3. Click the Change Spot Color button.

4. Select the Black and white only option.

5. Click OK twice.

Notice that both of the photographs and all of the color images are black or gray.

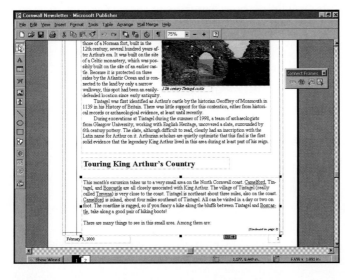

Figure 6.31
The page number and the current date have been added to the footer, and the photograph has been changed to shades of gray.

5. Using the Detect and Repair Tool

If you are using Publisher in a public lab or on a machine that gets a lot of use, it is possible that some of the program files are missing or damaged. Publisher has a tool that looks at the current program files and compares them with the original files. If any differences are found, the damaged or missing files are replaced.

Activate the Detect and Repair tool in the Help menu. The program will ask you to save your changes; then close your publication. Click Start to begin the procedure. If you are working in a lab, check with the lab manager first. If you are not working on a network, you may need the original Office disc at some point in the process.

If you are through with this exercise, close Publisher unless you are going to move on to the Discovery Zone.

Discovery Zone

Discovery Zone exercises help you gain advanced knowledge of project topics and/or application of skills. These exercises focus on enhancing your problem-solving skills. Numbered steps are not provided, but you are given hints, reminders, screen shots, and/or references to help you reach your goal for each exercise.

[?] 1. Adding an AutoCorrect Entry

There are probably long words or phrases that you type frequently. Publisher, has a feature called AutoCorrect, which is also included with most other Office applications. You can use this feature to add shortcuts that expand to full words or phrases when you type them into a document.

Goal: Add an AutoCorrect entry that expands a three-letter code into a four-word phrase.

You should do the following:

- Find and open the Pub-0603 file on your CD-ROM and save the file as **Cornwall Newsletter 2**.
- Create a shortcut called **chh** (because sometimes you might want to use CHHS in your text).
- Expand chh into **Cornwall Historical Heritage Society**.
- Type **chh** after the second word in the "Touring King Arthur's Country" article on the bottom of page 1.
- Print the first page of the newsletter.

Hint: You can find AutoCorrect help in the Help menu.

Save your work and close Publisher.

[?] 2. Investigating Commercial Printing

If you are going to use a service bureau and/or a commercial printer, you will have to investigate many things. It is a good idea to answer these questions before you create your publication. Some of the terms may be new to you, so use the Help menu to find out what you can about them.

Goal: Check with a service bureau, commercial printer, or graphic design department in your business or university to answer some of the following questions:

- How does the cost of printing vary based on paper weight and quality? the number of copies made? the resolution you want to print at?
- Should you use trapping to make sure problems do not occur?
- Can the service bureau use the character formatting of fonts you are using, or do they need separate italic and bold versions of each font?
- What is the best way to handle color?

Project 7

Building a Web Site with Publisher

Objectives

In this project, you learn how to

➤ **Create a Web Site Using a Wizard**

➤ **Set Page Width**

➤ **Add Text to Web Pages**

➤ **Insert Pictures on a Web Page**

➤ **Insert a New Page**

➤ **Preview the Web Pages**

➤ **Save the Publication as Web Pages**

➤ **Preview the Web Pages Using a Browser**

Key terms introduced in this project include

- horizontal bar
- host computer
- hyperlinks
- Hypertext Markup Language (HTML)
- Internet
- intranet
- layout guides
- pixels
- vertical bar
- Web browser
- Web pages
- Web site

Why Would I Do This?

Many organizations use the *Internet* to communicate with their members. The Internet is a worldwide network of computers that is available to anyone with access to a phone line. Because of the Internet's accessibility, it is not always suitable for publishing sensitive company information that is not intended for public viewing. Most companies also have an *intranet* that uses the same software and looks the same as the Internet but is available only to people within the company.

Publisher can create *Web pages* that are connected by navigation buttons. A collected of pages and their supporting files is called a *Web site.* A Web site can be transferred to a *host computer* where its pages are made available to the other computers. Web pages are screens that can be transmitted on the Internet or intranet and viewed by a *Web browser* such as Netscape or Internet Explorer. The host computer is connected to the Internet or the intranet and allows other people to view the pages. Web browsers are programs that communicate with your computer and the host computer to display Web pages.

Publishing information on Web pages has several advantages. The information is easy to change and keep current. In addition, there is little lead-time between writing and distribution, so late-breaking news can be incorporated and made available almost immediately. Publishing on the Web is cheaper than creating printed documents and has no practical limit on the number of viewers who can read it. A disadvantage is that the reader must take action to find the site and read it. If the reader is unaware of the site or does not have a computer that is connected to the Internet/intranet, the message goes unread.

In this project, you create a set of pages that communicates the same information that is contained in the company newsletter you worked with in Project 3, "Working with Text."

Visual Summary

When you have completed this lesson, you will have created a set of linked Web pages.

Figure 7.1
Page 1 of the Summer News Web pages.

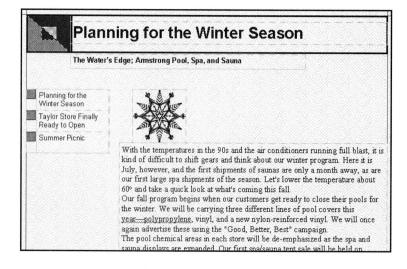

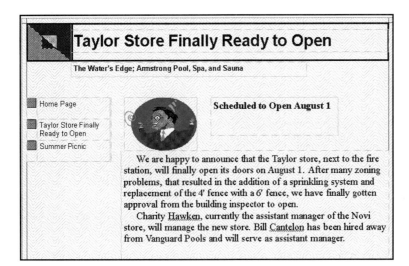

Figure 7.2
Page 2 of the Summer News Web pages.

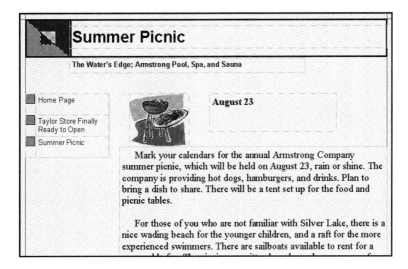

Figure 7.3
Page 3 of the Summer News Web pages.

Lesson 1: Creating a Web Site Using a Wizard

One of the programming languages of the Internet is **Hypertext Markup Language,** or **HTML.** You use HTML to write and create Web pages. HTML consists of a set of codes that any computer can use to display text onscreen. It describes what the result should be and lets the local computer use its own software to display the text. For example, an HTML code for boldface is <strong>. It is up to the computer that is displaying the text to figure out how to display boldface text on that machine.

Publisher does the HTML coding for you. If you can set up a flyer, you can create Web pages with Publisher. The best way to get started is to use the Publisher Wizard and choose a previously designed set of Web pages. You can then customize the Web pages with your own text and graphics.

In this lesson, you launch Publisher and select a design for your Web site.

To Create a Web Site Using a Wizard

1 **Launch Publisher. Select Web Sites from the list of Wizards in the column at the left.**
Dozens of designs are displayed in the frame at the right.

2 **Scroll through the various design options to see what is available and select the first choice, Accent Box Web Site.**
The Accent Box Web Site is the first option in the upper-left corner of the frame (see Figure 7.4).

Figure 7.4
Many designs are available for your Web site.

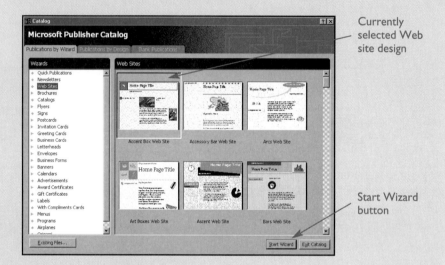

Currently selected Web site design

Start Wizard button

3 **Click the Start Wizard button.**
A sample page is displayed in the frame on the right and the Web Site Wizard is in a frame on the left.

4 **Click Next.**
A list of available color schemes is displayed on the left.

5 **Click on several different options to see how they would look on the sample page. Click Mahogany and then click Next.**
A list of optional pages are displayed in the frame on the left.

6 **Click Next.**
A list of optional forms is displayed.

7 **Click Next.**
The navigation bar options are displayed (see Figure 7.5). The *vertical bar* consists of buttons at the left side of the page. Additional pages will each have a button after they are added. The buttons are used to go to the page when pressed. The *horizontal bar* is a list of page names side-by-side that work like the buttons.

8 **Click Next.**
A sound option is offered. Accept the default choice of No.

9 **Click Next.**
A background texture option is suggested. Accept the default choice of Yes.

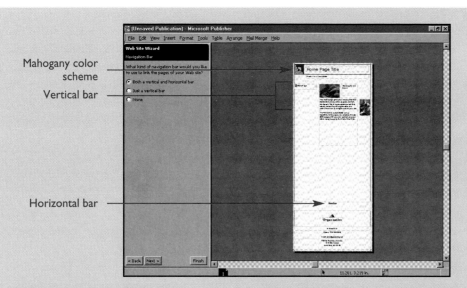

Figure 7.5
The Web Site Wizard is used to modify a standard Web page.

Mahogany color scheme

Vertical bar

Horizontal bar

⑩ Click Next.

A list of personal information options are displayed. Accept the default choice of Primary Business. This option will use the name of the organization and its logo if one has already been created.

⑪ Click Finish.

The sample page is displayed on the right and the wizard on the left.

⑫ Click Hide Wizard.

The sample page is displayed in the center of the screen. Notice that the default width is 6" and default length is 14" (see Figure 7.6). Leave the publication open for use in the next lesson.

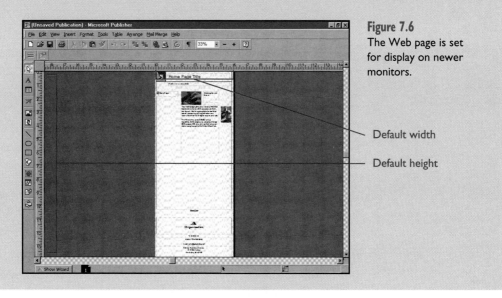

Figure 7.6
The Web page is set for display on newer monitors.

Default width

Default height

Lesson 2: Setting Page Width

When you create Web pages that will be viewed by many people on a mix of new and old computers, you need to decide whether you should design the web pages for most convenient viewing on new computers or on old ones.

The screen of a monitor is divided up into tiny rectangles called picture elements, or *pixels.* Older monitors could display only images that are 640 pixels wide and 480 pixels high. If a screen is wider than the monitor can display, scrollbars automatically appear to allow the user to view the portions that are offscreen. Newer monitors can be set to display images at a wide range of sizes but are commonly set at 800 × 600 pixels. Publisher uses a default page width that is most convenient for people who are viewing the page using a monitor set to 640 × 480 pixels. When these pages are viewed on a monitor set to 800 × 600 pixels, the page fills only part of the screen. If most of the computers in an organization are less than 3 years old, it is advisable to increase the page width for better display on the newer monitors. The people in the organization who have older monitors or people who have set their monitors on 640 ×480 pixels may need to use the scrollbars to see all of the page.

In this lesson, you change the page setup to make the pages wider for better viewing on newer monitors.

To Set Page Width

❶ Choose File, Page Setup from the menu.
The Web Page Setup dialog box is displayed. Notice the default is a page that is 6" × 14".

❷ Click Wide to increase the width of the page.
The width is changed to 7.5" (see Figure 7.7).

Figure 7.7
Wider pages fill more of the screen when viewed on newer monitors that are set to display more pixels.

Better choice for newer computers

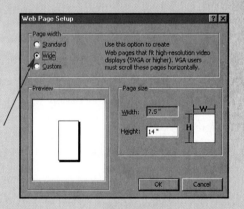

❸ Click OK.
The new page appears slightly wider onscreen.

 Computer Displays
There is a component of your computer called a video graphics adapter. Your monitor is plugged into this card. The capabilities of this card and those of your monitor determine how many pixels can be displayed and how many colors are used. Early models could display only 640 × 480 pixels in 16 different colors. This standard was called VGA, after the name of the card. The next improvement was called Super VGA, or SVGA, and could display 800 × 600 pixels and more colors. Video graphics cards have improved dramatically, allowing them to display images that are more than 1,000 pixels in both directions and in millions of colors.

4 **Click the down arrow next to the Zoom button and change the zoom to Page Width.**

The zoom feature controls the appearance of the page in Publisher but is unrelated to the apparent width of the page when viewed by a browser on the Web (see Figure 7.8).

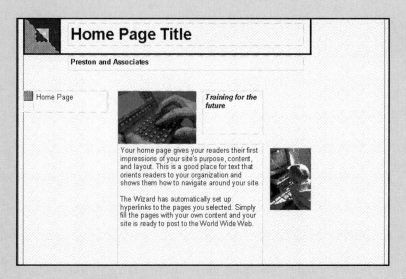

Figure 7.8
The page is displayed full width, ready for editing.

5 **Select the elements that make up the title (the rectangular border around the title at the top of the page, the text box within the rectangle, and the graphic in the rectangle at the left). Group them together and resize them so that the right side is aligned with the layout guide.**

The *layout guides* are lines that are visible on the screen but not on the final page. They are used to align objects on the page.

6 **Right-click on the frame to the right of the top picture and select Delete Object from the shortcut menu.**

7 **Delete the picture at the right of the main text box and then widen the text box (see Figure 7.9).**

Leave the publication open for use in the next lesson.

continues ▶

To Set Page Width   (continued)

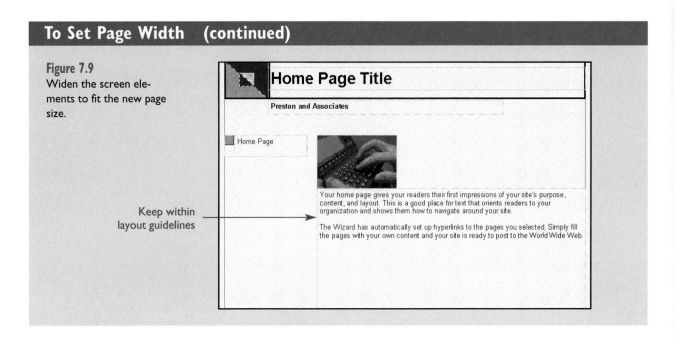

Figure 7.9
Widen the screen elements to fit the new page size.

Keep within
layout guidelines

Lesson 3: Adding Text to Web Pages

Adding text to the Web pages is done the same way as in other publications, but it is important that you avoid overlapping text and graphic frames. If frames are overlapped, the program will treat the text frames as graphic frames, which limits how the browser can display the text and, because of the larger file size of graphic frames, significantly slow down the display of the page.

In this lesson, modify the existing text in the title and copy text from a Word document into the text frame.

To Add Text to Web Pages

1 **Click on the Home Page Title to select it and type** `Planning for the Winter Season.`

2 **Click the text box below the title box. Select the existing text and type** `The Water's Edge; Armstrong Pool, Spa, and Sauna.`
The text in the title and subheading text boxes has been edited (see Figure 7.10).

4 **Select all the text in the large text box. Choose Insert, Text File from the menu. Find and select the Winter Season Article file from your CD-ROM and then click OK.**
The Microsoft Word file is imported into the newsletter, and a Publisher message box lets you know that the document is too big for the text frame. It asks if you want to use the AutoFlow feature.

5 **Click No.**
The text from the article is placed in the existing frame.

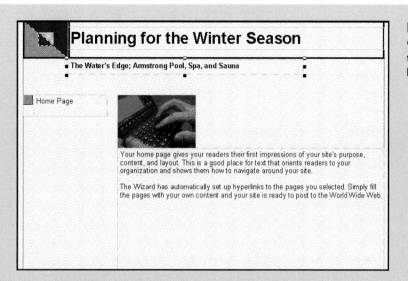

Figure 7.10
Change the text in the title and subheading text boxes.

![alert icon] **Inserting Large Amounts of Text**

If the text you insert is too large for the text frame, a message box appears offering the option of flowing the text into another text frame. This is not a good idea when creating Web pages because the text will not flow between frames on the Web pages the way it can in other publications.

---

6 **Change the zoom to Whole Page. Select the large text box. Use a handle at the bottom of the text box to resize the box downward until the text overflow indicator disappears (see Figure 7.11).**
Do not widen the text box to the left. This area will be used for navigation buttons.

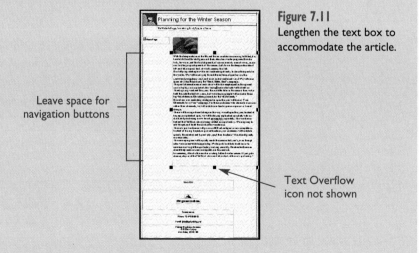

Leave space for navigation buttons

Text Overflow icon not shown

Figure 7.11
Lengthen the text box to accommodate the article.

8 **Change the zoom back to Page Width. Scroll up the page if necessary to display the picture at the top of the page.**
Leave the publication open for use in the next lesson.

Lesson 4: Inserting Pictures on a Web Page

Inserting pictures is done the same way in Web pages as it is in other Publisher publications.

In this lesson, you insert clip art into the existing picture frame.

To Insert Pictures on a Web Page

1 **Click the picture near the top of the page to select it.**
Handles indicate that the picture is selected.

2 **Choose Insert, Picture, Clip Art from the menu.**
The Insert Clip Art dialog box is displayed (see Figure 7.12).

Figure 7.12
Search for clip art that would be appropriate for the Winter season.

3 **Click in the Search for clips box and type** Winter. **Press** ⏎Enter.
Clip art that is related to Winter is displayed (see Figure 7.13).

Figure 7.13
Searching for clip art using keywords provides a variety of related pictures from which to choose.

Keyword

4 **Click a snowflake picture and then click the Insert Clip button on the resulting menu.**
The picture is placed on the Web page but is not visible behind the Insert Clip Art dialog box.

5 **Close the Insert Clip Art dialog box.**
The snowflake picture replaces the placeholder picture (see Figure 7.14).

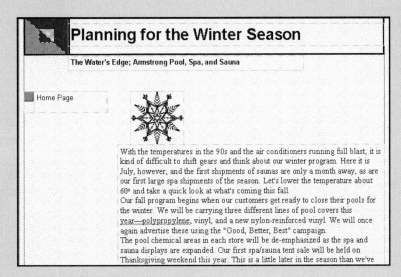

Figure 7.14
The placeholder picture has been replaced by clip art that is appropriate to the topic.

6 **Click the Save button to save your work. Save it with the name Summer News.**
Leave the publication open for the next lesson.

Lesson 5: Inserting New Pages

Web sites consist of related pages that are linked together with hyperlinks. **Hyperlinks** are addresses that are attached to words or objects, such as buttons, on the page. When you click on the hyperlinked words or objects, the browser goes to the attached address. Publisher creates the navigation buttons and their hyperlinks automatically.

In this lesson, you insert a new Web page that is a duplicate of the existing page and then modify it to hold information about the next topic.

To Insert a New Page

1 **Choose Insert, Page from the menu.**
The Insert Page dialog box is displayed (see Figure 7.15).

2 **Click More Options.**
Another Insert Page dialog box is displayed (see Figure 7.16).

continues ▶

To Insert a New Page   (continued)

Figure 7.15
A wizard helps create new Web pages and links between them and previous pages.

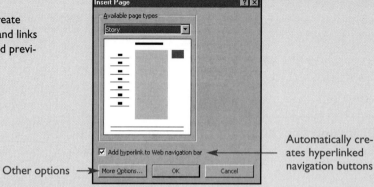

Other options ⟶

Automatically creates hyperlinked navigation buttons

③ **Confirm that Add hyperlink to Web navigation bar is selected. Confirm that After current page is selected. Select Duplicate all objects on page.**

These choices will produce a duplicate page after the current one. Both pages will have navigation buttons that will be used to navigate between them (see Figure 7.16).

Figure 7.16
The Insert Page dialog box creates a duplicate page with navigation buttons.

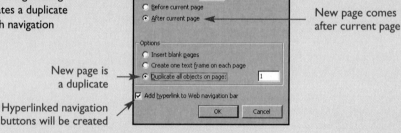

New page is a duplicate

Hyperlinked navigation buttons will be created

New page comes after current page

④ **Click OK.**
A second Web page is added (see Figure 7.17).

Figure 7.17
You have just created a second Web page.

Page 2

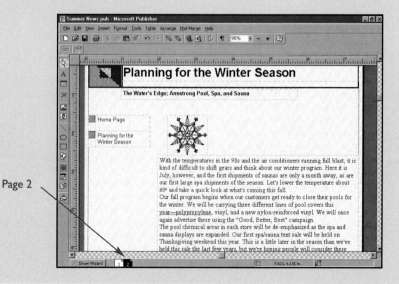

5 **Select the text in the title, and change it to** `Taylor Store Finally Ready to Open`**. Click in an unused part of the page to deselect the title.**

Notice that the text in the navigation button automatically changes to match the new page title.

6 **Click the Text Frame Tool and drag a text frame to the right of the picture. Change the font size to 14 point and click the Bold button. Type** `Scheduled to Open August 1`**. See Figure 7.18.**

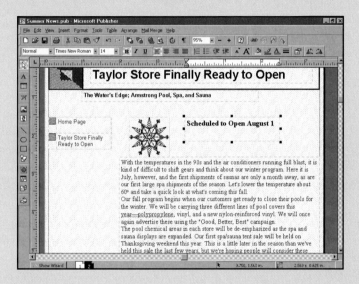

Figure 7.18
Add a text frame to the right of the picture.

7 **Select all the text in the large text box. Choose Insert, Text File from the menu. Locate the document Taylor Store Opening. Select it and click OK.**

8 **Select the inserted text and change the font size to 14 point.**

9 **Select the picture. Choose Insert, Picture, Clip Art from the menu. Search for the keyword** `Celebration` **and pick an appropriate clip art image.**

The second page now contains the story about the new Taylor store (see Figure 7.19).

10 **Repeat this process to produce a third page titled** `Summer Picnic`**. Insert the document Picnic for the main text and use an appropriate clip art picture. Put the date of the picnic,** `August 23`**, in the text box next to the picture.**

The third page covers the story about the summer picnic (see Figure 7.20).

11 **Click the Save button to save your work.**

Leave the publication open for the next lesson.

continues ▶

To Insert a New Page (continued)

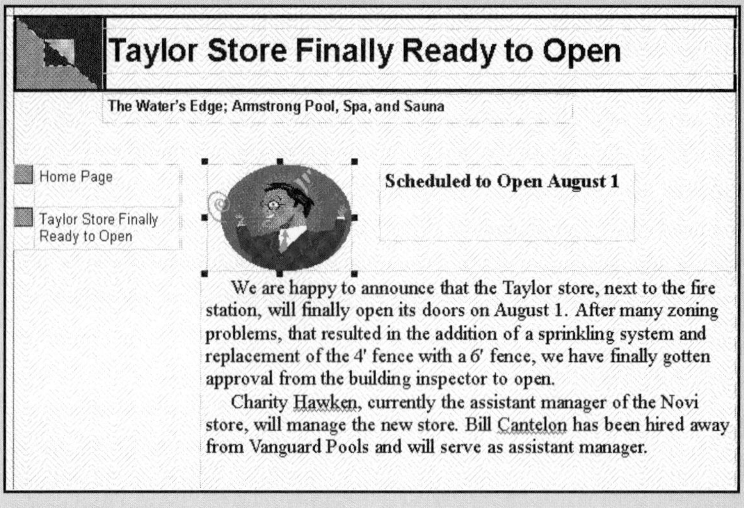

Figure 7.19
New text and an appropriate clip art picture has been added.

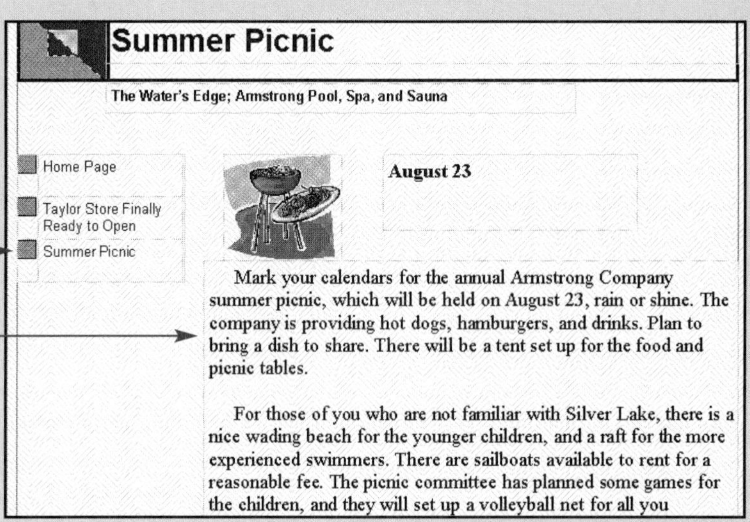

Figure 7.20
The third Web page announces the summer picnic.

New text for
navigation button

Text from Picnic
document

Lesson 6: Previewing the Web Pages

Before you convert your publication to HTML code and create the final Web pages, you can simulate the process and see what they will look like in your browser and test the navigation buttons.

In this lesson, you preview the Web pages before they are actually created.

To Preview the Web Pages

❶ Choose File, Web Page Preview from the menu.
The Web Page Preview dialog box is displayed.

❷ Select the Web site option, if necessary, and click OK.
Your browser launches automatically and displays the first page (see Figure 7.21).

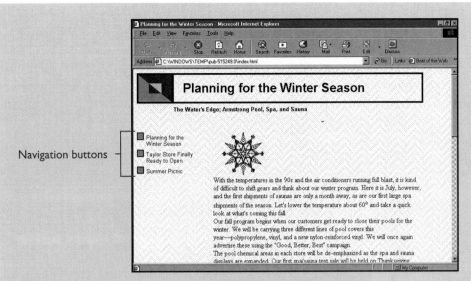

Figure 7.21
You can preview the Web pages in your browser.

Navigation buttons

3 **Click the second navigation button labeled Taylor Store Finally Ready to Open.**

The browser displays the second page. Notice the name of the first navigation button changes to Home Page.

4 **Click the third navigation button labeled Summer Picnic.**

The third page is displayed. Notice that the first page navigation button is labeled Home Page in the second and third pages (see Figure 7.22).

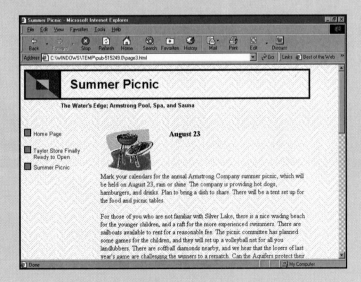

Figure 7.22
The first page is referred to as the Home Page in the other pages.

5 **Close the browser and return to Publisher.**

Leave the publication open for the next lesson.

Lesson 7: Saving the Publication as Web Pages

The Publisher program can produce a set of Web pages and their accompanying graphics so that they can be viewed by a browser on the Internet or company intranet. The program will assume that you want to create a subfolder named Publish in the folder where the publication currently resides. Allow it to create this folder for you and place all the files needed for the Web site in the same place.

In this lesson, you save the publication as a Web site that would be suitable for publishing.

To Save the Publication as Web Pages

1 **Choose File, Save as Web Page from the menu.**
The Save a Web Page dialog box opens. The program will create a subfolder named Publish in your current folder.

2 **Click OK.**
Each page is converted to HTML code.

3 **Launch Windows Explorer and open the new Publish subfolder.**
The navigation buttons, background patterns, and clip art are stored as images (see Figure 7.23).

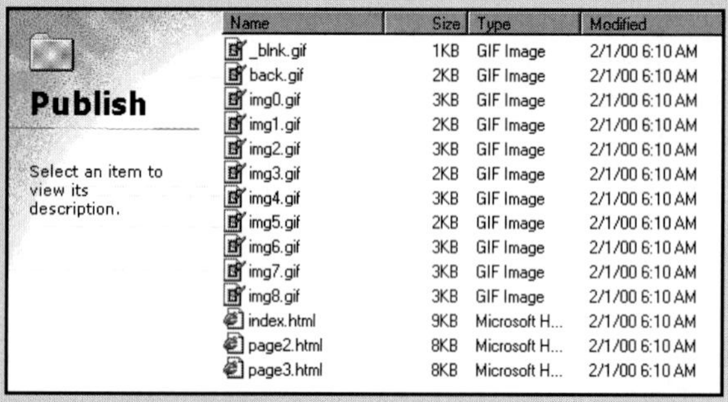

Figure 7.23
The publication is converted to a form suitable for publishing on the Internet/intranet.

4 **Close Windows Explorer. Close the Summer News publication.**
The Web pages cannot be edited easily. You need to keep the original publication so that you can make changes and generate a new set of Web pages if necessary.

Lesson 8: Previewing the Web Pages Using a Browser

You previewed the Web pages when they were part of Publisher, but it is still a good idea to test them again to make sure they were created successfully and to be sure you know where the new files are located. If your intended audience uses a mix of browsers such as Netscape and Internet Explorer, you should view your pages in both. If your audience is likely to view the pages using a mix of screen resolutions and colors, you can test the pages on these machines as well.

Netscape and Internet Explorer can view Web pages directly from disk as well as over the Internet. To do this, you provide the location of the home page in the address line. When Publisher creates a set of Web pages, it names the first page index.html and then names the rest of the pages sequentially such as page1.html, page2.html, and so forth.

In this lesson, you launch your browser and preview the Web pages.

To Preview the Web Pages Using a Browser

1 **Launch your browser.**
You do not have to be connected to the Internet for this exercise.

2 **Select the address box and type the location of the Index.html file.**
The Index.html file is located in the Publish subfolder that was created in the previous lesson.

The first Web page is displayed (see Figure 7.24).

Location on the computer's hard disk

Figure 7.24
You can view the Web pages with various browsers to simulate what your audience will see.

3 **Click the two navigation buttons to test them.**

4 **Close the browser.**
The last step to putting these files on the Internet varies considerably depending on who is providing this service. See the exercises in the Discovery section for direction on how to take this final step.

Summary

In this project, you used the skills you have developed to produce a set of Web pages that are suitable for publishing to the Internet or a company intranet. You modified the size to fit newer, high-resolution monitors and modified the text and pictures of an existing template to suit your needs. You learned how to add new pages, and you also learned how to check your work by previewing it before and after the pages were created.

Checking Concepts and Terms ✓

True/False

For each of the following statements, check *T* or *F* to indicate whether the statement is true or false.

__T __F   **1.** Publisher can create the individual pages of a Web site but you have to learn some basic HTML coding to create the navigation buttons. [L1]

__T __F   **2.** If a page is designed for a VGA monitor and you show it on a SVGA monitor, you will have to use horizontal scrollbars to view the page's width. [L2]

__T __F   **3.** You can insert text into a text frame on a Web page from existing documents. [L3]

__T __F   **4.** New Web pages can be created that are duplicates of existing pages. [L5]

__T __F   **5.** It is better if the pictures and text frames do not overlap on Web pages. [L4]

__T __F   **6.** You cannot see what the final Web site will look like until you save the publication as Web pages and view them with a browser. [L6]

__T __F   **7.** Once you save the publication as a series of Web pages and their associated graphics, you make changes to the Web pages by making changes to the publication and generating the Web pages again. [L7]

__T __F   **8.** Browsers can view only Web pages that have been transferred to an Internet host computer. The address must start with http://. [L8]

__T __F   **9.** A company intranet uses the same communications software as the Internet except it is not open to unauthorized people. [L1]

__T __F   **10.** If you change the monitor setting to show more pixels, the individual objects on the screen look larger. [L1]

Multiple Choice

Circle the letter of the correct answer for each of the following questions.

  1. The language used on the Internet to display Web pages is known by the abbreviation _____. [L1]

    a. URL

    b. UNIX

    c. OS/2

    d. HTML

  2. The Web Page Wizard provides two formats for navigation links between Web pages. They are _____. [L1]

    a. perimeter and horizontal bars

    b. vertical and horizontal bars

    c. virtual and literal bars

    d. monochrome and 256 color bars

  3. When the monitor setting is changed from 800 × 600 to 640 × 480, items on the screen look _____. [L1]

    a. larger

    b. the same

    c. smaller

    d. better in color

  4. If you insert text into the text frame from a Word document, what would be your best solution if there is too much text for the existing frame? [L3]

    a. Allow the text to flow to another frame as you would in a newsletter.

    b. Increase the size of the frame until the overflow indicator disappears.

    c. Do not use that article.

    d. Widen all the Web pages to make more room for text.

5. HTML stands for _____. [L4]

   a. Hyperactive Technicians Making Laws

   b. Hypertext Markup Language

   c. High Tech Meta-Language

   d. Howard-Temple Management Lab

6. VGA refers to a graphics standard that uses _____ pixels onscreen. [L1]

   a. 600 × 400

   b. 640 × 480

   c. 800 × 600

   d. 1024 × 760

7. A host computer _____. [INTRO]

   a. is used to create the Web pages

   b. is used to make Web pages available to the Internet or intranet

   c. is used to write Web pages in HTML

   d. is necessary only on a company intranet

8. The difference between the Internet and an intranet is that the intranet is _____. [L7]

   a. available to everyone

   b. much less reliable because of its size

   c. much more secure

   d. slow during the evening and weekends

9. Pixel is _____. [L2]

   a. an abbreviation for picture element

   b. about 64" × 48" of screen size

   c. a fanciful term related to Pixy dust

   d. the acronym for a famous graphics studio

10. Which of the following are true when you save the publication as Web pages? [L7]

   a. The program creates a subfolder named Publish to hold the files.

   b. The first page is named index.html.

   c. The images are saved as separate files.

   d. all of the above

Screen ID

Label each element of the Publisher screen shown in Figure 7.25.

Figure 7.25

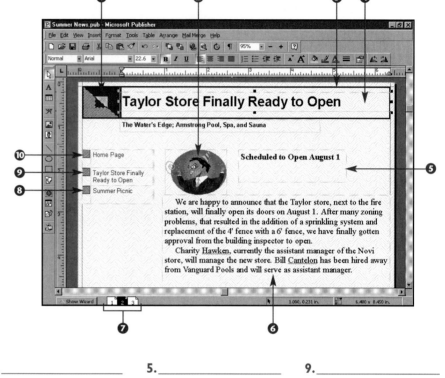

A. Clip art

B. Navigation button for third page

C. Graphic widened for larger screen

D. Navigation button for first page

E. Page navigation buttons used during editing

F. Text pasted from a Word document

G. Navigation button renamed to match current page title

H. Rectangle border widened for SVGA screen

I. Text box for page title

J. Text box for additional comments

1._____

2._____

3._____

4._____

5._____

6._____

7._____

8._____

9._____

10. _____

Discussion Questions

1. What are some disadvantages of being able to put your newsletter on a companywide intranet that were not mentioned in the introduction?

2. What type of information should be published on the company intranet versus the Internet?

3. If you plan to put an official company document on the Internet where everyone in the world can read it, what special steps should you take in proofreading or verification before you publish it? Why?

4. What types of people are likely to read a brochure that would not see the Web page? Who would see the Web page but might not see the brochure?

5. In your experience, when was the last time that a mistake was printed and distributed before anyone noticed? If the information was on a Web page and could be changed quickly, would it have saved any cost or embarrassment? How?

Skill Drill

Skill Drill exercises reinforce project skills. Each skill reinforced is the same, or nearly the same, as a skill presented in this project. Each exercise includes a brief narrative introduction, followed by detailed instructions in a step-by-step format.

The following exercises once again deal with the Helping Hands organization. You will develop a Web site that can be used to supplement the newsletter.

1. Creating the Web Site and Changing the Page Width

In this exercise, you create a set of Web pages that contain the same articles that were used for the Helping Hands Newsletter.

To create the Web site for the newsletter, complete the following steps:

1. Launch Publisher, select the Web Sites option, and start the wizard.
2. Choose the Sapphire color scheme. Accept all the other default choices and then hide the wizard when you are finished.
3. Choose File, Page Setup from the menu. Choose Wide and click OK.
4. Select the elements that make up the page title and widen them to fit the new page width.
5. Delete the small picture at the right side of the page. Select the small text box to the right of the larger picture and choose Edit, Delete Object.
6. Widen the main text box to fit the width of the page. Lengthen the main text box to fill the available page space below it.
7. Click the Save button to save your work. Save it as **Helping Hands**. Leave the publication open for the next exercise.

2. Modifying Existing Text

Modify the text in the title and subheading. Add a new text box to the right of the picture.

To modify existing text, complete the following steps:

1. Select the text in the title box and type **Busy Year Ahead**.
2. Select the text in the subheading and type **News & Notes: Helping Hands**.
3. Click the Text Frame Tool and drag a text frame to the right of the picture. Type **2001, Start of the New Millennium (according to some)**.
4. Select the text in the new text frame and change it to 12 point, bold.
5. Select all the text in the main text box. Choose Insert, Text File from the menu and locate the document Helping Hands Upcoming Events on your CD. Select the document and click OK.
6. Click the Save button to save your work. Leave the publication open for the next exercise.

3. Changing the Picture

You can use the Clip Art gallery to add an image that is related to the topic.

To change the picture, complete the following steps:

1. Select the picture. Choose Insert, Picture, Clip Art from the menu.
2. Search for the word **walk** or another keyword that is relevant to the topics talked about in the text.
3. Select an appropriate picture and click the Insert Clip button on the shortcut menu. Close the Insert Clip Art dialog box.
4. Click the Save button to save your work. Leave the publication open for the next exercise.

4. Inserting a New Web Page and Modifying It

Insert a new page by making a duplicate of the existing page.

To insert a new Web page and modify it, complete the following steps:

1. Choose Insert, Page from the menu. Click More Options.

2. Confirm that After current page is selected.

3. Choose Duplicate all objects on page.

4. Confirm that Add hyperlink to Web navigation bar is selected. Click OK.

5. Change the title of the new page to More Volunteers Needed!

6. Change the text in the box to the right of the picture to Let's try to add at least 20 first-time volunteers.

7. Select all the text in the main text box. Choose Insert, Text File from the menu. Locate the document Volunteers. Select the document and click OK.

8. Click the Save button to save your work. Leave the publication open for the next exercise.

5. Previewing the Web Site and Saving the Publication as Web Pages

Preview the Web site before you convert it into a set of Web pages. Confirm that it has two pages and that the navigation buttons work. Then save it as Web pages.

To preview the Web site and save the publication as Web pages, complete the following steps:

1. Choose File, Web Page Preview from the menu. Choose Web site and click OK.

2. The browser will launch. Test the navigation buttons and then close the browser.

3. Publisher will save the Web site files into a subfolder named Publish that is located within the current folder. This subfolder already exists and has the files you created in Lesson 7. Launch Windows Explorer. Choose File, New, Folder from the menu and create a new subfolder that will hold the Web site files. Right-click on the name of the new subfolder. Choose Rename from the shortcut menu. Rename the subfolder Publish2.

4. Choose File, Save as Web Page from the menu. Locate and choose the Publish2 subfolder. Click OK.

5. Save any changes and close the publication.

6. Previewing the Web Pages Using a Browser

Before your pages are placed on a host computer and made available to the world, you should preview them with different browsers set to different screen settings.

To preview the Web pages using a browser, complete the following steps:

1. Use Windows Explorer or My Computer to locate the Publish2 subfolder and determine where it is on your computer's disk. Open the Publish2 subfolder and observe that one of the filenames is index.html.

2. Launch a Web browser. Use a different browser or different screen setting, if possible.

3. Enter the address of the index.html file in the address box of the browser. An example might be C:\My Documents\Publish2\index.html

4. Press ↵Enter to activate the browser.

5. Observe how the page looks in this browser and screen setting. Confirm that the navigation buttons work.

6. Close the browser.

Challenge

Challenge exercises expand on or are somewhat related to skills presented in the lessons. Each exercise provides a brief narrative introduction, followed by instructions in a numbered step format that are not as detailed as those in the Skill Drill section.

In the following exercises, you create a Web site for a fictitious Cornwall Historical Heritage Society (CHHS). This Web site focuses on a small area on the north coast of Cornwall that is closely associated with the Arthurian legends. You will use this Web site to learn how to insert new types of Web pages, how to link to pictures rather than insert them, and how to create hyperlinks. You will also look at the Web pages in two different browsers or two different screen settings to see how it might appear to other viewers.

The first four Challenge exercises use the file Pub-0701, saved as **CHHS**. The exercises may be done sequentially or you may do any combination of individual exercises. If you do not do the first exercise, Open Pub-0701 and save it as **CHHS** for use in the other Challenge exercises.

1. Inserting and Resizing an Events Page

You can add several other types of Web pages to an existing Web site. In this exercise, you insert an events page, select all of its elements, and resize them to fit the SVGA screen size. The Publisher program does not have an easy way to rearrange pages, but there is a way to work around this short-coming.

1. Open Pub-0701 and save it as **CHHS**.
2. Select the third Web page.
3. Choose Insert, Page from the menu.
4. Click the down arrow next to the Available page types box and select Event. Click OK.
5. The Event page may not be placed last. Look at the pages and locate it. In this example, it is page 2. There are now four pages.
6. Select page 4. Choose Insert, Page from the menu. Click More Options. Select Duplicate all objects on new page and enter the page number of the new events page, **2**, in the adjacent box. Click OK. You now have two Events pages.
7. Select the original Events page (page 2). Choose Edit, Delete Page, OK, and Yes. You now have four pages, the last page of which is an Events page.
8. Save your work. If you plan to do the next exercise, leave the publication open.

2. Inserting a Calendar Page

Organizations are always sponsoring activities, and a calendar is a good way to organize the activities. In this exercise, you insert a calendar page and select the current month.

1. Choose Insert, Page from the menu.
2. Click the down arrow next to the Available page types box and select Calendar. Click OK. A calendar page is placed in the Web site as the second page. (See the previous exercise if you want to learn how to move the calendar.)
3. Click the calendar on the new calendar page to select it. Click the Wizard button at the bottom of the frame.

4. Choose Dates in the top pane of the window and then click Change Dates.

5. Select the current month and year. Click OK.

6. Close the wizard and save your work. If you plan to do the next exercise, leave the publication open.

3. Linking to a Picture

Pictures may take much more storage space than clip art. If the same picture is used many times, you can save storage space by linking to the picture from each Web page instead of inserting the picture in each page. If you have a logo or some other picture that occurs in many places but may change if the company changes name, you can use links to a single version of the logo so that you only have to change it once to be sure it is changed in all the official publications. In this exercise, you will link to the picture of Gwennap Pit.

1. Locate and view the page titled Gwennap Pit Provides Rich History.

2. Launch Windows Explorer or My Computer and locate the picture Pit.jpg. Copy it and paste it into the same folder where you store your homework files.

3. Switch back to Publisher and choose Insert, Picture, From File from the menu.

4. Locate the picture Pit.jpg in your homework folder and select it.

5. Click the down arrow next to the button labeled Insert and choose Link to file.

6. Move and resize the picture to fit in the available space near the top of the page.

7. Save your work. If you plan to do the next exercise, leave the publication open.

4. Inserting a Hyperlink

One of the great advantages of the Internet is the capability to hyperlink to related pages. In this exercise, you change selected text into hyperlinked text that connects to another Web site on the Internet.

1. Select the first page and read the text about King Arthur's castle.

2. Launch your Internet browser. Go to a search engine such as www.yahoo.com and search for **King Arthur**.

3. Find a Web site that you like. Select the site's address in the browser's address box and copy it to the Clipboard by using the keyboard shortcut for copy, Ctrl + C.

4. Switch back to Publisher. Select the words "King Arthur" in the first sentence.

 5. Click the Insert Hyperlink button on the toolbar.

6. Confirm that the beginning of an Internet address is selected in the Internet address of the Web site or file box is selected. Use the keyboard shortcut for paste (Ctrl + V) to paste the address into this box. If this does not work, type `http://www.britannia.com/history/h12.html`.

7. Click OK. The text changes color and is underlined. Place the pointer over the text "King Arthur." A ScreenTip displays the Internet address of the hyperlink. When this page is published, clicking this text will bring up the Web page to which it refers.

8. Save your work and close the publication.

5. Comparing Netscape and Internet Explorer

To do this exercise, you will need to use two different browsers—Netscape and Internet Explorer. Both browsers may be installed on the same computer, but it is more likely that you will need to find another computer that has the second browser installed on it.

In this exercise, you open the Web page that you created using Internet Explorer, capture the screen, and paste the screen image into a Word document. Then, you will repeat the process using Netscape. The resulting Word document will have an example of how the same Web page appears in two different browsers.

1. Use Windows Explorer to locate the Publish subfolder that you created when you saved the publication as a Web page in Lesson 7. Copy the folder to a floppy disk.

2. Determine the screen settings. Click the Start button on the taskbar and then choose, Settings, Control Panel. Double-click on Display and choose Settings. Write down the setting for Colors and the number of pixels in the Screen area. Click Cancel. Close the Control Panel dialog box.

3. Launch Internet Explorer. Type the location of the index.html file on your floppy disk into the Address box in the browser. For example, A:\Publish\index.html.

4. Press ⏎Enter to view the first page of the Web site.

5. Press the Print Screen button (PrtSc on some computers) on your keyboard to copy an image of the screen into the Office Clipboard.

6. Launch Word and open a blank document. Type **Summer News viewed in Internet Explorer**. Press ⏎Enter and type the information about the number of colors and pixels. Press ⏎Enter again.

7. Choose Edit, Paste from the menu. The screen image is placed in the Word document.

8. Close the document and save it on the floppy disk as **Comparison**.

9. Locate another computer that has Word on it and has the Netscape browser. Take your floppy disk with you and repeat steps 1 through 8 to capture the same Web page as it appears in Netscape.

10. When you are finished, you should have a Word document with two screen images on it. One displays the Web page in Explorer and the other in Netscape. Both images should be accompanied by information about the screen settings for color and number of pixels.

Discovery Zone

Discovery Zone exercises help you gain advanced knowledge of project topics and/or application of skills. These exercises focus on enhancing your problem-solving skills. Numbered steps are not provided, but you are given hints, reminders, screen shots, and/or references to help you reach your goal for each exercise.

Your computer must be connected to the Internet to do the following exercises.

If you want to post your Web pages to the Internet, you need to place the files on a host computer that is connected to the Internet and is running the type of software that is used to share Web pages on the Internet. Your school may have space on its computer for this purpose, and there are many services that allow you to place your Web page on their computer for free in exchange for some advertising privileges. The following Discovery exercises guide you in the process of locating a free Web hosting computer service and then publishing your Web site to that service.

1. Searching for a Free Web Hosting Site

Follow these guidelines to locate a free Web hosting computer service.

Goal: Find a service that will host your Web pages in exchange for placing advertising banners on your pages.

Launch your browser and go to a search engine such as www.yahoo.com. Search for `Free Web Page Hosting`.

Pick a site from those listed. Choose one that will host your Web site, not just provide a free home page that you can configure with stock quotes and news. These sites change often, but at the time of this writing, www.webprovider.com is a workable option.

Register to use this site. When you are done, you must have three things: an Internet address, a username, and a password.

Some sites will require that you use their method of uploading files so that they can attach the banner ads while others will let you upload files using other programs.

Print out the confirmation screen that shows your new address and user name.

2. Creating a Web Folder and Save the Web Site

If you have permission to transfer files to a host computer, you will have an Internet address where the files may be stored as well as a username and password for that computer. You need all three of these to do this exercise.

Goal: Create a Web folder and save Web pages to the folder.

Launch My Computer from your desktop. Double-click on Web Folders. Choose Add Web Folder and follow the directions for creating a Web folder.

Launch Publisher and open one of the publications that contains a Web site such as Summer News or Helping Hands. Choose File, Save as Web page from the menu. When the Save as Web Page dialog box appears, click the Web Folders button at the lower-left corner of the box. Choose the Web folder you created in My Computer and save the Web pages to that location. Enter the username and password when prompted.

Launch your browser and view the Web site. For example, if you had an address on your university's computer that looked like this, www.myschool.edu/myname, and you placed the files in the myname folder, the address of page one of your site would be http://www.myschool.edu/myname/index.html.

If the Web Folders method does not work, go to www.ipswitch.com and choose Download Evaluations. Download an evaluation copy of WS_FTP Pro. Follow the directions to connect it to your host computer and use it to upload the files from the Publish subfolder.

Task Guide

A book in the *Essentials* series is designed to be kept as a handy reference beside your computer, even after you complete all the projects and exercises. Any time you have difficulty recalling the sequence of steps or a shortcut needed to achieve a result, look up the task in the following table. If you would like more detail on a topic, turn to the page number listed in the third column to locate the step-by-step exercise or other detailed description.

To	Do This	Page Number
Project 1: Getting Started with Publisher		
Use the Publisher Catalog	Launch Publisher. Click the tab that you want to use and then select the design you want. Click Start Wizard if you are using a publication wizard or design set. Click Create if you are using a blank publication. Click the Existing Files button to open an existing publication.	3
Create a Publication Using a Wizard	Select the design from the Catalog and then click the Start Wizard button. Answer the wizard's questions. When you are finished, click the Finish button.	6
Create a Blank Publication	Select the layout from the Blank Publications tab of the Catalog and then click the Create button.	6
Update Personal Information	Click Update in the wizard, or select Edit, Personal Information from the menu. Select one of the four information sets, make your changes, and click the Update button.	8
Navigate the Publisher Screen	Use the page navigation control buttons to move from page to page. Use the Zoom In button to make the page larger, and use the Zoom Out button to make the page smaller. Use the vertical and horizontal scrollbars to move the document up and down, or left and right.	10
Resize Frames	Click on the frame to select it. Place the pointer over one of the selection handles and drag to resize. Use the corner handles to resize proportionally.	14
Move Frames	Move the pointer over the frame until it turns into the Move pointer. Click and drag the frame to its new location.	14

continues ▶

To	Do This	Page Number
Add Pages	Select Insert, Page from the menu. Choose the new page location and choose whether to insert a blank page or a duplicate of the current page. Click OK.	17
Remove Pages	Move to the page you want to remove. Select Edit, Delete Page from the menu.	17
Print a Publication	Click the Print button on the Standard toolbar. For more control, select File, Print from the menu. Select the page(s) you want to print and the number of copies; then click OK.	19
Save a Publication	Click the Save button on the Standard toolbar. If the publication has not been saved before, the Save As dialog box will prompt you to give the file a name and to specify where the file should be saved.	20
Get Help Using the Office Assistant	Click the Office Assistant, or select Help, Microsoft Publisher Help from the menu. Type your question and click the Search button. Find the appropriate topic and click on it.	21

Project 2: Adding Graphics

Open an Existing Publication	Launch Publisher, click the Existing files button, find the file you want to open, and click the Open button.	35
Save a File with a New Name	Choose File, Save As from the menu. Type a new name for the file in the File name box and specify the location to save the file in the Look in box. Click Save.	35
Insert Clip Art	Click the Clip Gallery Tool button, position the mouse pointer on your publication, and click and drag a frame. Select the image you want to insert from the Clip Art Gallery and click the Insert clip button. Close the Clip Art Gallery window.	37
Resize Object Frames	Click the object you want to resize. Move the mouse pointer on top of one of the selection handles until the pointer changes to a Resize icon; then click and drag to increase or decrease the size and shape of the frame. Use the corner selection handles to keep the object proportional.	40
Move Object Frames	Click the object you want to move. Move the mouse pointer on the object until you see the Move icon. Click and drag the image to a new location.	40
Insert Pictures	Click the Picture Frame tool, move the mouse pointer onto the publication, and click and drag a frame. Then choose Insert, Picture from the menu. Locate the file you want to use and click the Insert button.	43

To	Do This	Page Number
Crop Pictures	Click the image you want to crop. Click the Crop Picture button and position the mouse pointer over one of the selection handles. Click and drag toward the middle of the image to crop the parts you want hidden. Click the Crop Picture tool to deselect it.	44
Create WordArt	Click the WordArt Frame tool and click and drag a frame on your publication. Type the words you want made into a WordArt image and click Update Display. Close the WordArt dialog box.	47
Modify WordArt	Make sure the WordArt image has a hash-mark box around it. If necessary, double-click the image to activate the WordArt program. Use the buttons on the WordArt toolbar to change the shape, font, font size, and other characteristics. Click in an open area to return to the Publisher window. Click the WordArt image and use the buttons on the Formatting toolbar to make further modifications to the image.	48
Add a Drawing	Click on the shape you want to use and click and drag to place it in the position you want in the publication.	50
Add an Arrow	Click the Line Tool and click and drag a line. Click one of the three Add/Remove arrow buttons on the Formatting toolbar.	50
Color a Drawing Shape	Click the shape to select it and then click the Fill Color button. Click More Colors to see a wider range of choices. Select the color you want and click Apply. Click OK to close the Colors dialog box.	52
Layer Two Objects	Click the shape that you want in the back and click the Send to Back button.	52

Project 3: Working with Text

Replace Placeholder Text by Typing	Click on the placeholder text. Start typing; the placeholder text will disappear.	67
Replace Placeholder Text by Inserting Text from a File	Click on the placeholder text. Select Insert, Text File from the menu; then find and select a document from the Insert Text dialog box. Decide whether to AutoFlow the text, if asked.	67
Edit Existing Text	To remove letters one at a time, place the insertion point next to the letter and then click Backspace or Del to remove the character before or after, respectively. To edit words or groups of words, select the text and type over it.	69
Use AutoFlow when Inserting Text	Insert text. When prompted to AutoFlow, click Yes. When the program finds an empty frame, click Yes to place the rest of the text.	70

continues ▶

To	Do This	Page Number
Pour Overflow Text into an Existing Frame	Click on the frame with the overflow indicator. Click the Connect Text Frames button on the Connect Frames toolbar. Find an empty text frame and then click on it to pour the overflow text.	70
Reference Connected Frames on Different Pages	Right-click on the frame you want the reference to appear in. Select Change Frame, Text Frame Properties from the menu. Select the Continued on or Continued from note and click OK.	73
Add a Text Frame	Click the Text Frame Tool button in the Objects toolbar. Move to an open area on the publication and click and drag down and to the right. Release the mouse button when the text frame is the right size.	74
Create a Bulleted or Numbered List	Place the insertion point where you want the list. Click either the Bullets button or the Numbering button and then type the list.	76
Change Font Characteristics	Select the text you want to change. Click one of the formatting buttons (such as Bold, Italic, Font Color). You can also select Format, Font from the menu.	79
Change Paragraph Formatting	Select the text you want to change. Click one of the alignment formatting buttons. You can also select such things as line spacing or indents from the Format menu.	81

Project 4: Working with Frames

Group Frames as One Object	Select all of the frames in the group by dragging a box around the objects. Click the Group Objects button.	97
Ungroup and Rearrange Frames	Click the group to select it. Click the Ungroup button. Move the frames individually.	98
Group Several Shapes	Click on one shape, hold down ◆Shift and click on each additional shape to select it. When all the shapes you want grouped are selected, click the Group Objects button that is displayed near the selected objects.	98
Edit a Grouped Object	Click the frame that is part of the group to select it. Select and edit the text within a text frame.	100
Resize and Move a Group	Click the group to select it. Click and drag a handle to resize the group. Hover the pointer on the group until the pointer turns into a move pointer. Click and drag the group to move it to a new location.	102
Wrap Text Around Frames	Click the text frame to select it. Choose Format, Text Frame Properties from the menu. Choose the Wrap text around objects option and click OK.	104

To	Do This	Page Number
Change the Frame Border and Fill Color Characteristics	Select the frame. Click the Line/Border style button and select one of the options to change the border. Click the Fill color button and select a fill color from those listed.	105
Format Page Borders	Use the rectangle tool to draw a rectangle around the page. Select Format, Line/Border Style from the menu. Choose a border style. Choose More Styles if you want to make customized borders.	107

Project 5: Using Tables, Charts, and Mail Merge

To	Do This	Page Number
Add a Table	Click the Table Frame Tool and click and drag the table frame. Select the number of rows, columns, and table format.	121
Enter Data in a Table	Click in the first cell and type the information for that cell. Use the Tab key to move from cell to cell as you type.	121
Navigate a Table Using the Keyboard	Use the up- and down-arrow keys to move between rows, Tab to move to the next cell, and Shift+Tab to move to the previous cell.	121
Select the Entire Table	Click and drag across all of the cells in the table; choose Table, Select, Table from the menu, or click the Select Cells button in the upper-left corner of the table.	121
Add a Column in the Middle of a Table	Click the column selector above the row where you want to insert a new column; choose Table, Insert Columns from the menu. A column will be added to the right of the selected column.	125
Add a Row in the Middle of a Table	Click the row selector to the left of the row where you want to insert a new row; choose Table, Insert Rows from the menu. A row will be added below the selected row.	125
Add a Column to the Left of a Table	Select the entire table; choose Table, Insert Rows or Columns from the menu; select Columns; indicate the number of columns; and then choose Before selected cells option.	125
Add a Row to the Top of a Table	Select the entire table; choose Table, Insert Rows or Columns from the menu; select Rows; indicate the number of rows; and then choose Before selected cells option.	125
Resize a Table	Click and drag the resizing handles around the table to increase or decrease the overall table size.	128
Use Table AutoFormat	Select the table and choose Table, Table AutoFormat from the menu. Select the format you want and click OK.	128
Change the Formatting in a Table	Select the columns or rows you want to affect and use the tool bar buttons to change the font, font size, fill color, font color, or border style.	128

continues ▶

To	Do This	Page Number
Change a Row Size	Hold down ⬆Shift and then click and drag the dividing line between the row selectors for the rows that you want to resize.	128
Change a Column Size	Hold down ⬆Shift and then click and drag the dividing line between the column selectors for the columns that you want to resize.	128
Add Objects from Other Applications	Make sure nothing is selected and then choose Insert, Object from the menu. To insert an existing object, click the Create from File option button and then use the Browse button to locate the file that you want to insert. Select the file, click Insert, and then click OK.	131
Resize an Inserted Object	Use the resize handles that surround the object and click and drag to resize the object. Use the corner resize handles to maintain proportion.	131
Move an Insert Object	Use the Move icon to click and drag the object to the location you want.	131
Edit Microsoft Excel Chart	Click the chart to select it. Choose Edit, Microsoft Excel Worksheet Object, Edit from the menu. Exit the editing program and then reactivate it to reset the formats for the chart. Click the part of the chart you want to reformat and use the tools on the toolbar to change the formatting. Exit the editing program by clicking off the chart.	133
Create an Address List	Choose Mail Merge, Create Publisher Address List from the menu. Type the information for the fields you want to use. Click New Entry to begin a new entry. When all of the entries have been typed, click the Close button and save the file.	137
Merge a Mailing List with a Publication	Click the text box where you want the address to be inserted. Choose Mail Merge, Open Data Source from the menu. Locate the file you want to use, select it, and then click Open. Click the first field you want to include in the address and click the Insert button. Add a space, and then insert the next field. Use the keyboard to add a new line or other punctuation as needed. Continue this pattern until the mailing label is complete. Close the Insert Fields dialog box.	140
Merge Data with a Publication	After field placeholders have been inserted in a publication, choose Mail Merge, Merge from the menu.	143
Print a Mail Merge	After the data has been merged with a publication, choose File, Print Merge from the menu. Select the entry numbers you want to print and then click the Print button.	143
Test a Mail Merge Printing	After the data has been merged with a publication, choose File, Print Merge from the menu. Click Test.	143

To	Do This	Page Number
Project 6: Working with Publisher Tools		
Run the Spell Check	Select Tools, Spelling, Check Spelling from the menu. When you find an unrecognized word, choose whether to ignore it, add it to the dictionary, or change it to one of the suggested alternatives.	161
Turn Hyphenation On or Off	Select Tools, Language, Hyphenation from the menu. Click the Automatically hyphenate this story check box to turn it on or off. To check it word by word, click the Manual button.	163
Add a Design Gallery Object	Click the Design Gallery Object button on the Objects toolbar. Select an object from the Categories panel and then select the design from the panel on the right. Click the Insert Object button.	165
Add Headers and Footers	Choose View, Go to Background from the menu. Add a text box at the top or bottom of the page; then add text, the date, or the page number.	168
Run the Design Checker	Choose Tools, Design Checker from the menu. Select which pages to check and then evaluate the suggestions made by the program.	170
Embed Fonts	Choose Tools, Commercial Printing Tools, Fonts from the menu. Make sure all of the fonts are TrueType and that none of them have licensing restrictions. Choose to Embed the fonts and decide whether to use a subset of the fonts; then click OK.	173
Prepare Images for Color Printing	Choose Tools, Commercial Printing Tools, Color Printing from the menu. If you are going to print with Publisher, choose Composite RGB. If you are going to use commercial color printing, choose Process colors (CMYK). If you are going to use only one or two colors, choose Spot color(s). Click OK.	177
Set Publisher Options	Choose Tools, Options from the menu. Make the necessary changes in any of the four categories and then click OK.	178
Project 7: Building a Web Site with Publisher		
Create a Web Site Using a Wizard	Launch Publisher and select Web Sites from the list of Wizards. Answer the wizard questions.	192
Change Page Width	Choose File, Page Setup from the menu. Choose Wide and OK. Resize the frames on the screen as needed.	194
Add Text to Web Pages	Edit existing text as you would any ordinary text box. Insert documents into text frames but do not use the overflow feature. Expand text frames to accommodate all the text.	196

continues ▶

To	Do This	Page Number
Change Pictures on Web Pages	Change or insert pictures as you would in other publications except do not overlap text and figures.	198
Insert New Web Pages	Select the last page in the publication. Choose Insert, Page. Click the More Options button. Select After current page, Duplicate all objects on page, and Add hyperlink to Web navigation bar. Click OK.	199
Preview the Web Site	Choose File, Web Page Preview from the menu. Select the Web site option. Click OK.	202
Save the Publication as Web Pages	Choose File, Save as Web Page from the menu. Allow the program to create a subfolder named Publish within the current folder or specify a different folder.	204
Preview the Web Pages Using a Browser	The first page of the Web site is named index.html. Launch a browser and use the file's name and location on your disk as the address.	205

Glossary

All key terms appearing in this book (in bold italic) are listed alphabetically in this Glossary for easy reference. If you want to learn more about a feature or concept, turn to the page reference shown after its definition. You can also use the Index to find the term's other significant occurrences.

AutoFlow   A feature that enables you to automatically place overflow text in an empty frame when you insert text from another source. [pg. 70]

background   The area behind a page. You can add page numbers, dates, text, or graphics to a background, and they will appear on every page of the publication. [pg. 34]

border   The edge of the frame. [pg. 105]

bulleted list   A preformatted list that is used to display information that has no particular order. [pg. 76]

Catalog   A list of publication types and styles that Publisher will set up for you. [pg. 2]

cell   The intersection of a row and column in a table where you enter data. [pg. 123]

clip art   A collection of photographs, drawings, and other such graphics that can be "clipped" from the collection and inserted into your publication. [pg. 34]

clip art frames   Frames that contain images from the Publisher Clip Gallery or some other source of images. [pg. 13]

CMYK color model   A way of separating color graphics into cyan, magenta, yellow, and black so that commercial printers can print realistic pictures. [pg. 176]

color schemes   Sets of colors that are designed to work together to provide a pleasing overall effect. [pg. 106]

column selector   The bar at the top of a selected table that is used to select an entire column. When you point to this area, the ScreenTip displays "Select Cells." [pg. 123]

crop   To hide parts of a picture or graphic. [pg. 44]

data source   A listing of names, addresses, and other information that may be used to merge individual information with a publication to create a preaddressed publication. [pg. 137]

Design Checker   A tool that checks for layout and design problems in your publication. [pg. 169]

Design Gallery Objects   Preformatted frames that match the design of the publication. These objects can include mastheads, pull quotes, sidebars, or calendars. [pg. 160]

docked toolbars   Toolbars that are attached to the edge of the Publisher window. [pg. 31]

drawing tools   Shapes such as lines, rectangles, and circles that can be used to create a picture, image, or drawing. [pg. 34]

drop cap   An enlarged first letter (or letters) in an article, either set off or embedded in the text. [pg. 89]

embed   To store all the font information in the publication document. [pg. 173]

field   A term used to identify a category of information such as name or address in a database or address list. [pg. 138]

floating toolbars   Toolbars that are in a box, not attached to the edges of the Publisher window. [pg. 31]

footers   Information placed on the background that appears on the bottom of each page of the publication. [pg. 160]

frame   The container for an object on a Publisher page. All objects, including pictures, clip art, and text, are contained in a frame. [pg. 2]

Group   To combine two or more frames so that they can be treated as a single frame. [pg. 16]

headers   Information placed on the background that appears on the top of each page of the publication. [pg. 160]

horizontal bar   On a Web site, a list of page names side-by-side that work like buttons. [pg. 192]

host computer   A computer that is connected to the Internet or an intranet that allows other people to view Web pages. [pg. 190]

hyperlinks   Addresses that are attached to words or objects, such as buttons, on a Web page. [pg. 199]

Hypertext Markup Language (HTML)   A set of codes that any computer can use to display text onscreen. [pg. 191]

Internet   A worldwide network of computers that is open to everyone. [pg. 190]

intranet   A network of computers that uses the same software as the Internet but is available only to people within the company. [pg. 190]

layer   A technique used with graphics to place images on top of one another and control which one appears on top or at the bottom of a stack of images. [pg. 34]

layout guides   Lines that are visible on the screen but that do not print. They are used to align objects on the page. [pg. 195]

Mail Merge   A program that merges an address list with a publication or other document to create a personalized and addressed publication. [pg. 120]

masthead   The heading on the first page of a newsletter, usually containing text, a logo, the volume and issue number, and a graphic background. [pg. 32]

numbered list   A preformatted list that displays sequential information in numeric sequence. [pg. 76]

Object Linking and Embedding (OLE)   A feature that is part of Microsoft Office applications that enables you to share information between applications. The main difference between linking and embedding is where the data is stored. With a linked file, the original data is stored in the source file and is linked to the destination file. If changes are made to the source file, the changes are also reflected in the destination file. An embedded object does not maintain this link. Any changes to the source are not reflected in the destination file, and any changes in the object after it is embedded do not affect the original source file. [pg. 131]

Office Assistant   The interactive Help feature in Publisher. The Office Assistant enables you to type questions in sentence format. [pg. 20]

page navigation controls   The buttons at the bottom of a newsletter that enable you to move quickly from page to page. [pg. 13]

picture frames   A frame that contains a digitized photograph, clip art image, or drawing. [pg. 13]

pixel   Name for picture element into which the screen of a monitor is divided. [pg. 194]

placeholder   A temporary object placed in a frame by a wizard—it will be replaced by text or other object by the user; also identifies the field name of the specific data that will be displayed when the merge program is run. [pg. 14]

PostScript   A language, developed by Adobe, used to define fonts. [pg. 173]

pull quote   A box containing an important quote from the surrounding article. [pg. 165]

RGB color model   The way Publisher saves publication colors using red, green, and blue. [pg. 176]

row selector   The bar at the left side of a selected table that is used to select an entire row. When you point to this area, the ScreenTip displays "Select Cells." [pg. 123]

ScreenTip   The name or other information that displays when you hover the mouse pointer over a button or an object. [pg. 11]

selection handles   Little boxes around the edges of a frame, indicating that the frame has been selected. They are also used to resize a frame. [pg. 11]

service bureau   A company that takes your publication file and creates high-resolution originals to be used by a commercial printer. [pg. 172]

table frames   A frame that holds data in a row-and-column format; similar to a Word table. [pg. 13]

text frames   Any frame that contains text, including hyperlinks. [pg. 13]

TrueType   A language, developed by Microsoft, used to define fonts. [pg. 173]

Ungroup   To remove the grouping characteristic so that you can work with the individual objects that make up the whole. [pg. 98]

vertical bar   On a Web site, the navigation buttons at the left side of the page. [pg. 192]

Web browser   A program that communicates with your computer and the host computer to display Web pages. [pg. 190]

Web pages   Screens that can be transmitted on the Internet or intranet and viewed by a Web browser. [pg. 190]

Web site   A group of interconnected Web pages. [pg. 190]

wizard   A built-in program that asks you questions and then sets something up that conforms to your answers. [pg. 5]

WordArt   A program that enables you to transform text into fancy letters that are treated like graphic objects. [pg. 34]

WordArt frames   Frames that contain fancy text that is created using the WordArt program included with Publisher. [pg. 13]

Index